GUILLAUME DE PALERNE

GUILLAUME DE PALERNE

*An English Translation of
the 12th Century French
Verse Romance*

Translated and Edited by
Leslie A. Sconduto

McFarland & Company, Inc., Publishers
Jefferson, North Carolina, and London

LIBRARY OF CONGRESS CATALOGUING-IN-PUBLICATION DATA

Guillaume de Palerne. English

Guillaume de Palerne : an English translation of the 12th
century French verse romance / translated and edited by Leslie A.
Sconduto.
    p.   cm.
Includes bibliographical references and index.

ISBN-13: 978-0-7864-1964-7
(softcover : 50# alkaline paper) ∞

1. William of Palerne (Legendary character) — Romances.
I. Sconduto, Leslie A., 1950–   II. Title.
PQ1483.G6E5   2004
821'.1 — dc22   2004009595

British Library cataloguing data are available

On the cover: *Ruins of the Roman Theatre at Taormina, Sicily*, William Stanley Haseltine, 1889, oil on canvas (PicturesNow.com).

Manufactured in the United States of America

McFarland & Company, Inc., Publishers
  Box 611, Jefferson, North Carolina 28640
    www.mcfarlandpub.com

For Eugene,
who is still my romance hero

Acknowledgments

I first began to translate *Guillaume de Palerne* while I was writing my dissertation at Rutgers University and am especially indebted to Mary Speer for the invaluable guidance and assistance that she provided at that time. I would also like to express my gratitude to Armstrong Atlantic State University for the grant that funded the early stages of my work on this book and to Bradley University for the research grant that allowed me to complete the translation.

Contents

Introduction

"Ceste merveille est molt estraigne:
Comment le puet on ensi croire?" (8524–8525)[1]

— This marvel is very strange.
How can one believe it then?

Guillaume de Palerne tells the story of a young prince of Sicily who is kidnapped by a werewolf at the age of four. Woven into the story of the eponymous hero is the parallel story of Alphonse, the Spanish prince who was transformed into a werewolf by his stepmother when he was still a toddler. Offering a treasure-trove of hidden meanings to the seeker of literary treasure, *Guillaume de Palerne* is a remarkable *roman d'aventure*; only those who rely on first impressions and outward appearances will contest its merit. Certainly not the first and perhaps not the most important of the adventure romances that were composed at the end of the twelfth century, it nonetheless offers an intriguing story of love and war and the triumph of the human spirit over the vagaries of fate. Into its engaging plot the poet has skillfully woven humor, contemporary allusions, reworkings of traditional motifs, and a hidden moral lesson. Guaranteed to please its medieval audience, *Guillaume de Palerne* presents the modern reader and scholar with a complex portrayal of the constancy and changeability of identity that provides new insight into the medieval attitude toward individuality. The audience's search for the hidden meaning that the poet promises to reveal coincides with and mimics the characters' search for the hidden identities of Guillaume and the werewolf. The poet thus sets up a parallel between the evaluation of identity and the interpretation of the elusive truth that is concealed behind appearances. *Guillaume de*

---

1. All citations are from Alexandre Micha's edition of *Guillaume de Palerne* unless otherwise noted. All translations are mine unless otherwise noted.

1

Palerne is indeed a romance worthy of the attention of modern medieval-
ists.

Manuscript, Editions, Derivatives and Translation

The only surviving Old French version of *Guillaume de Palerne* can
be found in a thirteenth-century manuscript: Paris, Arsenal FR. 6565,
Folios 77–157. Folios 1–76 contain the only extant copy of the romance
L'Escoufle. *Guillaume de Palerne* consists of 9,664 verses in octosyllabic
couplets. The manuscript is complete at beginning and end. Although it
includes approximately seventeen lacunas, none seriously interfere with
our comprehension of the narrative. Red and blue initials break the narrative into passages of unequal length. Two editions of the manuscript are
available: the first, *Guillaume de Palerne*, was prepared by Henri Michelant
in 1876 for the Société des Anciens Textes Français; the second, *Guillaume
de Palerne: Roman du XIIIe siècle* by Alexandre Micha in 1990.

In addition to the two editions of the Old French verse romance, *Guillaume de Palerne* survives in many other versions and derivatives. Four editions of a Middle French prose reworking by Pierre Durand were published
in the sixteenth and seventeenth centuries. In 1976 John C. Manolis prepared a new edition of these reworkings: *Guillaume de Palerne: Les Versions
en prose*. Three editions of a thirteenth-century Middle English alliterative
verse *William* also exist: *Guillaume de Palerne: The Ancient English Romance
of William the Werwolf*, prepared by Frederick Madden in 1832; *The
Romance of William of Palerne (Otherwise Known as the Romance of "William and the Werwolf),"* prepared by W. W. Skeat for the Early English
Text Society in 1867; and most recently, *William of Palerne: An alliterative
romance*, prepared by G. H. V. Bunt in 1985. Furthermore, *Eachtra Uilliam:
An Irish Version of William of Palerne*, a seventeenth-century Irish translation of a sixteenth-century English prose version of *William*, was edited
and translated by Cecile O'Rahilly in 1949. Finally there are three modern
juvenile versions of Guillaume's story dating from the early twentieth century.[2]

The present translation, which is the first modern translation ever done
of the Old French original, is based on Micha's edition, unless noted otherwise, since his edition is generally more available to scholars than Michelant's. In order that my translation might also serve as an aid to reading

---

2. For titles of the sixteenth-century prose versions and titles of the juvenile versions, and for
further information, see Dunn (3–10), Sconduto (*Metamorphosis*, 1–3), and Williams (Versions.)

the original, I selected unrhymed verse as the medium rather than prose. I attempted to be as literal as possible and to remain faithful to the register and "flavor" of the original. Sometimes I found it necessary to reverse the sequence of two verses. Whenever possible, I respected the verb tense of the original. Due to the nature of Old French romance, however, which tends to combine past tenses and the historical present, even in one sentence, I sometimes found it necessary to change the tense of a verb.

Poet and Patroness

We know very little about the poet who wrote *Guillaume de Palerne*. Since the romance is written in the Picard dialect, he was either from that region or at least very familiar with its language. The knowledge of Palermo and Sicily that he demonstrates in the romance suggests that he may have visited the island, perhaps while en route to the Holy Land or while returning from the Third Crusade. He tells us that he wrote the romance for "la contesse Yolent [Countess Yolande]" (9656) at her request: "Cest livre fist diter et faire / Et de latin en roumans traire [She had this book written and made / And translated from Latin into French]" (9659–9660).

Pierre Durand, who prepared the prose version of the romance in the sixteenth century, identified Yolande in his prologue as the aunt of Baldwin VI, the Count of Flanders and Hainaut who became Emperor of Greece.[3] Yolande, the daughter of Baldwin IV, was born in 1131. In 1178 she married Hugh Candavene IV, the Count of Saint Pol, after her first husband died. During the autumn and winter of 1190-91, Yolande's husband traveled with the King of France, Philip Augustus, from Sicily to Palestine. The author of *Guillaume de Palerne* may very well have been a cleric in his entourage. The Third Crusade ended in 1192, at which time the Count returned to France. He later participated in the Fourth Crusade (1202–04), during which time he became Constable and Baldwin became the Emperor of Constantinople. Hugh died in 1205. Yolande was still alive in 1212. There are some indications that she may still have been alive in 1223, although she would have been 92 years old.

Both Yolande and her nephew had important literary connections. Baldwin was the son-in-law of Marie de Champagne, to whom Chrétien de Troyes dedicated *Lancelot*. He was also the nephew of Philip of Alsace, who gave Chrétien the book on which he based *Perceval*. In addition, *L'Escoufle*, the other romance contained in Arsenal 6565 with *Guillaume*

---

3. See Manolis' edition of *Guillaume*, 22. The passage is also quoted in Dunn, 31.

de Palerne, was dedicated to Baldwin VI. Besides the anonymous poet who wrote *Guillaume de Palerne*, we know of two writers who worked under Yolande's patronage: Nicolas of Senlis who translated the *Pseudo-Turpin* from Latin into French for her, and Peter the clerk of Beauvais, who had numerous translations of Latin works attributed to him.[4]

Composition Date

The parameters for dating *Guillaume de Palerne* are based on the life span of its dedicatee, Countess Yolande. Most critics agree that it was written prior to her death, sometime between 1188 and the end of the twelfth century. The most recent editor of the romance, Alexandre Micha, provides very little information regarding the composition date in the introduction to his edition, although he notes that it could have been composed as late as the 1220s (23). Charles Dunn, however, in his 1960 study of *Guillaume de Palerne*, links the events of the romance to contemporary events and personages and convincingly demonstrates that it was written between 1194–1197, particularly since this time would have been a happy one for Yolande. Her husband, the Count of Saint Pol, who had been in Sicily with other crusaders, including Philip Augustus and Richard the Lion Heart, from 1190 to 1191, was home from the Third Crusade and had not yet left with her nephew on the Fourth Crusade, from which they would not return.[5] Harry Williams also accepts 1194–1197 as the date of composition for the romance.[6] Most recently (1993), Douglas Kelly gives the end of the twelfth century as the composition date.[7]

---

4. For further reading on Yolande and her husband, see Dunn (31–38), McKeehan (803–804), and Fourrier. Sara Sturm-Maddox also discusses the historical context of the romance in her comparison of *Guillaume de Palerne* and *Floriant et Florete*, an Arthurian verse romance which was written approximately fifty years after *Guillaume* and contains some similar plot elements. Unfortunately, she errs when she states that *Guillaume* "dreamed that he would extend his right hand over Rome and his left over Spain," as it is Guillaume's mother Queen Felise who has this dream (vv. 4759–4772). Moreover it is Felise's son Guillaume — not Guillaume's son — who becomes ruler of Rome and Felise's daughter and Guillaume's sister — not Guillaume's daughter — who becomes the wife of the king of Spain. Nevertheless, Sturm-Maddox is correct about the dynastic outcome of the romance, since one of Guillaume's sons eventually becomes emperor and the other becomes king (v. 9649). See Sturm-Maddox, 484. McKeehan also compares *Guillaume de Palerne* and *Floriant et Florete*, although she relies on the plot of the English version in her discussion of the French and the inaccuracy of some of her details indicates that she has probably not read the French version.

5. See Dunn, 141.

6. See Williams (Review, 124).

7. See Kelly (*Medieval*, xvii). For further information and additional references, see Sconduto (*Metamorphosis*, 15–16).

Source

No specific source has ever been found for *Guillaume de Palerne*, although the poet certainly claimed to have one. In verse 9660 he states that he translated the romance from a Latin source: "Et de latin en roumans traire [And translated from Latin into French]."[8] As early as verse 20, in his prologue, he refers to "une anciëne estoire [an ancient story]" that he wants to relate according to his understanding and his memory.[9] Medieval authors frequently claimed to have a source in order to augment the prestige and/or authority of what they had written. Elsewhere, when the *Guillaume* poet recounts the story of the werewolf's original metamorphosis, he specifically refers to a written source — "l'escriture" (276) and "l'escris" (293), i.e., "the writing" — twice within the space of less than twenty verses. Given the marvelous nature of the story he is about to relate, it is not surprising that he takes advantage of this literary convention in such a way.

In spite of the fact that no source has been found, a close study of *Guillaume de Palerne* reveals that it combines elements from other werewolf tales, contemporary events, and other romances. First, the romance participates in the literary tradition of medieval werewolf tales. The corpus of the *Werewolf Tale* includes two short texts written in the vernacular, Marie de France's *Bisclavret*,[10] and the anonymous *Melion*,[11] as well as one written in Latin, *Arthur and Gorlagon*.[12] The *Guillaume* poet avails himself of their motifs, playing with them, adapting them, and weaving them into the strands of Guillaume's story to create the precise literary actualization that becomes *Guillaume de Palerne*. Radically transforming the traditional image of the werewolf, the narrative literature of the twelfth and thirteenth centuries portrays the creature sympathetically as a victim, rather than as the perpetrator of violent and bloodthirsty deeds. Written against the popular image of the werewolf, they all reflect the Christian interpretation of metamorphosis with their insistence on the opposition between appearance and reality. Each narrative varies in the manner in which it plays with the tension between the human and bestial sides of the werewolf. It is in *Guillaume de Palerne*, however, that we find the fullest treat-

---

8. Dunn suggests that Yolande may have possibly provided a Latin manuscript to one of the poets working under her patronage that contained "at least the germ of the story of *Guillaume*" (38).
9. For other references in the romance to this *estoire*, see also vv. 280, 327, 8398, 9653.
10. For the French edition, see Marie de France.
11. The Old French edition can be found in *Les Lais anonymes des XIIe et XIIIe siècles*. A bilingual Old French-Modern French version can be found in *Lais féeriques des XIIe et XIIIe siècles*.
12. For an English translation of *Arthur and Gorlagon*, see Otten, 234–255.

ment of the *Werewolf Tale,* as well as the most complete metamorphosis of the werewolf. As Philippe Ménard points out, Alphonse the werewolf is "doux comme un mouton [gentle as a lamb]."[13] His werewolf identity is merely a disguise that he has been forced to wear; it never has any effect on his behavior.[14] Indeed, Guillaume and Melior see him as an agent sent by God; he is the answer to their prayers.

In addition, the poet alludes to many contemporary events and personages in the romance with which its readers/listeners would have been familiar and which would have aroused their interest. When reading or hearing of Queen Felise's predicament, trapped in Palermo and besieged by the Spanish, they would immediately have thought of Joanna, the sister of Richard the Lion Heart, who was married to King William II of Sicily. Richard and Philip Augustus, accompanied by Yolande's husband, the Count of Saint Pol, arrived in Sicily approximately one year after William's death to find the throne in the possession of Tancred, William's cousin, and Joanna being held against her will. In order to secure her release, they sacked Messina and defeated Tancred. Similarly, the werewolf's name Alphonse and the circumstances concerning Guillaume's kidnapping would have made the reader/listener think of Alfonso VIII of Castille. At the age of four, Alfonso was carried off by a servant and hidden in order to protect him from his uncle, who had seized the throne after the death of the boy's father. These and other allusions would have made *Guillaume de Palerne* a medieval "best seller."[15]

Finally, the poet was also obviously well read and very familiar with *Énéas,* Chrétien de Troye's *Cligès,* and the legend of Tristan and Iseut. His depiction of the awakening love between Guillaume and Melior is obviously heavily influenced by *Énéas* and *Cligès,* where we find the same complaints and the same physical symptoms, the same worries and the same inner debates. The poet also borrows and adapts a major plot element shared by *Tristan and Iseut* and *Cligès.* Like Tristan and Cligès who both fall in love with their uncle's wife, Guillaume falls in love with a woman who is betrothed to his uncle. Guillaume's familial tie to her fiancé is not revealed, however, until the end of the romance. More important, since Guillaume and Melior flee Rome before her marriage, their love is never adulterous.

13. See Ménard, 214.
14. For further reading on the *Werewolf Tale* and the werewolf motif in *Guillaume de Palerne,* see Kittredge, Ménard, and Sconduto (Blurred, *Metamorphosis,* 273–308; Rewriting).
15. Irene McKeehan described the romance with these words. For further information, see McKeehan, 803–806.

Content and Structure

The plot may be briefly summarized as follows: Guillaume is a young prince of Sicily who is kidnapped by a werewolf at the age of four, brought up by a cowherd, and later taken to Rome by Nathaniel, the Emperor, and given as page to his daughter Melior. After falling in love, the two young people flee Rome, disguised in bearskins and aided by the werewolf, who leads them to Palermo, where Guillaume helps Queen Felise defeat the Spanish armies besieging the city. The King of Spain, who has been captured by Guillaume, then recognizes the werewolf as his long lost son Alphonse. After he recovers his human form, Alphonse reveals Guillaume's identity as Felise's son and everyone rejoices. Guillaume marries Melior and is crowned King of Apulia and Sicily. Later, after the death of Nathaniel, Guillaume becomes the new emperor of Rome.

The following presents one possible way to divide the narrative:

vv. 1–22	Formal Prologue
vv. 23–78	The plot against Guillaume
vv. 79–186	The werewolf kidnaps Guillaume
vv. 187–260	Guillaume is found by the cowherd
vv. 261–358	The story of Alphonse, the werewolf
vv. 359–646	The emperor finds Guillaume
vv. 647–816	Guillaume becomes Melior's page
vv. 817–1782	Guillaume and Melior fall in love
vv. 1783–2562	Guillaume becomes a knight and defeats the Saxons
vv. 2563–2936	Melior is betrothed to the son of the emperor of Greece
vv. 2937–4390	Guillaume and Melior flee Rome in bearskin disguises and travel south, led and aided by the werewolf
vv. 4391–7190	Guillaume and Melior arrive in Palermo, where Guillaume helps Felise and defeats the Spanish army
vv. 7191–7982	The werewolf recovers his human form
vv. 7983–9649	Alphonse reveals Guillaume's identity; Guillaume becomes king and marries Melior
vv. 9650–9664	Informal Epilogue

Genre

Guillaume de Palerne has been categorized as a *roman d'aventure* or adventure romance. Critics who have studied the genre comment frequently on the difficulty of determining which romances belong to this category. In 1988 Daniel Poirion challenged the very concept of the *roman d'aventure* as a generic category, saying that *aventure* is an essential element in all medieval romances.[16] Nevertheless, adventure does not play the same role in each romance. Most scholars accept the *roman d'aventure* as a separate genre or subgenre, albeit loosely defined, into which they place some non–Arthurian romances. Important distinctions exist between the *roman d'aventure* and the *roman arthurien*, ones that influence heroic identity and are worth keeping. First, the Arthurian romance typically has a mythical setting that incorporates elements and creatures of the Celtic Other World, whereas the setting of the adventure romance is much more realistic and usually more specific: the poet frequently provides a specific geographical location for the romance. Second, in the Arthurian romance the adventure is deliberately undertaken as part of a quest, while in the adventure romance the *aventure* happens to the protagonists. Chance, or Providence, in the case of *Guillaume de Palerne*, is in control, rather than the hero. Third, in the Arthurian romance as typified by Chrétien de Troyes, the knight generally has two major concerns—acquiring an identity and establishing his reputation—and frequently a third—serving his lady. In the adventure romance, however, the knight is almost totally preoccupied with facing fate. The Arthurian romance focuses more on the love relationship, whereas the *roman d'aventure* concentrates on the removal of the obstacles to love and accords only an ancillary role to the relationship between the knight and his lady. The Arthurian knight, then, intentionally uses the adventure quest to prove his love for his lady and to establish or re-establish his identity; the knight in the *roman d'aventure*, however, establishes his heroic identity by the manner in which he confronts *aventure*, the unexpected hazards of life. The adventure romance thus accentuates the innocence of the protagonists and their triumph over adversity. Fourth, *aventure* plays a central role in the adventure romance by creating "narrative variety and complexity."[17] Indeed, the narration itself of the adventure may play a central role in the romance, as it does in *Guillaume de Palerne*, with its multiple retellings of Guillaume's story by various intradiegetic narrators who mirror the activity of the poet.[18] The emphasis is on what happens, rather than on the character portrayal and development depicted in Arthurian romances. Nevertheless, the protagonists of the *roman d'aventure* are not presented as caricatures; they are portrayed as textual individuals, that is, individuals within the context of

16. See Poirion, 111–112.
17. See Kelly (Fortune, 6).
18. I call the repeated renarration of an adventure the "clerical adventure."

one specific romance such as *Guillaume de Palerne*, yet they are also generic types—the hero and the heroine—since they have their counterparts in other romances.[19]

The Author's Purpose

In his prologue the poet announces a didactic purpose, declaring that he plans to reveal his knowledge so that he will not waste it:

> Que tot li mauvais puissent fondre
> Et cil qui me vaurront entendre
> I puissent sens et bien aprendre. (9–10)

> And so that all who are evil might perish
> And those who would like to hear me
> Might learn what is good and true.

Like any other work of literature, a *roman d'aventure* must entertain its listeners or they will lose interest; even so, it is much more than simply a work of fiction "simplement destinée à plaire" as Gaston Paris suggested in 1898.[20] The *Guillaume* poet sets up the protagonists of his romance as a model for others to follow and offers them a lesson; more specifically, he attempts to influence the attitudes of his audience by arguing for the willing subordination of the aristocrats to an ideal and, ultimately, to a king who embodies that ideal.[21] With its numerous examples of both positive and negative conduct, as well as its confessions, scenes of repentance, and explicit exhortations to behave properly, the romance demonstrates a noble code of behavior which combines virtue with prowess and to which knights are expected to conform. Thus the romance becomes a handbook for chivalric behavior in which the poet defines Guillaume's core identity as the ideal against which noblemen may measure themselves. Although Guillaume's virtues can best be realized in a kingly role and not every knight can be king, the romance nevertheless demonstrates that individual merit is recognized and rewarded. Paradoxically using his hero's status as a unique individual to encourage conformity and obedience, the *Guillaume* poet also demonstrates the problematic of core identity. Any deviation from the noble code, such as the lack of a noble appearance or a confirmed

19. For further information on the *roman d'aventure* and additional references, see Sconduto (*Metamorphosis*, 139–146).
20. See Paris, 760–761.
21. *La Chanson de Roland* functions similarly.

noble lineage, does not necessarily mean that the individual is not noble, nor does beauty or high birth guarantee true nobility if unaccompanied by noble behavior. Dramatizing their obsession with lineage, identity, and function at the end of the twelfth century, *Guillaume de Palerne* offers its aristocratic listeners a *miroir des princes*[22] concealed within a delightful and entertaining *aventure*. The romance not only challenges them to conform to the high standards set by Guillaume and Alphonse, but also reminds them of the unreliability of appearances and the need for thoughtful, careful interpretation.

---

22. For a detailed survey of the twelfth- and thirteenth-century moral guides and theoretical writings of John of Salisbury, Giraldus Cambrensis, Gilbert of Tournai, Thomas Aquinas, William Perrault, and Aegidius Romanus, see Born (*Education*, and "The Perfect Prince").

The Romance of Guillaume de Palerne

No one should hide or be silent
If he knows something which might please others,
But does not explain it clearly;
For he truly conceals and wastes his knowledge,
When he does not reveal it openly
In the presence of the people.
For this reason I will not hide what I know,
And so that all who are evil might perish
And those who would like to hear me
Might learn what is good and true.
For hidden wisdom which is not heard,
Is, it seems to me, exactly like
Walled-up treasures,
Which do no good nor bring no profit
As long as they are locked away.[1]
Secret knowledge is just like that:
For this reason I do not want to keep mine concealed.
Thus it pleases me to relate,
According to my understanding and my memory,
The facts of an ancient story
That happened long ago in Apulia[2]
To a king who held that land.

4
8
12
16
20

---

1. The idea that knowledge is wasted if it is hidden is a common rhetorical topos in prologues. For a discussion of this topos, see Curtius, 87–88, and Uitti, 139–141. In *Guillaume de Palerne*, however, the revelation of secret knowledge is more than a just a reason for telling the story; it is a major theme that will be developed throughout the romance.

2. Apulia, a region of southeastern Italy on the Adriatic Sea, was part of the Kingdom of Sicily.

The king was called Embron.
24   He was very powerful.
He maintained peace in his region
And he was of great renown.
Embron had as his wife a beautiful queen,
28   A gracious lady of noble birth
And the daughter of the wealthy emperor
Who held dominion over Greece.
The lady's name was Felise;
32   She was loved very much in her realm.
They had only one child,
A small boy not very big.
Four years old was the young noble lad
36   Who was wondrously beautiful.
His name was Guillaume.
Now the queen had expressly
Entrusted his care to two ladies
40   Whom she had brought from her country.
One of them was named Gloriande,
The other was called Acelone.
She ordered them to watch over him,
44   To teach him, to instruct him,
To show him and school him in the law,
As must be done for the son of a king.
In them she placed her confidence,
48   But she was horribly betrayed,
Tricked and deceived.
Just how much you will hear.

King Embron had a brother
52   Who would inherit the kingdom.
This brother gave and promised so much
To the nursemaids who were guarding the child
And pursued them and did so much for them
56   That they finally told him that they would kill the child
As well as the king himself.
They have already procured the herbal brew
From which both will receive death,
60   If God, the King of the world, does not do something.[3]

3. Notice the switch to the present tense in the last verse (60). In Old French, it is very common to find a mixture of both past and present tenses within the *(continued on next page)*

In Palermo they had been residing
For an entire month in the city,
In the company of the king and queen.
64   Beneath the principal marble tower
There was a marvelously beautiful orchard,
Completely enclosed by a wall and by cement.[4]
There were many wild beasts there.
68   Now one high feast day
The king came there to amuse himself.
His knights and his men from the city
And many barons had come there;
72   The queen herself was there.
The women who have the child in their care,
The ones whom evil inflames and the wicked fire burns,
(But in spite of this they do nothing to him)
76   Have brought him there with the other people.
If they had known the grief
That would come that day because of the child

[5]

In the orchard the king is resting in the shade
80   And the queen is very happy,
But they do not know that their great grief
Is about to appear before their very eyes.
The child is gathering flowers;
84   From one flower to another he goes playing.
At this moment they are looking at the foliage:
A great wolf jumps out, his mouth gaping open;
He comes rushing like a tempest.
88   Everyone turns away because of the beast;
Right in front of the king himself
The wolf takes his son in his mouth.
Away he goes; now the cry
92   Was raised very quickly after him.
The grieving begins, the cry is raised,

same narration, often within the same sentence. Here the use of the present tense transports the past action of the narrative into the listeners' (or reader's) present. In my translation, I respect the tense of the original when it does not sound awkward in English.

4. In medieval buildings, the thick walls of castles and city walls usually consisted of a core of rubble made of cement poured over stones and gravel, with a façade of cut stone blocks. See Newman, 49.

5. This is the first of approximately seventeen lacunas or gaps in the narrative.

For the son of the king who has been dragged off.
The queen screams over and over:

96   "Help! Help! Holy Mary!
Household of the king, what are you doing?
I will kill myself now, if he is not rescued."

The king asks for his horse
100 And has all his vassals mount up.
The whole city is in an uproar;
Each man runs there as fast as he can.
The king charges after the wolf.
104 They surround the park,
But the wolf has jumped out of it,
He had set out for the country.
The child often cries out and wails;
108 The king following him hears him.
He watches and sees the wolf go up a mountain.
The king summons his people to go there quickly;
All of them try hard then,
112 But the wolf escapes with the child.
The wolf runs off, followed by those
Who are determined to capture him;
From that spot to the Strait of Messina[6] they chase him.
116 He jumps in the water with the child
And crosses the strait. They have lost him,
The king and those who are with him.
Thus in this manner the fierce beast
120 Went off with the child.
The king turns back;
His heart is very sad and mournful
For his child that he has lost this way.
124 To the city they returned.

The queen is grieving so much
That to be dead would be her desire;
She weeps frequently and cries out and wails.
128 She describes her son with the beast:
"Son, sweet beloved," says the queen,
"With your tender, rose-colored mouth,

---

6. The Strait of Messina, which separates Sicily from mainland Italy, is three kilometers wide
at its narrowest point.

Divine, celestial creature,
132   Who would have believed that a beast or wolf
Would devour you? God, what luck!
Woe is me! Why am I alive? Why do I outlast him?
Son, where are your beautiful eyes now,
136   So beautiful, gentle and without pride,
Your noble brow and your beautiful hair,
Which all seemed to be made of fine gold,
Your tender face and your bright countenance?
140   Ah, heart, why do you not leave me?
Son, what has become of your beauty,
Your pretty body and your radiance,
Your nose, your mouth and chin,
144   And your face and your countenance,
Your beautiful arms and white hands,
And your beautiful loins and hips,
Your beautiful legs and your feet?
148   Woe is me, what grief and what a regrettable event!
Indeed you were supposed to be made
For pleasure and for desire;
Now, you are food for a werewolf,[7]
152   My child. What a horrible adventure!
But I do not believe for anything
That any savage beast might be so bold
As to dare to harm your beautiful body,
156   To wound it, make it bleed, or injure it.
I will never believe that it would please God
Nor that He would cause such cruelty to be done."

In this way, the lady torments herself;
160   In this fashion she laments for her son,
Thus she weeps for him, and so she regrets his loss.
But the king chastises her and constrains her so much
That soon he makes her set aside
164   Her grief and her expressions of mourning.
So the lady calms down.
But now it is right that I tell you
About the wolf who escaped with the child.
168   He carried him so far both day and night

---

7. Felise is the first to label the wolf a werewolf, a "leu garoul."

And crossed so much land
Until in the countryside near Rome
He stopped in a great forest
172 Where there were many savage beasts.
There he rests eight entire days.
Whatever the child needed
The noble beast provided for him;
176 Never did he experience any discomfort.
In the ground the wolf dug a den;
He carried and placed grass within it
And ferns and reeds
180 That he strewed inside.
At night next to himself
The werewolf puts the king's son to bed
And embraces him with his four paws.
184 In this manner he tamed the son of the king,
Who is pleased by everything
That the beast does for him.

A cowherd who was watching his cows
188 And who was living in that forest,
Was in the woods with his herd.
He had his dog on its leash.
Coming back from pasture at night,
192 The dog catches the scent of the child and sniffs.
He barks so much that the cowherd shouts and releases him.
The child, who had come out of the den,
Had such a fright
196 That he darted back inside.
The werewolf had gone in search of food;
The child had remained behind all alone.
When he hears the dog barking so,
200 He is very frightened;
He cries out so loudly
That the whole forest resounds with his voice.

When the cowherd hears the child,
204 He runs in that direction;
He hears him crying in the laurel grove
And he marvels greatly.
He really thinks and believes that the child was left there

208   By a beast who had carried him off.
       He bends down over the child and calls to him;
       He cajoles and caresses him repeatedly.
       So gently does he entice him
212   That away with him goes the son of the king.
       The cowherd picks him up in his arms
       And then he leaves quickly;
       To his house he returned.
216   Never did anyone see greater joy
       Than that demonstrated by the cowherd's wife.
       She asks the child his name and he told her
       That Guillaume was his name.
220   The virtuous woman and honest man[8]
       Are very happy because of him and give him a good welcome.
       They set great store by him and praise
       The beauty with which he is so endowed.
224   They had never had a child.
       They say now that they will make him their heir;
       Thus he will have their land and their manor.
       So they said. But now hear
228   About the wolf who had returned
       With the meat that he went in search of
       In the villages and through the land
       For the child; he had so much meat
232   That he carried it with great difficulty.
       When he did not find the child,
       Never did any man born of a mother
       See a beast demonstrate such grief.
236   Whoever might have heard him shriek and howl
       And see him wring his feet together,
       Bite and plunge his mouth into the ground,
       Tear out and scratch the grass,
240   Lie down and get up again,
       And see how he is almost dying of chagrin and how over-
           whelmed he is,
       How he searches low and searches high,
       Tears flowing from his eyes,

---

8. The cowherd is referred to as "li preudom," his wife "la preude feme." *Preudom* was often used as a synonym for noble in the courtly romance. In other romances these terms would normally be reserved for nobles. In *Guillaume de Palerne*, however, *preudom* also acquires the connotation of a nobility of virtue that is indifferent to social rank.

244   That person might well have said that such great grief
Had never been expressed by any other beast.
Then he jumped into the marsh
And put his nose to the ground;
248   Just exactly as the child had gone,
From that spot to where the peasant took him,
The wolf follows him full of rage.
He charged after him at such a high speed
252   That he came to the house
Where the child had been carried.
Through an opening in the wall
He looked and he saw him;
256   They had seated him next to the fire.
They are caressing him with their hands,
Both the cowherd and his wife.
They do for him whatever they might think
260   He wants and they give to him whatever they might have.

         When the werewolf sees the child
And that they are making him very happy,
That he will be well cared for
264   And that he is staying with a good host,
He is very happy about it and shows his great joy.
The werewolf bows down low and goes on his way,
I know not where, off on his adventure.
268   May the King of all creatures
Preserve him from evil and from sorrow!
Now you can hear about him,
Who he was and what he became,
272   And how it all happened.
No one has ever heard such a marvel!
The werewolf that I am telling you about
Was not at all a beast by nature.
276   As the writing tells it,[9]
He was formerly a man and the son of a king.
I can tell you why,
How it happened to him and who did it.
280   So, as the story tells us,
He was the son of the king of Spain,

---

9. The poet first alludes to his source, an ancient story, in verse 20. This allusion to a written source adds authority to his narrative.

The firstborn of his wife.
His mother had died giving birth to him;
284 The king his father took a new wife,
The daughter of the king of Portugal.
Now that lady knew trickery and evil very well;
Much sorcery and magic
288 She had learned from her childhood.
Well I know that she was named Brande.
By many people was she praised.
By her lord she had one son,
292 A handsome young man, noble and generous.
His name was Brandin; so says the writing.
He was young in age and small.
Hear now what that wicked woman did.
296 She saw how her stepson would reign;
She has such a strong hatred for him
That she will take away his life, if she can,
Or she will put him in such a position
300 That he will never rule the kingdom.
She anoints his body with an ointment
Which was very strong and powerful;
It was so very potent that
304 As soon as the child was anointed with it
His condition and appearance changed;
A wolf he became and he was transformed into a beast.
At once he became a werewolf;
308 Everything that was visible of him
He has lost, he believes.
He wants to flee immediately,
For he knows very well that if he is taken now
312 He will not escape and might be killed.
But before he leaves that land
Against his stepmother he begins a war;
Toward her he runs, his mouth stretched open.
316 He would have hurt Brande had her people not run to her;
From death they truly protected her.
Now with a shout
They assail the wolf in order to kill him;
320 They are angrily shouting and chasing him.
Making a great deal of noise throughout the city,
They pursue him more than three miles from town.

The wolf, who is truly making haste, escapes;
324 He exerts himself and pushes himself so much
That with great effort he gets away from them.
And so they followed him from early in the morning to late at
    night until,
Just as I find in this story,
328 To Apulia after one season came
The one that you hear me talking about.
Tired he was and in great pain.
He had been in that land for two years
332 Where he grew very fierce, strong, and big.
He found out about the guilty deed and the serious wrong
That was to be done to the son of the king
By his uncle, that treacherous thief,
336 To his nephew and his brother.
He could not tolerate this great suffering,
Nor the arrogance of the traitor.
Because of this he kidnapped the child,
340 Just as you have already heard.

At this moment I want to leave him;
Well we know how to come back there later.
Another time we will return to him,
344 When the moment is right. But now we will talk
About the son of the king, about the young nobleman
That those people are raising well
And are doing whatever they can do for him
348 That should be useful or pleasing to him
And just exactly as they would do
If he were their own child.
The more he grows and the more perfect he becomes,
352 The more they find themselves caring about him.
And the child serves them with such gentleness,
As if they were his mother and his lord;
For he truly believed that the cowherd was his father
356 And that the cowherd's wife was his mother.
Oh, God! How his condition has changed
From that of the king's son that he was supposed to be!

They took good care of him for seven years;
360 He was already both very virtuous and very tall

And he was marvelously noble and beautiful.
To the fields would go the young nobleman
With his father the cowherd,
364 Who loved him very much and cherished him.
He already knew very well how to watch his beasts,
How to drive them ahead and turn them around
And lead them to better pasture.
368 He knew more than any other man about archery
And how to shoot and hunt and use a bow and arrow.
At night when he returns to their dwelling,
The young gentleman comes back all laden down
372 With hares, with rabbits, with birds,
And with partridges and pheasants.
He was loved very much by all the children,
For when he had taken his birds,
376 For his own amusement and because of his merit
He would give them immediately to his companions.
Never did he keep any for his own use
Until all those who were
380 In his company had some.
He was very good to them and very loyal
And he did it very willingly.
Therefore the sermon is true, according to which nature
384 Tests all creatures
In a suitable manner according to its own purpose.
So the child was in the grove
Where his father kept his cows,
388 Until one day when the emperor
Who then governed Rome
Came to that forest to hunt.
This time he took along
392 With him many people from his household,
But very soon they had left him alone
Because they had seen a boar
That the dogs, who were hunting
396 In that forest, had pursued.
They had all wandered so far away from him,
The men on horse and those on foot,
That he cannot hear anything at all of them,
400 Neither the clamor of the dogs nor the blowing of horns.

So he was going through the forest
Carefully listening to see if he could hear
The baying of the dogs or the sounding of the horns,
404   For he was not at all pleased
That he had been left behind alone this way.
On a path he stopped.
Just at this moment while he is totally alone there,
408   Here comes the werewolf
Chasing a stag in front of him;
He is following closely on the heels of the stag
And the emperor runs after them.
412   He followed as fast as he could
Until by chance he came upon the child.
He does not know what has become of
Either the stag or the werewolf,
416   So he turns to the boy with great chagrin.
The emperor looks at him and stops.
With great wonder he made the sign of the cross
Because of the child's beauty, his appearance,
420   And because of his noble countenance.
He marvels who the boy might be,
Who his people are and what their situation is.
He believes that the child might be an enchanted creature
424   Because he sees him alone in that place.
Very kindly he speaks to him
And he says to him very gently:
"What is your name, good brother?
428   — Guillaume, my lord." — And the emperor
Said to him: "And whose son are you?
— In the name of God, my lord, who made us all,
Do not trouble yourself, please:
432   A cowherd of this forest,
Whose cows these are that I am watching here."
Said the emperor: "Where is he, in what direction?
Have him speak to me now.
436   — No I will not, my lord. — And why not?
— Because I know not what you want,
Who you are or what you are seeking,
Or if you want anything that is not good.
440   — May God never pardon me,
Beautiful sweet friend," says the emperor,

"If there be any trouble or difficulty for your father.
Now be completely reassured and go to him at once.
444   — My lord," said the boy, "I will, happily."
As fast as he could he ran to him.
"Good father," says he, "get up,
And come here to a lord
448   Who is asking for you right now.
Never anyone more handsome than him have I seen.
— Did you tell him that I was here?"
Says the cowherd who is very displeased.
452   "Yes, dear sir. — A curse
On you when you thought it
And when you informed him about me!"
Said the cowherd to the son of the king.
456   And the boy responded: "My lord, why?
Indeed now you are very wrong;
An oath he made to me so strong
That, in order that God might pardon him,
460   Never will you have anything but great profit from this."
When the emperor hears them,
Toward them he quickly went.
The cowherd gets up to greet the emperor,
464   Very troubled and grieving
From what the boy had told him.
The emperor spoke to him
And said: "Cowherd, do you know me?"
468   And the honest man[10] responded:
"No, my lord, so help me God,
I have never set eyes on you before.
— Do you not know the emperor?
472   — No, my lord, in the name of the Creator,
I am not able to go near enough to him
That I might be able to recognize him;
I have never yet seen him."
476   The emperor said: "You see me here;
It is he who is speaking to you.
Now I beg of you, by the faith
That you owe to your most prized possession,
480   Tell me if you fathered this child,

10. "li preudom"

Whose son he is, yours or another's,
And, so that you might rejoice for him,
Who raised him; tell me honestly.
484   I want to know the truth about him."

    The cowherd trembles with fear
When he hears the emperor speak,
Whom he had never seen before.
488   Trembling all over, he responded,
For this honest man truly fears
That the emperor might not keep his word.
He stepped back a bit from him
492   And said: "Good sire, if it pleases you,
I will tell you the truth about him.
In this forest I found him
Rather close to where we are now.
496   It has been seven years or even more
Since I brought him to my house,
For I found him completely unguarded.
And we kept him and raised him
500   Since never did I hear news
In a village, or town, or castle
Of anyone asking for this young man.
Never has there been a creature that was more noble,
504   As long as the heavens and the earth have existed,
Better brought up or more courtly,
More obliging in all situations,
More generous or more gentle
508   In the entire sanctuary
Of the esteemed Saint Peter of Rome.
Now I have told you the story
Exactly as it happened."
512   The emperor responded:
"You have done well, my good sir.[11]
You will receive a good reward
Before many days pass.
516   But now tell me what garments
He was wearing when you found him,
What he was clothed in and how the fabric was made.

11. The emperor refers to the cowherd as a "preudom."

— Sire," he says, "truly the most beautiful

520   That ever had any young nobleman.

Entirely vermilion with flowers

And a great number of stripes of gold around it.

No man ever saw anything more beautiful."

524   The emperor told him

That he wants to take the child with him

And the cowherd, who is grieving greatly about it

But does not dare contradict him, responds

528   That he may do as he wants as lord,

Whatever he pleases and whatever he desires.

The child marvels very much

When he hears that he is not at all

532   The son of the cowherd; tears flow from his eyes

And he weeps out of great tenderness.

Said the emperor lovingly:

"Dear Guillaume, do not fear

536   That you will not have enough wealth and honor.[12]

But mount up here, do not delay,

Behind me on my charger.

Thus we will leave, for I have been here too long."

540   And Guillaume responds: "Sire, thank you.

I do not know indeed what I should do.

I do not want to harm my lord,

Or my lady at home.

544   — Oh yes you will go, son," said the honest man,[13]

For great good can come to you from it.

So be ready to merit it;

And to do whatever he wants

548   And everything that you know

That one must do at such a high court.

So be noble and gentle

And obliging and moderate;

552   Do not be arrogant

Or outrageous, treacherous or proud

And make yourself loved by all.

Do not rid from your right side

556   Anyone more esteemed than you in court,

---

12. My translation is based on Michelant's edition, since the verse was omitted from Micha's edition. The verse numbered 536 in Micha's edition is actually verse 537.

13. Again, the cowherd is being referred to as "li preudom."

So that together you might well prevent
You from being in the wrong or at fault there.
Watch your words and what you say
560 So that you will not be attacked
And so that no man in the street or on the square
Might be able to blame you.
To the poor humble yourself
564 And against the rich help them.
In such a high imperial court
Some vassals are very sly.
Many truly want their words,
568 Be they wise or foolish,
To be well-received, to be heard,
Held dear and savored.
Let no one there catch you in the wrong;
572 But let them find you strong in the right.
You will not find anyone who will teach it to you.
Sweet son, in the name of God, remember.
My father heard this account told.
576 In his time he served a count;
For a long time he was in his household,
And he often told me this sermon.
I have told it to you; now remember it.
580 May this God who makes the whole world His
Keep watch over you." Then he takes leave.
They are tenderly crying out of pity,
The young nobleman and the cowherd.
584 And the boy tells him: "Dear sweet sir,
Say goodbye for me to my gentle lady.
May God watch over you and make restitution to your souls
For the nurturing that both of you have
588 So loyally given me.
I truly believed that I was your son,
In the name of the Lord who caused me to be born.
And if ever God in his pleasure
592 Consents that honor come to me,
You will not have raised me in vain.
Say goodbye for me to Huet the dwarf
To Hugenet and Aubelot
596 To Martinet the son of Heugot,
And to Akarin and Crestiien

And to Thumassin the son of Paien
And to all my other companions."
600 When the emperor hears the names,
He laughs heartily because of them and is very joyous.
He makes Guillaume mount and then goes on his way.

Through the forest he wanders
604 And the cowherd remains behind crying
For the boy whom he sees leaving
That the emperor is taking away.
His heart is greatly saddened because of it.
608 To his wife he returned,
His cheeks all wet
From hot tears and from the news,
Because of which he is moaning very much and is devastated.
612 The cowherd tells his wife exactly
How the emperor took away the boy.
She is distraught with grief and almost loses her mind
When she hears his news.
616 Very tenderly she mourns for him,
His great beauty and his kindness,
His prowess and his generosity,
His great intelligence and his moderation.
620 Very much did she curse this adventure,
That the emperor had taken him away in this way.
Because of everything she might have killed herself and died;
Never would her mouth have eaten another bite,
624 If her husband had not comforted her;
He told her about the emperor,
Who in a short time without long delay,
Was supposed to give them what they merited.
628 Never another day will they experience poverty.

Thus she puts her mind at rest.
The emperor meandered haphazardly
Through the forest
632 With the child who was behind him
Until he found the men from his household.
They were burdened and laden down now
With four wild boar that they had taken;
636 They had already set off on their return,

When they saw approaching
The emperor with the child
That he was carrying behind him.
640   Because of the great beauty that he had
Most of them marvel
And they ask the emperor
Where he had taken such a prey.
644   "My lords, God, who does not forget me,
Through His mercy gave him to me."
Then they all got under way.

       To Rome they returned straightaway.
648   The emperor had a daughter
Who was called Melior.
Never before was there anyone born of woman
More beautiful or more clever.
652   She was even of about the same age
As Guillaume might well be.
Very courtly and honest was she,
Full of generosity and honor.
656   At this moment behold the emperor
Who gives the child to her as a present.
Melior is grateful and thanks him
More than one hundred times and begs of him,
660   If it pleases him, to tell her
Where this young man was taken,
Who is so very noble and beautiful,
And if he was the son of a king or duke or count.
664   And the emperor recounts to her
How God had sent the boy to him
And that all his men had left him alone
And had abandoned him,
668   And how he met the child by chance
Because of a wolf that was chasing a stag,
How the boy was in the forest watching
The cows of a good man,[14]
672   How he told him the story
Of exactly how he had found the child,
And also dressed well

14. Here the emperor again refers to the cowherd as ".I. preudome." It is significant that the person occupying the top of the social hierarchy appears to be erasing social distinctions.

In rich cloth beaten with gold,
676   Just as if he were the son of King Alphinor
Who is the sovereign and king of Hungary,
Who is so very abundantly wealthy.
And how then at that time
680   He was not more than four years old,
How he was raised by him for seven full years,
And that the peasant[15] grieved exceedingly
When he took the child away.
684   He told her absolutely everything and recounted it to her
Just as he had heard it spoken,
And how the child had begged the cowherd
To say goodbye for him to his mother who had raised him
688   And to all his companions also,
And how he named each one by name.
"Daughter, Guillaume is the name
Of the young man," says the emperor.
692   "I believe by the venerable holy Father
That he is from a very high lineage,
For he is both very handsome and noble
In body, in face and in comportment.
696   We may still hear perchance
From what people he was issued and born.
My sweet daughter, now provide for
This child whom I bring to you here.
700   —Let great thanks be yours for this,"
Said Melior, "good father dear,
"I will take him on very gladly."
Then she takes the child and leads him
704   Into her own chamber.
She has some garments brought to her
And has him dressed and outfitted.

When he was appareled in the clothing
708   And garbed in shoes and hose to her liking,
Then so courtly and so handsome
And so noble was the young man
That one would not find his equal

---

15. Here the emperor re-establishes the social hierarchy with his use of the term "li vilains," which stands in marked contrast to his earlier use of "preudom(e)" as well as his reference to King Alphinor and the child's clothing.

712   In beauty or appearance
        Beneath the brightness of the sun.
        Melior, who is so very noble,
        Had one of her servants
716   Bring him a meal,
        Which he ate because he was hungry.
        Now he returns a bit to what is suitable for him;
        Because, if he is the son of a king,
720   There is no dishonor, as I believe it,
        If he serves at the emperor's court
        And a maiden of such worth
        As was the beautiful Melior.
724   Thus Guillaume remained with
        The maiden, as you can hear.
        He truly endeavors to serve her
        And others all in the same way;
728   He learns to do it very graciously,
        Just as the man who was not at all
        Raised at court or in the middle of a great household,
        But Nature reveals his qualities.[16]
732   And he, more than any other creature,
        Tries hard and wants to put his whole heart into
        Whatever must be undertaken by
        Any young nobleman in service
736   At a court so high and so rich.

            The child truly put his heart into it
        And was so attentive and learned so much
        That before the year had passed
740   He was so expert and knowledgeable
        That there was no man who could reproach him,
        As much as he might watch and be attentive
        For anything that he could see,
744   Since Guillaume did nothing wrong nor did he dishonor him-
            self.

---

16. Guillaume's true character, his nature, is revealed by his actions. In spite of having been raised in a peasant environment, Guillaume's nobility and high birth will reveal itself. In the debate in medieval literature between nature and nurture, the poet clearly positions himself on the side of the former and agrees with the proverb "Meulz vaut nature que nurreture" ("Nature takes precedence over upbringing"). See Morawski, no. 1273. For further reading on the courtly treatment of the topos in medieval literature, see Berkvam, 73–95; Cosman; Frappier; and Kennedy.

For a long time you have heard it said
That birds of noble birth
Train themselves all alone
748   Entirely without the correction of others.[17]
As you will hear now,
Guillaume educated himself in exactly the same way.

     So Guillaume is at court.
752   In everything he merits that others honor him,
For he does nothing which might displease.
He is very noble and gentle,
Obliging, courtly and virtuous.
756   He makes himself loved very much by everyone
And is generous with all that he has.
And know this well, there was no need
To chastise him for his words
760   For being disagreeable or foolish;
For they were always well placed and charming.
And he knows more about chess and backgammon,
More about birds, the woods, and hunting
764   Than anyone who might be in Lombardy.
Nor is there anyone in all the territory of Rome,
Whether he be a valet, the son of a great man,
Or by birth a rich prince,
768   When Guillaume sits on a horse,
His shield at his neck and his lance in his fist,
Who is as fierce in appearance,
As noble or as skillful as he.
772   I do not know what more I can tell you,
Except that all seem to be peasants compared to him,
Both the Lombards and the Romans.
He truly seems to be the sovereign of everyone;
776   In the entire realm and empire
There is not a single person, of low or high condition

Who possesses, of this I boast,
His qualities, which are recounted by the people.
780   Each one speaks of them and tells stories about him.
All the people with a common accord,

17. The narrator is referring to the proverb "Oisiax debonaire par soi s'afaite" ("The noble-born bird educates itself"). See Morawski, no. 1434.

And the emperor in a similar manner,
Honors him, loves him and holds him as dear
784   As if he were the son of his own wife.
When he goes out for amusement,
He always takes Guillaume with him;
For great events or on an errand,
788   He always goes along, whether near or far.
And those of the realm all around,
The great lords and the barons,
Out of love for the emperor
792   Love him and bear him great honor,
And still even more because of his generosity,[18]
For which each one praises him and values him so much.
And what could I say about the maidens,
796   The ladies and the damsels?
Indeed, and if God might give me joy,
I believe that there is none who might see him
Or might hear his praises told,
800   As high as her condition might be,
However beautiful, courteous or esteemed,
However noble her lineage,
And however wise, proud, and gracious,
804   Who would not value being his sweetheart.

He has a very good reputation throughout the country;
His renown spreads everywhere.
So Guillaume was at court three full years
808   Among the Romans
As you have heard me say.
The young man grew well
And became strong and handsome,
812   Robust, of beautiful stature, and fair.
In the chamber he is wonderfully accomplished;
The maidens above all else
Because of his nobility of character and his valor
816   Bestow on him great honor.

When the sweet Melior
Hears recounted the praises of the valet

---

18. Guillaume's generosity is one of the essential attributes recommended for noblemen in the twelfth- and thirteenth-century *miroirs des princes*.

And the great qualities that are in him
820   And sees that there is none so fair in the world,
Nor is there a youth with his merit,
Whether he be son of king or emperor,
Nor of such great renown,
824   All her heart and her thoughts
She immediately turns toward him.
Now she is so very pensive and sad
That she does not pay attention to anything else.
828   She accuses and blames and reprimands her heart
And often says: "Heart, what is wrong with you?
What have you looked at or seen?
What have my eyes shown to you or done
832   That you have pushed me into such a state
That I do not know what might be wrong with me
Or what burning desire makes me suffer so
And complain more than I am wont?
836   God, what malady is it from which I am suffering so,
Which makes me stretch so much
And sigh and yawn
And become cold and hot,
840   Change color and perspire
And tremble all over in such a way,
As if I were taken with fever?[19]
I am truly transformed into another state;
844   And when this malady pains me the most,
It is when I hear named the one
Who cannot be compared to anyone else.
Truly there has been of his stature,
848   As long as the world has been turning,
No other young man, it seems to me.
Nor is there any angel in paradise as beautiful
As he is, to my knowledge.
852   I marvel about this so much
That I always carry his image inscribed

---

19. Melior is of course experiencing symptoms of Ovid's *amour-maladie* ("love-sickness"). For other romance lovers who have suffered from this same illness, see Lavine and Énéas in *Énéas*, vv. 8073–80, 8919–34; Soredamors, Alixandre, Fenice and Cligès in Chrétien de Troyes' *Cligès*, vv. 456–57, 533–35, 2954–59, 2971–72; and Galeran and Fresne in *Galeran de Bretagne*, vv. 1327–55, 1511–27. At the time of Lucien Foulet's edition of *Galeran de Bretagne*, the romance was attributed to Jean Renart, but the identity of the author is now in question. The narrator calls himself Renaut in the text. In my bibliography, *Galeran de Bretagne* is listed under Renaut.

Inside my heart, so enmeshed there
That I am not powerful enough or strong enough
856   To be able to tear it out.
Above all, I do not have the will
Even though I have the ability,
To throw or tear it out,
860   While it torments me and harms me.
Rather it pleases me that it be so.
Therefore I am wrong to blame
My heart for anything, it seems to me.
864   Who therefore? My eyes that put my heart there
On that path and led it there,
From whence comes this lament to me here
And this burning desire that I feel.
868   And yet I am wrong to complain about my eyes.
Why? Because: they have no culpability.
Who therefore? The heart to which they belong.
Are they my heart's? Yes, in truth,
872   And they do everything according to its will;
They are its servants and its envoys.
In this they are so well taught and wise
That they will do nothing
876   If the heart has not previously summoned them.
Therefore I really ought to leave them in peace
And seek reparation for these damages
From my heart, which wounds me this way
880   Because of its pride, because of its nobility,
And resists so against me.
God, how foolish and weak I am
That I deign to seek no reparation,
884   Since I myself do not undertake it!
Do I not have my heart under my jurisdiction?
Do I not have sovereign authority over it?
Do I not have such great power over it
888   That if it does me harm or torments me
I might take reparations for it?
No. Why? Because I have put myself too much
Into my heart's power and have abandoned myself.
892   I do not know why I am controlled so much
That I cannot hide anything from it.
Now I belong to my heart; it is my lord.

Thus I must do its will.

896   And I know well that
        If the people of my country find out,
        I will certainly be strongly blamed for it.[20]

            I am certainly destroyed and beaten down;
900   Fortune has really confounded me.
        It has truly taken me from high to low,
        When my servant and my valet
        I have made my lord and myself his slave.
904   I have fallen on the wheel[21]
        Without being able to get up again, so I believe,
        If the one to whom my entire heart
        Gives itself has no pity for me."
908   In this way she reproaches herself
        And then says: "Now I am very wrong
        To blame Adventure
        When I am trapped and abandoned,
912   For I have pulled down on myself the net
        That I threw to capture another.
        Now I am taken there and there I am caught;
        I have fallen into my own trap.
916   God, how weak and mistaken I am
        When I complain about what is pleasing to me,
        And grieve about my health,
        And am angry about my joy!
920   There where my heart draws and pulls me
        I must go without long delay:
        It is to the most fair and to the best
        Who ever was or ever might be.
924   Therefore my heart is right and correct when
        It bows down to him and is drawn toward him.
        So I pardon my heart for all the misdeeds
        And the distress and all the sorrow

20. In this passage replete with feudal imagery, the poet presents Melior's heart as a prideful vassal who has disobeyed her and caused her great harm. Heart can also be read here as a metaphoric double of Guillaume, who is also a servant. This analogy continues in the next five verses, with both her heart and Guillaume playing the role of the servant who has changed positions with her.

21. Melior is referring to the Wheel of Fortune. Using the image to convey both the reversal in Melior's situation and the vacillating nature of her mood, the poet reveals, without equivocation, the depths to which the emperor's daughter feels she has sunk as a helpless victim of Fortune and Love.

928   That I was complaining about.
       According to his will I now speak and command,
       For I am ready henceforth
       To do all that pleases him.
932   But I do not know how the young man
       Might know it. Who will tell him?
       Never indeed will he know it from me.
       And if it were perchance
936   I might be heard without compromise
       And if I should be so outrageous and so foolish
       As to address a word to him,
       Then I do not know what I ought to say to him.
940   If I say that I am sick,
       If I reveal the burning desire that possesses me
       And how it has hold of me and is making me suffer,
       Then my situation will worsen, or so I believe.
944   "Damsel, this grieves me."
       How could he respond otherwise?
       Now my ship sails without a rudder.
       Thus it drifts through the high seas,
948   Navigating without a mast and without a sail.
       May God allow it to come to a good port!"
       Thus, as you can hear,
       The beauty torments herself.
952   What she said she now denies again
       And says that she never had him in her thoughts;
       Her heart is so troubled
       That what she has said she immediately
956   Says she never saw or perceived.
       What once pleased her, she now refuses
       And then tries to conceal her declaration.
       The person that she holds most dear
960   She pushes further away.
       Therefore she begins to chastise herself more
       And she frequently reprimands herself.
       She does not know what is tormenting her.
964   Thus she is on such a path
       That she does not know which one to take.
       But finally, whatever might come to pass,
       She says that without fail she will take the path
968   Toward which her heart is drawn and expends all its efforts,

And that now she never wants to step away from it.
In this manner Melior laments.

Thus for a long time she leads such a life.
972   So her body suffers great pain
And she loses her appetite for drinking and eating;
The maiden begins to fast
And she does not sleep.
976   She loses the color from her cheeks,
Which had been so bright red and beautiful.
She puts all her effort into thinking
And from that is pleased and soothed.
980   Oftentimes her cousin,
A maiden by the name of Alixandrine
Who is the daughter of a count of Lombardy,
Speaks to her.
984   She frequently appeals to Melior
And says: "My dear sweet friend,
Because I see you so
Colorless and so very pale and wan,
988   I am touched by a malady so great
That my whole heart trembles and is overwhelmed.
Dear, in the name of God, the King of the world,
What is wrong with you? What can it be that troubles you so?
992   Before I truly believed I was the one
Maiden of all those who are here inside the palace,
Indeed of all the maidens in the world,
Who would know your business,
996   Or even a need, if it were given credence by you.
On top of everything, says the young noblewoman,
I am your close cousin,
Your confidant, your friend,
1000 And I have always taken care of you.
Thus I truly marvel that you have
Concealed from me this great malady that you have,
Which is destroying you in every way.
1004 But never fear,
If there is something which merits being hidden,
No man will ever know it by me.
Tell me what is wrong,
1008 Just as you would to the one whom you well know

Would try to obtain absolutely everything
For your great profit, if she could,
And very gladly for your honor,
1012   So that God might give me His love."
When the beautiful Melior
Hears the words of the maiden
Who promises her so much and wishes so much for her
1016   And offers to serve her
As much as she could in this world,
She breathes a long sigh from deep in her heart.

With a very good heart she looked at Alixandrine,
1020   For greatly pleasing and agreeable are
The words that she has heard.
So Melior replies: "My sweet friend,
Beautiful cousin, sweet dear,
1024   I am in truth terribly
Tormented by a very great malady.
But you are so good and wise
And noble and worthy and courteous;
1028   And I know well that you are truly grieving
About this malady which so strongly afflicts me,
So I will tell you all my heart now.
But I truly believe, when you know it
1032   That immediately you will think less of me
And perchance you will be right.
This malady, which is disfiguring me
And destroying me so,
1036   I cannot say anything more about it except
That a thought has come to me
Which is torturing and bothering me so much
That it is causing me to lose sleep
1040   And to totally stop eating,
Thus changing my color and making me quite sick.
Dear friend, I would like to tell you absolutely everything
And to whom I am attracted and drawn:
1044   To the youth, to the young gentleman
Who is so very virtuous and courtly,
And noble, generous, and honest,
And the one whom everyone adores.
1048   Indeed, so help me God,

Every day it seems that I see him.
I do not know how to turn from his path
Nor can I avoid him,
1052 Because immediately I find him in front of my eyes.
Thus my body is joined so tightly to him
And my heart is so attached to his
That I cannot in any way
1056 Separate them or pull them apart;
I have grievously suffered many times about it,
But my body and heart have turned me so upside down
That they deign to do nothing for me;
1060 They are so contrary to me in all things
That they refuse all that pleases me
And what I want to hide they declare:
They go about saying what I want to conceal,
1064 There they wound me where I suffer;
They want what cannot be
And neglect what must be done;
They seek for me that which is harmful to me.
1068 That is the malady that is destroying me,
That is imprisoning and manipulating me
And making me so pale and weak.
I marvel greatly what it can be.
1072 Sweet friend, in the name of God the heavenly King,
Now you know my heart, now counsel me
About this ardent desire, about this trouble,
Just as you know that one must do
1076 And as you have heard me describe it."

Alixandrine was very pensive and contemplative;
She knows and sees very well the explanation for
What Melior said and revealed to her.
1080 She was quiet for a while and then she answered
Like a truly thoughtful woman:
"Melior, my well-born lady,
For the love of God and for His cross,
1084 Now do not be in such a fright
Nor in such fear nor in such agitation.
I know an herb that I have:
If only one time
1088 You see it and try it

From the sweetness of the root
You would be completely healed and cured,
Free from this malady and at ease
1092   All the days that you would have to live."
She does not want to tell Melior anything else
For she does not dare
Blame her lady's desire or her will.
1096   She would first like to know, if she can,
The sentiments of the young man,
Like one who is truly very wise
And virtuous and endowed with goodness.
1100   And Melior above all else
Begs her and tells her to hurry
And to procure this herb for her
And bring her its medicine
1104   Or otherwise she will be dead,
Know this, very soon.
And Alixandrine very gladly
Promised her that she would do it all.
1108   In this way they ended their conversation.

        Now they did not say anything more at that time.
Alixandrine was truly in a state of great agitation,
For she did not know what she could do
1112   Nor how she might attract the attention of
The young man so that he might know
The heart, the thoughts, the desires
Of the emperor's daughter
1116   Who is in such painful uncertainty because of him;
But soon he will learn it, I believe.
Now hear what happened one night
To Guillaume, when he was lying
1120   In his bed, and while the young man
Was sleeping alone without any companions:
Thus there came to him in a dream
Right in front of him, in his presence,
1124   The semblance of a being appeared.
No man has ever seen one better made
Better sculpted or drawn,
As colorful or as beautiful.
1128   It was in the form of a maiden,

Except for an instant
Her beautiful eyes were sad and tearful
And her face was wet with tears.
1132   She said to him, or so it seemed to him:
"My love, my love, look at me,
I have come here before you;
Open your arms, receive my body,
1136   I am the beautiful Melior
Who is beseeching your mercy and pleading
That you make me your sweetheart.
To your nobility I abandon my whole
1140   Body for your service and mine.
Receive my love without opposition,
For otherwise without much delay
I will die, for I will not be able to live
1144   If I do not have your love and you do not have mine."
Then he was kissing her, it seemed to him,
Her mouth and nose and eyes and face;
And in such a way,
1148   As if he held her openly
Naked flesh to naked flesh in his arms,
He is kissing her face again,
Her white neck and her breast.
1152   But he saves the honor of the young girl, for
Often he embraces his pillow,
When he believes he is kissing Melior;
Often between his arms he took it,
1156   Often he pressed it against his chest,
Often times he hugs it and kisses it,
He does not know which place pleases him most;
But he uses all his efforts and behaves in such a way,
1160   And trembles and carries on and stretches
That he is awakened and aroused.
For quite a while afterward it seems to him
That the pillow that he is holding
1164   Might be the beauty herself.
Often times he embraced it,
Pressed it, hugged it, kissed it,
Forty times, I believe, and more,
1168   Before he realized what he was doing.

When he perceives that it is not at all her,
Then his joy is changed for him;
To the contrary it is turned for him
1172 From where joy had led him,
Now he has nothing except anger and torment.
Then at that moment he feels around him
At his bedside, at its feet and its side,
1176 To see if the beauty might not be hidden there
To mock him, for he still does not believe
That she herself is not there;
And when he sees that he is seeking in vain
1180 And that it was a dream and deception
Illusion, nothing, just vanity,
At his bedside he leaned on his elbows
And marveled what it was.
1184 For quite a while he kept silent
And then the young man said
"Glorious Father Jesus Christ,
Lord and Master of the whole world,
1188 Where am I, and what can it be?
Who was it that spoke to me?
Then was this not the daughter of King
Nathaniel, the emperor?
1192 Yes, if I have the honor,
It was certainly she.
Did she not indeed tell me
That I should take her in my arms?
1196 Yes, may God forgive me,
And that she would become my sweetheart
Or otherwise she would not heal.
It was she, that is no lie.
1200 No it was not. Why? Now this is a dream
And while sleeping it came to me
What I believe to have seen.
It was a dream, now I truly know it:
1204 She would not come to me for anything.
Would she come? Not really: why would she?
God, what madness there is in me!
How my heart is full of great rage
1208 Who has ever been so presumptuous,
Who has dared to feel such desire

For the daughter of the emperor
And my lady herself!

1212 She is no common girl or peasant girl,
But the one whom no one in this empire,
Whatever he might be able to say
However powerful he might be,

1216 Rich in land or in possessions,
Would ever be able to triumph over
Whatever he might be able to do,
So much that he would not know how to recover from it:

1220 Therefore I must indeed set aside
And abandon this great desire
Which can harm me rather than help me;
Especially since I am the kind of man

1224 That does not know whose son I am
Nor from what land I was taken and born.
Thus I must be much more careful
Than those who are on their own lands

1228 And whose good friends are there with them.

If something happened because of me and
If word of this went out
Which might cause trouble at court,

1232 I would not find my friends
Nor my relatives who for love of me
Would speak to the emperor
About anything which might be bothering him.

1236 Thus I must be much more careful,
Take back my heart and instruct it
Turn it from its path and redirect it,
So that I might not undertake something

1240 For which the emperor might blame me and not be sympa-
    thetic.

Thus Guillaume corrects himself
For he truly believes he is on another path
And that he is aiming his heart elsewhere

1244 And extinguishing the fire that is burning.
But whatever he might be able to do
He cannot withdraw his heart
From the path that it has begun,

1248   Whether it be wise or foolish,
        Whether bad or good, whatever might come from it,
        He has to hold himself to this path
        That he does not want to abandon for another,
1252   Whoever must live or die because of it,
        Whatever anyone might say or not;
        Thus he makes a comparison of himself
        And says: "I seem like the wild boar:
1256   When he sees the lance turn toward him,
        He heads straight that way;
        So he hurries forward and throws himself on the spit,
        Just as one who does not fear death,
1260   So that the lance completely pierces his entrails
        And separates his heart from his chest,
        And he drops dead elsewhere.
        It is just the same with me:
1264   I am on the lance and on the spit,
        So I have killed myself with certainty.
        But what is troublesome for me about this is
        That she will not know, if I were dead,
1268   Who put the lance in my body.
        Oh, God, how would she know
        And who would dare to tell her?"

        Thus as you can hear
1272   The young man tormented himself,
        He has no idea what to do,
        For he cannot remove from his heart
        The one who has the beautiful body.
1276   From his bed he gets up quickly,
        Puts on his shoes and gets dressed,
        And leaves the room.
        He covers his head with his cloak;
1280   Into a wondrously beautiful garden,
        Beneath the bedchamber of the young girl,
        He enters, his head lowered.
        Beneath an apple tree he is seated;
1284   Toward her room he turns his face,
        So that he can plainly see
        Those who seat themselves at the windows,
        But never will they see him,

1288   He is so careful that they will never spot him.
        His head he points in that direction,
        There he puts his eyes and his gaze
        And then he remembers once again
1292   Both his adventure and his misfortune,
        And makes his laments and his responses
        And then his judgments all alone.
        He does not know what to do or say;
1296   Often he cries, often he sighs,
        Often he trembles, often he perspires,
        Often his color changes and is transformed;
        His body undergoes much torment and pain.
1300   Thus that day he led such a life
        That he never drank nor did he eat.
        That night he went to a lodging
        Near the emperor's palace
1304   At the home of a lady without a lord,
        She was a noble and loyal woman.
        There the youth came,
        For he was acquainted with the lodging,
1308   And he said that he was painfully ill.
        In a bed he had himself lie down,
        But never so much did he tell
        The good lady that he wanted
1312   To eat or to drink, thus he said to her:
        "My lady, for the love of God, leave me in peace,
        I will not be able to eat for anything
        From this moment on, but thank you."
1316   And she left him thus
        Until daybreak the next day;
        And he got up and got dressed,
        Like one who wants to set out on his way;
1320   But his good hostess pleads with him so much,
        Because she is very worried about his sickness,
        That in spite of himself it is necessary
        That he eat and drink just a little bit.
1324   And when he had to leave from there
        And he was hidden from the people,
        He reentered the orchard
        And sat beneath the apple tree.
1328   Toward the bedchamber he turns his face,

His heart and all his thoughts
Until nightfall when it is too dark to see a drop,
And the next day in the same manner
1332   And the entire whole week.
Each night he returns to his lodging;
The noble lady makes him eat and drink
As much as is in her power,
1336   Either in the morning or in the evening.

He is becoming much more sick and weak,
His color that had been so beautiful and so rosy
Has become pale and ashen.
1340   Melior wonders greatly
Why she has not seen him in such a long time.
So she said to Alixandrine
Who knew her entire situation:
1344   "Dear friend, she said, why is it
That we never see Guillaume?
The time seems long to me
Since I have seen him come here,
1348   A year and more has passed
That he has not been here with us.
Alas, how I am out of my senses,
When I have put myself in such painful uncertainty!
1352   Sweet friend, have you obtained for me the herb
That you promised me the other day?
— Dear friend, do not be troubled,
Alixandrine responds to her,
1356   In the name of the One who made the world
I have truly tried hard many times,
And I have not yet found it,
But in time we will have it, I believe.
1360   Regarding what you were just speaking to me about,
Truly it has been eight days and more
That he has not been here with us,
So I marvel exceedingly:
1364   Good friend, for your pleasure,
May God in time send him to you!
Let us go, if it pleases you,
Into that orchard to distract you;
1368   It can help you and harm nothing,

For it is extremely pleasant and beautiful.
And you will hear the songs of those birds,
You will see those herbs and those flowers
1372 Whose colors are so fresh."
And thus Melior gives her consent.
They got up, started on their way,
Descended by means of a staircase,
1376 They entered the orchard
Through the door of the chamber beneath:
They have no companions except each other.
Inside the orchard they rest in the shade,
1380 Look at the flowers and the herbs;
Of the nightingale they hear his song,
As well as that of the turtledove and the thrush;
It is quite agreeable and pleases her enormously.
1384 They are seated beneath a tree recently grafted
Which was very beautiful, its branches dense with foliage,
And on the green and luxurious grass
There they took their repose.
1388 Many words they related to each other there,
One talked about joy and the other about anguish;
But I cannot tell you absolutely everything.
Thus their talk kept them there
1392 Until by chance it happened
That Alixandrine the Lombard
Looked up toward the end of the orchard:
She saw the young man there
1396 Beneath the green flowering apple tree
Which was truly beautiful with its branches profuse with leaves.
By the clothing that he had put on,
By his shining and golden blond hair
1400 And by the shape of his body
That was so well made and noble
She recognized that it was he.
There he was asleep all alone.
1404 That beautiful lady was both very wise and very virtuous.
She pointed him out to Melior.
"My lady, she said, listen to me.
There I see lying beneath an apple tree
1408 A valet or a knight, I am not sure which,
But he is sleeping, or so it seems to me."

Melior sees him and trembles with fear,
For she recognizes well the valet.
1412 There is on her body no limb that does not jump,
Her color changes in many ways.
She sees him; she is surprised and trapped,
Surprised because she did not know
1416 In what manner she should conduct herself,
And enslaved by her will
That she thought she no longer had.

Alixandrine who was extraordinarily wise
1420 Knew well all of her sentiments and thoughts
From the change of color that she sees in her.
She no longer wants to pretend or conceal anything from her,
But quite openly tells her
1424 That it is Guillaume who is lying there,
Her own valet who is so noble
And virtuous and wise and worthy.
"He is not looking well, I believe.
1428 He probably came here as a diversion,
But fell utterly asleep because of sadness.
My lady, let us please go to him,
Because of your pity, to find out what he is doing,
1432 And if he has a sorrow or is in distress."
And Melior very graciously
Told her that she would do what she wanted.
So they set off from there,
1436 And went to the young man.

They sat down before him then,
And when the beautiful Melior
Sees the valet and his face,
1440 His nose, his mouth and his chin,
His body that was slender and noble
And all his limbs as well,
As if he were made according to her wishes,
1444 With the young nobleman
The young lady was quite overcome and inflamed.
If she did not think she would be blamed,
I believe, she would have kissed him
1448 More than one hundred times, if she had had the chance,

Because she was making him suffer.
He was sleeping, and it seemed to him
That from the bedchamber issued forth
1452   Alixandrine and Melior.
They were coming straight to him here,
They were bringing him a rose;
As soon as he received the rose,
1456   He did not feel any sorrow or pain,
Fatigue, sadness or distress.
In his sleep he becomes so happy
That the young man wakes up.
1460   He is truly amazed
When he sees the maidens.
"Welcome, he says,
My ladies, both of you.
1464   — God bless you, sweet friend,"
Melior answered him.
Guillaume clearly heard
That Melior is calling him friend:
1468   For a great while he was thus
Like the man who is taken by such a malady
That he neither speaks nor hears.
For a long time he was in such a state,
1472   The word 'friend' that he had heard
The maiden say arouses his heart.
Often he trembles, often he sighs,
And he blushes often and perspires,
1476   Often his color changes and is transformed,
He does not talk nor does he say a word.
Alixandrine who had seated herself near him
Begins to address him.
1480   She took notice of his appearance
Which for the valet was truly dreadful.
She told him very softly
"For God's sake, my lord, what are you doing?
1484   — Beautiful lady, I am dying straightaway.
— You are dying? — Truly, I am dying at last.
If God might take me forever,
Sweet lady, I do not believe that I will see another month.
1488   — Are you therefore in such anguish,
Dear sweet friend? said the maiden.

　　　　　— Indeed, my gentle young lady,
　　　　　Yes, much more than I can say.
1492　　— What, says she, is it so?
　　　　　— Yes. — How did it take hold of you then?
　　　　　— On one night that to my misfortune I once saw
　　　　　That she came to me, in my opinion.
1496　　— How did it seize you? — Dear lady, while sleeping.
　　　　　— And where does it hold you? — By the loyalty that I owe you,
　　　　　Sweet lady, all over my entire body.
　　　　　— All over your body? — Indeed. — How?
1500　　— A great marvel takes hold of me
　　　　　Which truly keeps me in great discomfort:
　　　　　One moment I am hot, another moment I am cold,
　　　　　One instant I am perspiring and the next trembling,
1504　　My heart separates from me and sneaks off
　　　　　I know not where it is going or where it arrives,
　　　　　I do not know who is holding on to it.
　　　　　Often it strikes me, often it pierces me
1508　　Often it causes me distress in my heart
　　　　　Often I yawn and stretch
　　　　　Seldom do I sleep and often I stay wakeful.
　　　　　Thinking is killing and intoxicating me.
1512　　Thinking? No, on the contrary, it makes me live.
　　　　　If I were not able to think,
　　　　　I would have been dead a long time ago,
　　　　　For I can neither drink nor eat.
1516　　Dear lady, to distract myself
　　　　　I therefore came here.
　　　　　Fifteen days have passed and more
　　　　　That I have not slept as much as I was sleeping just now.
1520　　— Indeed, I would truly and gladly likely to know,
　　　　　Said the maiden, about the occasion,
　　　　　How it took hold of you and what it is called,
　　　　　This malady that has afflicted you.
1524　　— Sweet lady, he said, do not trouble yourself,
　　　　　Because as long as I have a soul in my body
　　　　　I will reveal it to neither man nor woman."

　　　　　Alixandrine understands that he is hiding something,
1528　　That he does not want to reveal the affair to her,
　　　　　Thus she said to him, dissembling her true motives:

"Guillaume, that is bad luck.[22]
— Luck? Sweet lady, it is assuredly.
1532   By chance man lives,
        By chance he finds his destiny,
        By chance he dies and comes to an end,
        By chance a man gets himself out of a spot
1536   From which a thousand others die.
        Chance causes a man to perish
        Or causes a thousand to heal.
        Dear lady, now hear this: by chance
1540   A ship comes at high speed
        Across the sea, that a tempest chases,
        Until by chance it breaks up,
        And all those within escape
1544   Except two or three who perish there,
        Whom the sea totally engulfs and swallows up.
        And all those who are saved there
        Were not saved by their strength
1548   Or by their prowess or their intelligence,
        Those others were not for their bad actions
        Or for their intentions or desires drowned;
        They did not perish because of their laziness,
1552   The others did not survive because of their courage,
        But chance happens thus.
        Beautiful lady, of the three who perished
        I am one of them; know it well.
1556   I am at sea and shipwrecked,
        Adrift on the waves, I
        Know no protection for my life.
        Too long I have been at sea and too far from port;
1560   In my life I know no comfort,
        But chance wants it that way,
        For which many a good man complains and grieves.

22. In this verse Alixandrine tells Guillaume "c'est maus d'aventure. He replies (v. 1533) "D'aventure?" I translated *aventure* in both verses as "luck," since no other word worked as well with "bad." In subsequent verses of this passage, however, I translated the common adverbial phrase *par aventure* as "by chance." The poet's use of anaphora, or repetition, in verses 1532–1535 accentuates the domination of chance or fate over man. The passage also sets up a contrast between Guillaume and Melior with its echo and modification of an earlier comment of the princess in which she blames *fortune* for causing her to fall in love with her page (899–900) but later reproaches herself for accusing *aventure* of having done something that was caused by her own weakness (vv. 909–910). Melior thus rejects her role as a passive pawn of fate. Such different attitudes toward aventure reflect the different social positions of the lovers.

           Melior heard extraordinarily well

1564   Everything that Guillaume said to Alixandrine;
           Often she said between her teeth:
           "God, said she, Father all powerful,
           This is like this malady which has hold of me,

1568   And so each day it comes to me
           And I see it greatly worsened.
           But, alas, he does not realize
           The pain that I endure for him,

1572   The agony, suffering, and grief,
           Nor what price I am paying because of him.
           Never has any maiden of my lineage
           Of my merit and worth

1576   Ever put her heart in such a place
           As I have done, I can honestly say.[23]
           The world is truly correct to hold me in contempt
           When I have set aside dukes and counts

1580   And kings and sons of emperors
           And those by whom I was honored
           For a valet from another country,
           No one knows, not even he himself,

1584   What land he is from or from what people;
           He never knew the mother who bore him
           And he never saw the man who fathered him.

           Love takes over her consciousness,

1588   Against her remarks it debates and quarrels
           And Love says: "I am not all like that,
           I do not judge according to the authority of the lord
           Or according to his noble birth or greatness,

1592   But there where my will directs itself,
           For I have power over everyone:
           Thus I choose according to my desire,
           So I prefer the generous and the noble,

1596   The virtuous, the wise, the worthy,
           The well educated and the courteous
           Over all these princes and all these kings
           And these evil wicked counts.

1600   And nevertheless is it a misdeed

---

23. Melior sees herself as unique and thus is self-conscious of herself as an individual.

If I caused you to fall in love with that one?
Is there anyone in the world more handsome than he,
Who has more good qualities in all places
1604 Or is more worthy or more courteous?
What is it that he must lack,
Beauty, prowess, or wisdom?
Because if you do not know where he is from
1608 Or how he happened to come into the world,
You can surely see by his appearance,
Just as he demonstrates
Through his works and through his deeds,
1612 That he is of high noble birth.[24]

Now tell me your opinion
And give me an honest judgment:
If you had just now found
1616 A mark of fine pure gold
And did not know whose it was
Nor who had lost the mark,
Because of this would the gold be worth less
1620 Than if it had been taken from your treasury?
Never would the gold lose its value
Nor the fact that it came from the king's treasury.
Nevertheless we are all from one father,
1624 All of us were created by one single Creator,
We are all made from one substance
And all born of one lineage."

In this manner the young lady was thinking.
1628 Alixandrine, the maiden, hears
What the young man is explaining to her.
She is very attentive to him and thus replies
As one who is extremely wise:
1632 "My lord, I truly know your desires,
They have held you in their grip for a long time and have lasted
    too long;
There is no longer any need to conceal them.
Along two banks you are swimming,
1636 I can see you very well.

24. Love has just stated one of the major themes of the romance: although it may be concealed, noble birth always reveals itself through noble deeds.

Of what value are concealment and declaration?
I quite understand in which direction hangs the balance,
But I believe that I can do enough for the other
1640   That I will bring it to the same level."

      Guillaume hears that the young girl
Knows and is aware of his entire situation.
There is no need to hide anything from her,
1644   For she sees through the deception.
She has found what he had lost
And she has blown on the fire until
The flame has leapt out from it.
1648   Very softly he asks her for mercy.
"Dear lady, he says, I beg mercy of you.
— Mercy, Guillaume? For what?
— For me, sweet lady, and for my life
1652   That you have in your power,
In your power truly, and so
In the name of the Lord who does not lie
If you do not help me soon
1656   With the one whom you have told me
Holds the balance in her hand,
If the weight does not come toward me
So that my side draws from the other
1660   This wound will have no need of medicine.
But I have such great confidence in you
And your heart is so very noble and gentle
That I know you will bring the weight to the same level,
1664   Just as you have made me understand."

      Now what she hears pleases her very much
And she says: "Friend, now do not torment yourself.
You can have confidence in me,
1668   And you will be helped to the best of my ability."
He bowed his head deeply to her.
Alixandrine called to her damsel
And she said to her:
1672:   "My lady, in the name of Jesus Christ
And for mercy's sake and out of love
Have pity for the pain
That this valet is suffering for you."

1676   Melior said: "My dear, why?
    — My lady, for you he is languishing at last,
    For you he is dying and is coming to such an end.
    — In what manner, beautiful sister?
1680   — He has given you, my lady, his heart,
    He entered and put it there.
    If he does not become your sweetheart,
    By the Lord who caused me to be born,
1684   I do not believe that he will see tomorrow's vespers.
    Help, my dear, your lover."
    But she does not believe he will even last that long
    If she does not immediately allow
1688   Him to make her his sweetheart.

      Melior looked at him sweetly
    And said: "Dear one, as God is watching me,
    I would not want to be
1692   His murderer or the murderer of anyone else
    Nor a sinner in any manner.
    Because of you and because of your plea
    And for him whom I see in such peril,
1696   Before he dies this way for me,
    I grant him all my love and myself,
    Let this never again be in doubt."
    And then she said: "My love, come forward,
1700   For I am yours from this moment on.
    I am entirely yours and want to be,
    Without seigniorial authority and without pride."[25]

      When the damsel had said this,
1704   His heart jumped with joy.
    "God, said he, Father above,
    These are truly miracles and wonders
    That You are doing for me."
1708   His hands joined together he pays homage to her.[26]
    He surrenders and gives himself to her,

25. Although she is the emperor's daughter, Melior relinquishes her position of authority over Guillaume when she agrees to become his sweetheart. She symbolically rejects her social identity.

26. Joining one's hands together is part of the feudal ceremony of homage. For a description of the ritual, see Bloch, 145–6.

And she in turn abandons herself to him
So that she may do all that pleases him.
1712   Then they take hold of each other
Like those who have loved each other for a long time.
The love that they have between them is so great
That it reassures them and makes them bold,
1716   They kiss each other on the
Eyes and nose and mouth and face.
Alixandrine the maiden
Sees that now they will do very well without her,
1720   So she leaves them there and goes off
Into the orchard collecting flowers.
They declare their love
And how each one so many times
1724   Has been so distraught because of the other.
Both of them marvel about this:
Each believed to have because of the other
The illness and the pain that he suffered
1728   And then the other said that he had more.
Guillaume said: "I almost died.
— But I, my love, said Melior,
If this action had not been taken,
1732   Soon I would have been dead."

      In this way the two lovers speak,
They hug and kiss each other
And take their pleasure together so much
1736   That they are not aware that night has come.
Alixandrine observes evening fall,
She understands well that they can be there too long;
So she called to Melior;
1740   "My lady, this day
Is not tiring you, I believe.
Let us leave; here is the night,
I truly fear that we might be too long here,
1744   And that evil people might come here.
— Alixandrine, what are you saying?
Has it come time to go then?
— Yes, it has been time for a while."
1748   They stood up on their feet,
Observed that the day is drawing to an end,

And they determined how
They will handle their affair from now on.
1752 Then they kiss each other and depart.
Guillaume does not forget himself,
He thanks Alixandrine very much
And said: "My very beautiful sweet sister,
1756 You have returned above all my heart to me;
My reason and my life and my joy
And finally everything that I had lost,
But you have won everything back for me."
1760 Then they separated.

    To their bedchamber returned
The joyous and happy maidens.
The young man in turn made his way
1764 To his lodging most joyfully.
His good hostess asks him
How he is doing and if he is improving.
He said: "I am totally cured and healthy."
1768 And she raises her hands toward God,
Praising Him greatly and giving Him thanks.
That night he was well served
And the young man was provided with what he needed;
1772 His bed was prepared for him,
He went to bed and fell asleep.
He never woke up that night
And when it was day, he got up,
1776 He dressed and adorned himself handsomely;
To court he goes, just as he used to.
Just as it pleases him and as he wants
He has all that he desires from his sweetheart
1780 Without reproach and without villainy,
For he would do nothing
For which one might blame him.

    They love each other faithfully so very much.
1784 And so they remained for a long time
Until at the court there arose a situation,
In which the powerful duke of Saxony
Out of pride, out of arrogance
1788 Had revolted against the king

And by force had entered his land.
Castles and towns and cities
He had already taken and destroyed
1792   And the poor people expelled.
When the emperor hears the news,
You know he was not pleased.
He sent his messengers everywhere
1796   So that all his barons will come to him.
As soon as he could and as quickly as possible
He assembled his entire army.
When Guillaume sees and hears
1800   That the emperor has need of men,
Before him he kneeled,
He truly humbled himself before him,
And he begs of him that, if it pleases him,
1804   That he make him a new knight.
This pleases the emperor:
Who arms him that day
Along with eighty sons of princes
1808   Whom he makes knights because of his love.
He gives arms and horses to all,
Lords and princes he makes of them.

Then the army assembled
1812   They did not stay there any longer,
But all of them got on their way.
They are well instructed in how to fight wars,
And have whatever may be useful to them,
1816   Provisions, arms and destriers,[27]
They never speak of rest,
And so the army comes to the frontier.
When they arrived at the frontier
1820   The emperor was attentive to
The complaints of the people cast out,
The devastation, the damage, the loss
That the duke had done to him:
1824   He was truly very unhappy and rightly so.
Now he took his counsel
With his barons and with his marquis

---

27. Destriers are warhorses, horses that are used in combat.

As to how he will be able to avenge his shame.
1828   They advise him, his dukes and his counts
       And the other men together,
       That he and his men ride until
       They have ensnared the duke
1832   In a village, a town or a city
       And not to leave until they have laid siege
       And have taken him by vigorous force.
       Each one consents to this counsel.
1836   At daybreak the army was getting ready,
       And then they set off.
       There you would have heard many horns,
       Drums and tambourines and bugles,
1840   Flutes, bronze trumpets and other kinds of trumpets.
       They make a lot of noise, when they leave.
       They will threaten the duke, if they find him,
       And they will make him pay for his pride.
1844   The duke had a tremendous throng
       Of good men, fierce and bold,
       And such vassals in his power
       Who have very little regard for Germans
1848   And the Lombards and the Tuscans
       And the emperor's entire army.
       Because of his pride, because of his folly
       The duke sends a message to the emperor
1852   That he should not come,
       But that on a named day he will be waiting for him,
       So let him be prepared, let him defend himself,
       If he dares to engage in battle with him.
1856   The envoy does not rest
       Until he has given the message to the emperor.
       Without hesitation, the emperor
       Agrees to the day for the battle
1860   And expresses great joy to his men.
       He calls for my lord Guillaume.
       "Hear, dear friend, this news:
       The duke announces from over there
1864   That he will meet us in battle.
       — Sire, Guillaume replies to him,
       May this God who made the world
       Lead us to an honorable outcome

1868   That we might destroy their pride
            And his arrogance which is so great."
            So they remain there now
            Up until the day of the battle.
1872   They have carefully acquired without fail
            All that they might need.
            On the appointed day they all came,
            They have arranged their battalions,
1876   And separated and organized their men.

            There you could have seen that day
            So many dukes, so many princes, so many counts
            So many vassals of great holdings;
1880   Never were so many great people seen,
            And you would have seen across the battlefield
            So many banners, so many ensigns,
            So many lances and so many pennants,
1884   So many swords of good sharp steel,
            So many helmets of gold and so many shields
            And so many hauberks[28] with tightly woven mail,
            So much equipment and so many horses
1888   And the bodies of so many brave vassals.

            The duke was extremely fierce and aggressive,
            He incites his men from all sides:
            "Now do well, my barons!"
1892   At this moment they spur on their horses
            And attack the Lombards so vigorously
            That beneath them the earth trembles.
            And the Lombards received them well,
1896   In the mêlée they strike with all their might
            And truly deafening were the shouts
            And the clashing of the lances
            And great was the loss of vassals
1900   Who fell from impetuous horses,
            Dead and wounded, cold and bloody.
            They do not spare each other for anything.
            If they have lost their lances,
1904   They draw their swords.

---

28. A hauberk is a long tunic made of chain mail.

Then they strike each other with a single blow,
They slice their feet and then their arms,
They split their face right through to the brains.
1908 Brains, entrails and intestines
Are spread all over the meadow.
God! Such noble men lost their lives there,
Which caused great grief and great pain
1912 For most of them and their friends.

    The battle is very fierce
And horrific and truly quite difficult.
The wounded are moaning loudly
1916 And are dying painfully, crushed
By the warhorses stepping on their bodies.
The battle is so ferocious that
Whoever falls there is unable to get up.
1920 The Lombards are beginning to falter,
For they cannot suffer any longer.
Now it is necessary to abandon the field.
When the Tuscans arrive attacking
1924 With swords in their hands,
Then they rush into battle.
There is no hauberk with strong enough mail
Nor is there a strong enough helmet, or a strong enough shield
1928 That can resist or be effective
Against the blows of the swords they have readied.
So great is the fighting
That they are killing each other by hundreds and by thousands.
1932 The duke's people who are truly good and
Fierce vassals help each other very much.
There you would have seen many good destriers
From Lombardy and Germany
1936 Wandering here and there through the countryside,
Their broken reins between their feet,
Their saddles turned upside down,
That day their lords died
1940 In the battle most painfully.

    Along with his men the duke
Maintains a fierce combat
With the naked sword that he has drawn.

1944   He comforts his people around him.
        He is causing such destruction to the emperor's army
        That the least valiant and the most cowardly
        Among his entourage are very bold.
1948   They treat the emperor's men in such a way
        That they do not know what they can do
        Or where they can retreat to safety.

        When the emperor sees that
1952   His people and his men are being ill-treated and are dying,
        He grieves so much that I do not know what to say.
        "God, said he, Father, sovereign Lord,
        Who was born of the Virgin,
1956   Sire, in the name of Your worthy power
        Do not allow wrong to stand up
        Against right or prevail over it any longer.
        The duke was my liegeman,[29]
1960   He held nothing except what he received from me.
        He had not demanded anything of me
        Nor did he through his peers ask for an accounting
        Of anything that I might have done to him.
1964   And in spite of this he has wronged me,
        He has burned and devastated my country!
        Sire, for the sake of Your holy pity,
        Do not allow this disloyal man
1968   To harm me or my men."

        Guillaume hears the emperor
        Who is invoking God and is afraid.
        He calls his men around him:
1972   "Barons, he says, hear me.
        We are all newly armed
        Knights and young men.
        The emperor, our protector
1976   Has armed us according to his need;
        Now we have arrived at that need.
        So let us not be considered
        In the mêlée or in the battle
1980   As mere boys or useless knaves

---

29. A liegeman is a feudal vassal, a man who has taken an oath of allegiance to a lord.

But as good and fierce vassals
And men truly expert at their work.
We must all forget death,
1984   Prowess must be our only thought.
The duke is so very presumptuous
And the Saxons fierce and courageous.
They have fought so well in the battle
1988   That they value our boldness very little.
I see our people abandoning the place,
You see that they are being pursued.
They will be defeated, if they do not get help now.
1992   Lord barons, let us not delay."

Then they all charge together.
Beneath them the earth shakes and trembles.
Their shields together in front of their chests,
1996   They go to attack their enemy.
In the assault they strike them in such a way
That the shields break and shatter
And the strong doubled hauberks
2000   Are no protection against the steel,
For they thrust the rigid and solid lances
Right through their bodies
So that on the saddle pommels
2004   They spill out their intestines.
In this attack they fight so hard
That I do not know how to make a count
Of the number of souls departing their body.[30]
2008   All around the earth is covered
With the fallen and the dead.
Then they draw their good cleaned blades,
Thus they have begun the sword combat.
2012   The vanquished, the pursued
Hear the shouts and see their men
Who have come back into the mêlée.

"They are suffering the weight of the charge,
2016   And we are fleeing like cowards!

30. The *Guillaume* poet frequently refers to the impossibility of being able to count or describe something. See also vv. 3436–3440, 3471–3474, 3485–3488, 4666–4668, 8597–8598, 8827–8828, 8934–8936, 9376–9380. For a discussion of this topos of inexpressibility, see Curtius, 159–162.

Let us turn back, we are ashamed,
Against them all we will do our best.
If we have been shamed by fleeing,
2020   Now we will show them how to fight well.
Such shame ought to increase our anger
And double our audacity.
We have no need to talk about this any longer
2024   But each one must avenge his shame."
Then they turned quickly around
And pulled out their naked blades,
Thus they charged into the mêlée.
2028   There you would have seen so many blows
Struck against helmets and shields,
So many heads severed from trunks
And the earth covered in blood
2032   And so many vassals lying face down,
Eyes troubled, flesh blackened,
Whose souls had left their bodies.
Guillaume is in the mêlée,
2036   In his fist he holds his naked sword.
His eyes are red like those of a dragon,
His face is fierce like that of a lion
Inflamed with anger and rage.[31]
2040   He has completely transformed his color
From what it used to be before;
His gentle appearance has totally changed.
There truly appears on his face
2044   The great fierceness of his intentions,
His heart is full of audacity.
He drops his good warhorse's bit,
Spurs him on and urges him forward,
2048   He lets fly more than his men's quarrels.[32]
Wherever he sees the need greater
And where they are the strongest
And where the crowd is the thickest
2052   He rushes in to fight,
His naked sword in his right hand.

31. The poet uses epic clichés to describe Guillaume's figurative metamorphosis in battle from knight to beast.
32. Quarrels or bolts are somewhat similar to arrows and are the stone projectiles of a crossbow. For a discussion, see Newman 231–232.

Now the Saxons will find their master.
So he strikes Terri on his pointed helmet,
2056   Which he totally breaks and splits.
He brings the blow down with such force
That he completely slices through the face
That was never protected by armor.
2060   From here to the chest he puts his sword,
The torso and the chest topple over,
With a downward thrust he totally splits his spine.
Then he pushes himself forward into the mêlée
2064   Where their press is greater.
Thus he strikes Josson du Pré,
With his sword he separates from his body
Both his liver and his lungs
2068   Which he spills out over the pommel.
That one falls dead and he leaves.
Then he strikes a third with such force
That his soul no longer stays in him
2072   And he sends flying the head of a fourth
And strikes the fifth with his sword:
His children have become orphans.
Then he pushes himself forward into the mêlée
2076   Where they are exerting the greatest pressure.
There you would have seen blows flying,
Severing and slicing napes and necks,
Chests and clavicles and torsos,
2080   Ribs, entrails and spines;
And intestines falling from bodies,
Heads flying and people dying
And red blood spilling on the field.
2084   Never since the time of King Alexander
Who was so intelligent and powerful
Was there a vassal of his goodness.
Against his blows there is no defense.
2088   Thus the Saxons flee
Like the lark before the sparrow hawk,[33]
They fear him more than the devil.
The young knights fight well,
2092   With their swords they bring about great carnage.

---

33. The lark (the Saxons) fleeing before the sparrow hawk (Guillaume) is an epic metaphor.

The Saxons, who are both strong and fierce,
In return make their bodies bleed.
On both sides they fight well
2096   Until they are splitting each other in the chest.

A nephew of the duke, his sister's son,
A young knight of great valor,
Whose name is Terri, is very angry.
2100   When he sees his people so beaten
And killed and vanquished
He believes he will become mad and collapse from grief.
He is well armed with a fiery horse,
2104   He has a good lance, strong and sharp,
And he sees Guillaume in the mêlée,
Where he does not stop or cease
Emptying the place of his people.
2108   There is no Saxon, as fierce as he might be made
Or valiant, or brave or daring
Who has not turned his back to him.
They all fear his blade of steel;
2112   They do not dare come toward him.
Terri sees him, moves in his direction,
Now he will make him pay, if he can.
He sets off that way,
2116   The young man saw his great prowess become his misfortune.
Guillaume sees Terri coming
All ready to strike him.
Toward him he rushes headlong,
2120   Giving his horse the spur.
Thus the barons come together.
Terri strikes him so impetuously
With his hard lance through his shield
2124   That he totally broke it and split it.
If the hauberk had not been so strong,
It would have passed through his body.
Guillaume holds his sword drawn
2128   With which he had made many attacks.
He struck Terri with such a blow
That he split him through to his backbone,
So that he falls dead from his horse.
2132   Afterwards he said to him: "Unfortunate vassal!

You might have been very brave, I think,
If you had lived a little longer.
Often I saw you strike
2136 And separate the great crowds.
Often today you mistreated our people,
But now you have lost your life for it.
May your great strong boldness
2140 Accompany you with the dead."
When he had said this, he turns back.
The Saxons become sad and mournful.

When the duke sees his nephew dead,
2144 For his grief he knows no consolation.
Courage is of no value; he does not know what to do.
From his eyes run down
Hot tears along his face.
2148 He fell in a faint from his horse,
When his men greeted him.
For the sake of his nephew that he had lost
He frequently faints in their arms.
2152 He mourns him very gently:
"Ah, sweet nephew, you were truly ill-fated
And how unfortunate for you were your great strength
Your great prowess and your great intelligence
2156 And your beauty and your youth!
The one, dear nephew, who killed you
And who took you away from me
Indeed must be my enemy.
2160 *From the grief that I have my heart is leaving me.*[34]
Leaving? Indeed it will leave,
If I can no longer avenge you."
He calls his men around him,
2164 To them he complains about his distress:
"Ah, barons, what a dishonor!
See what loss and what pain
We are receiving today because of that vassal
2168 Who is seated on that black horse!
If only he did not exist, then for a long time they might have
          been

---

34. This verse is not in the manuscript. The translation is based on a conjecture by Michelant.

Either dead or captured, they would have no protection.
But his prowess makes all of them

2172   Fierce and bold and courageous.
Now he has killed my nephew,
For which I carry such anger in my heart
That I will no longer have joy in my life

2176   As long as he has life in his body.
You who have always loved me
And have deserved the honors
That you want me to give to you,

2180   All that will now be evident in this combat.
Avenge, at least, your friend
That this vassal has killed.
Let us attack, too long have we waited."

2184   Then together they charged,
Everyone trying to outdo the other, spurring their horses for-
     ward,
They hurry greatly and push themselves
Because of their lord's entreaty.

2188   They see Guillaume in the fracas of the battle
Massacring their people,
They strike him with such intensity
That the vassal and the destrier

2192   Toppled to the ground.
He angrily stood up,
In his fist he held his drawn sword,
He pulled his shield in front of his chest.

2196   *He sees the duke hurry toward him:*[35]
They run toward each other.
Soon he will have problems
And he will either loose his blood or his life

2200   If he does not receive help from his men soon,
For he is surrounded on all sides.
They throw darts and javelins
And good lances, sharp and pointed.

2204   His shield is broken and pierced,
His hauberk broken and losing its mail,
And he has received seven wounds in his body
So that blood is running down him.

---

35. This verse is not in the manuscript. The translation is based on a conjecture by Michelant.

2208	Guillaume, however, is not frightened,
	With his steel blade he gives them such blows
	That he splits them and cuts them in pieces,
	He strikes and kills and massacres them,
2212	Their faces turned down on the moors,
	Like a wild boar he gives them battle.
	God, what a baron and what a vassal!
	Against what a misadventure he defends himself!
2216	He was doing well, I believe.
	No longer would he have to worry about all of them
	Were it not for the traitor, the arrogant one,
	The duke who was menacing his barons,
2220	Because this vassal is keeping them at bay,
	And he says: "Great shame on all of you.
	What are you doing that you do not take him?
	I am amazed to see that one single man
2224	Is safe from all of you.
	He is certainly making you all look bad."
	Then they all run up at great speed.
	You should have seen the vassal turn,
2228	Defend his body and strike at them!
	How he often thrusts into them,
	How he kills them, how he slaughters them,
	How he defends himself, how he cuts them in pieces,
2232	How he disputes by arms his life with them!
	There is not one single soul, as well as he fights,
	Who hastens any more to hurt him;
	He defends himself well, but it is to no avail.
2236	The duke sees him and cries out:
	"Vassal, vassal, soon you will pay for
	The harm that you have done me
	When you killed my nephew."
2240	And he replied: "You are wrong.
	I much prefer, by the faith that I owe you,
	That I have killed him than he me,
	And to defend myself I did it."
2244	The duke shouts: "Surrender,
	Surrender to me soon, let yourself be taken,
	And I will have you hanged in the morning."
	And he replied: "I am still here.
2248	Never have pity on me.

I know well, if you can take me,
That I have arrived at a bad port;
But as God is protecting my life
2252   And my sword to which I am promised
And is, I believe, chastising you
And acquainting you with this news,
When you will know it, you will have no desire
2256   To take me, in my opinion.

The duke calls over his barons,
Once again he has summoned them.
With great anger he warns them
2260   To take the vassal's head.
Therefore they insult and surround Guillaume.
They do not hesitate to kill him because of lack of courage.
He defends himself, but to no avail,
2264   For on him descend three counts
And so many vassals and so many barons
That in their hands they take him, whether he wants it or not.
His warhorse had escaped,
2268   Like a tempest he was fleeing.
With his broken reins between his feet
Among the troops he flees.

When the young man's troop
2272   See Morel returning without him,
The bloody saddle on his back,
Each one becomes alarmed and is fearful.
They cry and shout because of their lord,
2276   Who they believe died in the battle.
Toward a slope they look and
See him being led away rapidly.
Like a thief they were taking him away,
2280   They had tied his hands
And bound both his eyes.
Toward him his men rush, each trying to outdo the other,
One advancing in front of the other,
2284   Each one wants his deliverance so much,
They hunt for him with so much ardor and desire him so much.
Soon it will be evident if they love him above anything else
And if they fear danger or death.

2288   They charge angrily and spur on their horses,
       Each one raises his naked sword,
       Right into the middle of them they rushed.
       They make a great din in the attack.
2292   There you would have seen blows being exchanged,
       Helmets cracking and their circles breaking,
       Shields separating, hauberks being damaged,
       Heads being cut through the middle and split,
2296   Brains flying and blood spilling,
       So many feet severed, so many intestines,
       So many entrails, so many guts,
       So many feet, so many fists, so many bowels,
2300   So many knights falling from their saddles
       Who never again got back up on their horses.
       Never since the King of the world
       Was made incarnate in the Virgin and was born
2304   Has there been a battle more without mercy.

       The emperor came there.
       With him were forty-three men,
       Because of whom the cries grew louder
2308   And the combat stronger.
       Guillaume's men fought so
       And maintained the great sword combat
       So that they emptied the place up to him,
2312   Whether it pleases anyone or not.
       When they reach their lord,
       They put the guards in pain,
       Whoever cannot flee from there
2316   Must die on the spot.
       They untied and unbound him,
       They put him back up on a destrier
       That was whiter than a lily,
2320   They put a steel sword back
       In his right hand now.
       When the valet felt the sword
       And he was back on a good warhorse,
2324   Then one would have seen him put into flight
       And attack his enemies
       As the falcon does to the partridge.
       He has no pity for them,

2328   A very bitter ransom he pays them.
          He sees the duke among his people,
          Toward him he thrusts himself angrily.
          A lance had been given to him
2332   By a knight from his household;
          He strikes him with such intensity
          On the shield on his chest
          That he completely shatters it and puts it into pieces.
2336   He breaks the duke's hauberk and its ring.
          He hits him on the shoulder
          And strikes him with such great force
          That he sends toppling to the ground
2340   Both the lord and his destrier.
          On him he puts his drawn sword
          And tells him angrily:
          "Sire, here is your prisoner
2344   Ready to pay his ransom.
          It was not so long ago that you wanted to take me,
          Now you can expect it from yourself.
          Such is your destiny now:
2348   For me you will do this duty."
          The duke hears him, cries for mercy,
          And that he not kill him, please,
          For he sees no help from his people.
2352   Whether he wants to or not, he gives him his sword.
          Guillaume bends down over his horse,
          Takes him by the nasal of his helmet,
          Leads him to the emperor,
2356   Gives him to the emperor as to his lord.
          The emperor praises God,
          Runs with joy to the young man,
          And kissed him and thanked him one hundred times
2360   For the duke that he had taken
          His enemy, the traitor,
          And promises him great honors.
          The Saxons see that their master was captured,
2364   They are discouraged; it cannot be otherwise,
          For their sire and their leader is a prisoner.
          Therefore they have not drawn or thrown a lance since,
          Or touched a man or struck a blow;
2368   Because they have lost their lord

They all flee together.
Happy is he who is seated on a good horse.
In retreat are the great companions,
2372   They flee over the mountains
And through the valleys and across the plains,
Each one trying to get ahead of the other.
Anyone who had a cousin, nephew or brother,
2376   Good friend, uncle or father
Does not wait for him anymore than for another;
Each one has too much to do for himself.
After them follow the emperor's men,
2380   Motivated by a desire to kill, with the vassal
Who chases them before him
And keeps them in such a disarray
That very soon he has his pleasure with them.
2384   I do not want to make a long discussion about it.
All the Saxons were finally destroyed,
Very few escaped, I believe,
All would have been killed or captured without fail,
2388   If the battle had lasted a little longer.
But night came and they went away,
And those who pursued them
Returned with their prisoners
2392   And presented them to the emperor.
There were of these prisoners
Five hundred or more high barons.

The emperor took counsel
2396   From his barons and from his marquis
That he will return to the prisoners their domains
And that he will take from them their promises of fidelity.
Thus they said, except the duke
2400   Who was well guarded and held well.
The emperor does his duty
Throughout the realm of Saxony,
The entire land submitted to him,
2404   Just as he wants it to be.
The old, the young, the hoary
All came asking for his mercy.
Absolutely everyone surrenders to his mercy
2408   And receives their fiefs back from him;

Then he puts guards in the towers,
In the cities, and throughout the land.

When the matter was finished
2412   And he had established peace throughout the country
And he had accomplished his duty,
Then he returns to Lombardy.
He puts in his prison the duke
2416   Who frequently cries and expresses his grief,
He repeatedly deplores the loss of his friends
Who died and were captured because of him,
His nephew, his land and his honor
2420   That he lost in such dishonor,
And he grieves for his situation even more sadly.
"God, said he, all powerful Father,
It is right that I suffer.
2424   Ever disastrous for me was my great pride,
My great crime, my excess."
He curses the hour that he lives so long,
He has so much pain and so much anger,
2428   And the huge wound that he had in his body
Was making him feel worse,
That at the end he is suffering.
I do not know how to tell you any more about the duke,
2432   His soul departed from his body.
The emperor knows that he died,
In a church he has the body
Very richly shrouded
2436   And interred and buried.
In a coffin of grayish-brown marble
They placed and sealed the body,
They have made him a very rich sepulcher.
2440   When they have given him the sacraments,
They set out on their way again;
Together they are all very happy,
So they never spoke of resting,
2444   Thus the army returned to their country.
They returned to their households
Who were joyous and happy.

The emperor selected messengers,

2448 To his daughter he sent them,
Informing her that they are returning safe and sound.
They carried out their task so well
That the messengers came
2452 To the maiden and told it to her.
When Melior hears the news,
Know that it was truly beautiful to her.
She holds up both of her hands toward God
2456 And with a good heart gives Him thanks.

Then she asks the messengers
About the barons and about the knights
How they are doing and how it is going for them.
2460 ....
"Did you find at any time anywhere
Anyone who gave you trouble?
— Yes. — Who was it? — That duke
2464 Who assembled such a people
Who were not less in number than us.
— Did they want to move against you?
— Move against us? What did you say?
2468 Such a great battle no one ever saw,
As painful or as strong,
Where so many good men received death.
— What happened to you? Tell me.
2472 — Good lady, by faith we would have all been
Vanquished and killed and the army would have perished,
If the one who does not forget prowess,
The good vassal, the strong, the fierce
2476 And the noble knight
Who is so very bold and valiant
And lord and master of all
Had not rescued us
2480 And protected and defended us.
If it were not for he himself
And his prowess and his efforts
Neither the best nor the worst
2484 In our empire would have escaped.
Thus we were saved by him
And the others died and perished.
Said the maiden: "Good sir,

2488   By the loyalty that you owe the emperor,
Who is this vassal that you have been talking about so much?
— My lady, the newly dubbed.
— Guillaume? — Indeed. — He is the one, then?

2492   — By faith, my lady, yes.
— So he is of such very great valor?
— No he is not. — What? — He is of greater valor.
We would not know how to tell

2496   How more valiant and courageous he is."
Afterward, they told her without fail
What happened in the battle to Guillaume,
How he killed the duke's nephew,

2500   And then how the duke in turn captured him,
How he defended himself from being taken
And how the duke wanted to hang him
And how he was fiercely rescued

2504   By his men from the Saxons
And how he captured the duke in turn
And gave him to the emperor
And how the Saxons were vanquished

2508   When they had lost their lord,
And how the duke was wounded bodily
And how he died in prison
"We do not know how, they said, to tell you any more,

2512   There is no vassal like him all the way to Russia."

      Said the maiden: "Good sir,
Is he coming with the emperor?
— Yes. — Is he healthy? — My lady, no,

2516   For he has some wounds that are hurting him.
— Will he heal? — Yes, without a doubt.
He is riding very well and is coming by the road."

      Melior hears that her sweetheart

2520   Was esteemed above everyone else.
He had the reward; he had defeated everyone.
And in her heart she was so happy
That she never had a greater joy.

2524   Now here is the emperor
Who dismounted at the great step,
He and his men and his barons.
The young lady goes to greet him.

2528   She expresses great joy about her father
        And similarly about her friend
        But she does it so courteously
        That no one can note anything wrong.

2532   The maiden says to the vassal
        Discreetly and in secret:
        "My love, this same day speak to me
        In my chamber, do not neglect to do it."

2536   And by signs he grants it to her,
        For he does not dare do it otherwise.
        I cannot tell you everything
        About how the Romans

2540   Received the emperor with joy and honor
        Nor the rich preparations
        That they made for his arrival.
        They expressed great joy

2544   And cried many tears there,
        Throughout the city, throughout the country,
        For their relatives, for their friends
        Who died in the battle.

2548   But this gives them great comfort
        That they were victorious
        And that they killed and destroyed the people
        Who had revolted against them.

2552   My lord Guillaume spoke
        As much as he wanted to his sweetheart.
        The lovers lead a very beautiful life
        For a long time together

2556   Until a great feast
        That they say was held at Easter,
        For which the emperor stayed
        In Rome awaiting that day.

2560   To him had come many
        Of his princes and his barons
        Whom he had summoned to this feast.

        The court and the assembly were enormous.

2564   Thereupon behold the entire procession;
        Thirty barons from Greece were there,
        Straight to the emperor they were coming;
        Each is carrying an olive branch

2568   To signify joy and peace
        And in order that one might know they are messengers.
        They ride up the street
        Until they come to the great step, where they descend
2572   And give their horses to the squires.
        They were adorned very well
        And richly mounted,
        Their garments are all in gold.
2576   They go up into the main hall
        And do not want anyone to consider them ill mannered:
        They remove their cloaks from around their necks
        And put them on their shoulders.
2580   Their bodies are noble and their faces fierce,
        They have hats of fine gold on their heads,
        Their hair is blond and cut,
        They have white, hoary beards,
2584   They do not seem to be desperate people.
        They have rich rings on their fingers
        And straps of fine gold on their hands
        With stones as clear as ice;
2588   Thus as they walk the place sparkles.
        They do not seem at all like young men,
        Each holds on to the other by his cloak.
        Those in the court escort them,
2592   Up to the emperor they go.
        First they saluted him by bowing their head,
        For it is the custom of their kingdom,
        Then the messengers greet him
2596   And the assembly of his barons very nobly
        On behalf of the magnificent emperor
        Who reigned over Greece
        And also on behalf of his son.
2600   The emperor briefly responds:
        "My lords, may God bless you
        Both you and your company."
        Afterward, one of them spoke,
2604   All the others listened to him.
        His name was Joathas,
        In Greece he was a very rich man.
        He drew a little forward
2608   And said: "My lord, have peace now."

The court became silent and the one
Who told his message spoke well,
Then he said to the emperor:

2612 "Listen, sire, and my lords.
We are truly messengers
Of the emperor who is so very rich
And noble and to whom belongs

2616 All of Greece and Constantinople,
The islands and the regions
And the great dwellings.
Thus he sent us to you

2620 And so hear why, sire
And my lords, said Joathas:
Because of a daughter that you have.
He has a son, a young man,

2624 I do not know any on earth so handsome.
Because there are no other heirs, he will be emperor.
For him, he is asking for your daughter.
If you give her to him, I believe,

2628 You will have more gold than you have silver
And more cities, towns, and castles
Than you have farms or small houses.
You must especially know as true

2632 That there was never
A woman who was more wealthy or noble
Than a lady of Constantinople.
In a happy hour was born the one

2636 To whom such an honor will be given.
May there be no fear of refusal:
Here are your princes and your people,
Advise yourself as to what you will do,

2640 If you will approve this accord."

The emperor took his counsel,
What they have asked for he grants them;
He agreed to the marriage

2644 And from them in turn he takes their solemn promise
That what they have said to him will be done
And that at the feast of Saint John[36]
The two lords will come to make their wedding.

36. Midsummer (the summer solstice) was celebrated the eve of the (continued on next page)

2648   He agrees to it, which must be very pleasing.
          Behold the court animated with joy,
          They make a great noise and tumult;
          Throughout the city spreads the news
2652   That their young lady is betrothed.
          Great joy is expressed in Rome
          By the poor people and the rich men.

              My lord Guillaume was then
2656   At a joust outside
          Where young men were amusing themselves,
          They were striking at a mannequin target.
          When he heard the news
2660   That his sweetheart was promised in marriage,
          He lost his color and his vigor,
          He almost died of grief.
          He abandons his palfrey's neck,[37]
2664   Leaves the game and the entertainment.
          Then he goes away, lowers his head,
          Until he gets to the inn he does not stop,
          He makes himself lie down in a bed.
2668   Now there is in him only affliction,
          For himself he knows no comfort,
          For himself he asks for death.

              In his palace, on the main floor
2672   Were the emperor and all his barons,
          His dukes and his princes and his peers.
          He had his daughter brought to him.
          They say, when they have seen her,
2676   That never has her equal been seen,
          Never was there such a beautiful woman,
          Above all others she is the gem.
          They praised her very much for her great beauty.
2680   Back to her room went
          The maiden who is very displeased
          By what her father has done to her.
          Truly she says to herself

feast of the Birth of Saint John the Baptist (June 24). In medieval romance, major events frequently coincide with important feast days.
    37. A palfrey is a parade or saddle horse, used for riding rather than for combat.

2684   And swears to God, the sovereign King,
        That this accord will never be accomplished
        And that she will have no one other than her beloved.

        The emperor marvels greatly
2688   Where my lord Guillaume was,
        When he had not come to the court
        And had not seen the men from Greece.
        He sends for him, but they tell him
2692   That he is lying sick at his lodging.
        The emperor is very troubled by this,
        For he loves him very much and with great love,
        But because of the Greek messengers
2696   He does not reveal his worry at this time.
        That night they left him thus.
        Very well were the Greeks served
        And treated courteously and entertained.
2700   Until the third day the Greeks
        Stayed with the emperor.
        They are very pleased with the way
        That the emperor has honored them;
2704   It will be recounted faithfully in Greece
        If God allows them to return to their land.
        The messengers do not want to delay
        Any longer, they took their leave,
2708   They go back to their country,
        To their lord, joyous and happy,
        For they have accomplished what they wanted to do.

        Here we will leave the Greeks,
2712   We will not say any more about them at this time;
        But let us not be negligent now,
        Thus we will speak henceforth
        Of Guillaume who is so distressed.
2716   He pays little attention, but does not speak,
        He hears with difficulty, but does not understand.
        He is gently beseeched by
        All the people of the city
2720   And the country and the realm
        Who all say: "God, what unhappiness!
        Ah, good vassal, full of valor,

Full of nobility and honor,
2724   And of great and gentle character,
What a great pity it would be,
If something unfortunate happened to you!
Sire, more valiant than all others,
2728   You are of such high birth and so very noble,
Generous above all other creatures,
Full of great wisdom and moderation,

....

2732   Young and handsome and gracious!
Was there ever of your age
A man who had so many qualities of a vassal?
You have more of these than a thousand men.
2736   May God save us all from this danger,
For the pain would be too grave,
If you, good lord, should die."
Thus they were saying throughout the city;
2740   More than one hundred thousand lament his loss.

The emperor is so troubled
About the young man, he does not know what to do;
Because of his suffering he is sad.
2744   He went there to see him,
And he asks him how he is doing.
Guillaume replies: "Sire, it is going badly for me.
— Badly? — Indeed, extremely. — Friend, how?
2748   — Sire, I know well with a certainty
That I am approaching the end without any recourse,
In me there is no longer anything but death.
Now may God through His cherished delight
2752   Reward you for the great love
That you have shown me, if it pleases you, sire."
Then he became silent, he cannot say anything else.

When the emperor hears this,
2756   He almost splits from grief;
He almost breaks, he is so sad,
When he sees him suffering from his malady.
He has such pain for the vassal
2760   That water runs down from his eyes,
Wets his beard and his chin

And the facing of his fur-lined cloak;
There can be no more pity than what he expresses.
2764 From the young man he took his leave.
He left and Guillaume remains,
Who is complaining about his enormous grief.
Within his heart he calls for the one
2768 For whom he lives and whom he loves so much,
But the beautiful lady does not know anything about it.
When she heard the news,
Concerning him she knows no comfort;
2772 If he dies, she truly wants to die,
If he leaves, she desires death.
To herself she begins to say:
"Lord Guillaume, sweet friend,
2776 Flower of beauty, valiant and wise,
More worthy than anyone, the most distinguished above all,
May it not please the king of paradise,
That, if you die, I live."
2780 Then she declares herself a poor wretch,
According to her desire she would like to be dead.
Thus she truly dared to show her grief.
Because of the modesty of the people,
2784 She showed too much, I believe.
Now that is why she hesitated
And thus doubles her torment.
Then she said: "Oh God, counsel me!
2788 I will go to him. No. Why not?
If I go there, everyone will say,
I believe, and right will they be,
That I am far too frivolous and foolish.
2792 So will I abandon him because of what they might say?
No indeed I will not, but because of my honor.
Does he not have my heart and my love?
If he has my heart, can I live without him?
2796 I do not know who will be troubled by it,
I will not abandon him because of evil hatred,
Nor for anything that people might say
Will I not go to my lover.
2800 Without him my life is not worth a glove."

Thus she assured herself,

And to the young man she went.
She takes with her as many

2804   Of her people as she desires.
Melior enters his room.
The others remained outside,
With the exception of only Alixandrine.

2808   Melior goes with the young woman,
Comes to the young man, and hugs him,
Cries tenderly, and speaks to him.
"Lord Guillaume, sweet lover,

2812   For the love of God, what are you doing?
I have come here alone to you.
Beautiful sweet lover, speak to me.
What will become of this abandoned woman

2816   Who is so frightened for you?
Now I am your dear love."
He was lying facing the wall,
He turns around and he saw her.

2820   "You are very welcome, he says,
My beautiful and very sweet and dear lover.
Lover? Alas, now enemy,
Enemy at the same time.

2824   Sweetheart, for God's sake, because of what misdeed
Have you thus killed and murdered me?
You have sinned and done a great wrong.
More than anyone I loved you;

2828   Always, sweetheart, I desired you;
In you I had put my spirit,
All my joy and my delight,
And so it will be as long as I shall live.

2832   But since I have lost you,
My life will be short and brief.
May God be thanked one hundred times
That you came here to me, my lady,

2836   For now your soul will be better for it."

When she hears her sweetheart,
She almost breaks from grief.
Very gently she replied:

2840   "My lord, for the sake of God the King Jesus.
Do you therefore believe that this wretched girl

Will live if you die?

No, may God not consent

2844 That this unhappy one should survive after you.

And thus you say that I have killed you:

Indeed I have not, you are wrong,

And that you have lost me.

2848 Indeed. — How? — You know it well.

— No indeed I do not, may it never please God

That I, my beautiful sweet love, ever know it.

— In truth, are you not betrothed?

2852 — Since my father did his folly,

Do you therefore believe that I will keep it?

Assuredly, I will not, whatever might happen,

I will never have a duke or count,

2856 A baron or the son of an emperor,

For anything that man might do.

I would allow myself to be torn apart

Or flayed or buried alive

2860 Than to be separated from you.

I will not leave you, my love,

And I will not belong to anyone but you.

Of this you can truly be sure.

2864 — Sweetheart, for the sake of God the celestial King,

If I were sure of this,

I would never feel any pain,

Then I would be completely healed.

2868 — Yes, of course, my fair sweet love,

You will no longer want anything that I will not do for you."

Then they take each other in their arms,

And kiss each other loyally

2872 And do together what they desire

As long as it pleases them, but the hour arrives

That they need to go back.

They took leave of each other joyous and happy,

2876 Straight to the lodging they returned.

He stayed at his inn

Now feeling neither well nor ill.

From his bed he got up quickly,

2880 He dresses himself well and richly,

He is totally healed; he is in completely good health.

The people are so very happy about this,

They all know the news
2884   That the maiden has healed him
And they all say that she is very wise,
Because she knows how to heal such an illness.

      The young man comes to the court,
2888   The emperor Nathaniel
Hugs and kisses him and is very pleased
By what his daughter has done for him,
For he does not know the truth.
2892   Now it is right that I tell you
About the Greek messengers. They rode their horses until
They returned back to Greece.
To the lords they tell the news,
2896   Which is very pleasing to them and good;
The two lords are very happy about it.
No man has ever seen such preparations and such ornaments
As those that they have made.
2900   The time comes for this matter;
They do not want to wait any longer.
The knights had arrived
Who had been summoned:
2904   There were many princes and barons,
Kings, dukes, counts and lords,
The companies are enormous.
The emperor and his son mount their horses.
2908   The company of Greeks is so large
That I cannot tell you whether there were hundreds
Or whether there were thousands of people there.
They set off with great joy.
2912   They went by such a direct route
That the Greeks arrived in Rome
On their palfreys before a month had passed.

      The emperor hears the news,
2916   You can know it is very pleasing to him.
He goes to greet them; he does not stop.
He greets them warmly and celebrates very much,
For the two lords he expresses happiness,
2920   To honor them he takes great pains.
They turn back to the city,
Which truly had a grand appearance

And was beautifully and richly decorated.

2924   In anticipation of their arrival
The streets are strewn with flowers
And hanging from above are
Curtains and cloths of silk

2928   There you would have heard great joy,
Young men and maidens singing,
The sounding of rotes, hurdy-gurdies,
Trumpets, flutes and frestelles,

2932   And buisines and small horns,[38]
The reverberating of tambourines and drums,
And bears and wrestlers fighting.
They make such a noise and such a racket

2936   That the whole city resounds and is in an uproar because of it.

To the lodgings come the lords,
There they are received with great honor,
Very richly and honorably.

2940   Such are the preparations
That the Greeks make throughout the city
That it cannot be calculated for you.
The Romans honor the Greeks very much:

2944   Destriers and mules and palfreys,
Jewels of fine gold, dogs and birds
Are sent to them by their hosts.
Great is the joy that they cause.

2948   Now it is right that I tell you
About Guillaume and about his life.
He was in his room with his sweetheart,
Often he complains and says to her:

2952   "In the name of God, dear one, it was my misfortune that I saw
            you,
Woe to me that I made your acquaintance.
The promise that you have given me has stolen my confidence
And know that because of it I will die.

2956   And thus I know well that I am wrong,
Sweetheart, when I ask anything of you,

---

38. Rotes, hurdy-gurdies, frestelles and buisines were all medieval musical instruments. A rote was a five-string harp, a hurdy-gurdy was a stringed instrument played by turning a wheel with a crank and depressing keys that held down the strings, a frestelle was a flute that resembled a panpipe, and a buisine was a large horn with a turned up bell.

But I have so much grief in my heart
That I do not know how to behave;
2960   It seems to me that absolutely everything causes me harm.

       She was very wise and very clever,
Thus she said to him: "Fair sweet friend,
Please, all this is not useful,
2964   But now let us think about exploiting it,
Examining it and researching
How we might get out of the realm
Without being seen,
2968   Found or captured or detained.
It is most fitting that we be attentive to this,
For it is not possible to wait any longer.
He responds to her: "My gentle sister,
2972   And I would grant it with a very good heart
If I were happier and more joyous.
May the King of the world, the all powerful,
Allow us to find such guidance
2976   Which would allow both of us to rejoice."
Then they spoke in various ways
And took and gave many a counsel.
In many ways they deliberated
2980   How they will leave the country,
But they cannot find any means
Where they will not be captured, this they see well.
They summoned Alixandrine
2984   Who was so very tearful for them
Because they want to go away thus,
That both her eyes were causing her pain.
They truly overwhelmed her and begged her
2988   That if she knows in any way
Anything that might be useful to them,
That she do it now according to her ability.

       She answers: "I have a lot of grief.
2992   According to my desire, I would never want this,
But when it cannot be otherwise,
I will tell you well my advice.
It seems to me that you want to go away
2996   And that for no reason will you remain.
But when the two emperors

Learn of this dishonor,
That you have left the realm this way,
3000 They will search for you everywhere:
They will guard all the passes,
The seaports and the riverbanks.
There will never be any condemned man,
3004 Clerk or bourgeois, noble or peasant,
In secret or otherwise,
That one will not know his situation.
And if you are recognized,
3008 Absolutely all the gold that there ever was
Would not be able to save you from death.
This is a painful and difficult counsel.
But hear now, says the young noblewoman,
3012 Down in the great kitchen
They have skinned several animals,
Goats and deer and stags and bear;
Those are beasts that are greatly feared.
3016 No one sees them who does not distance himself
Rather than dare approach them;
They are so cruel and strong and fierce.
No other counsel can I see.
3020 But if you can obtain these skins
And if you were sewn into them,
Never would you be recognized.
In such a way, I believe, you will be able to protect yourselves
3024 And depart from the land.
I do not see any other defense.
But, and may God pardon me,
About your meals I do not know what to say."
3028 Guillaume begins to smile
And says: "My dear sweet sister,
Do you therefore believe in any way
That I might suffer from any privation
3032 As long as I am with my sweetheart?
We will live well off our love,
From grass, from leaves and from flowers.
But now think how it might be done so,
3036 We have no need of further discussion."
The maiden began to say to them:
"Sir Guillaume, dear sweet lord,

What will this miserable girl do
3040 Who will stay behind after you?
Immediately the emperor will make me
Die a violent and pitiless death.
He will accuse me of this affair,
3044 So he will cause me to be vilely torn apart
And killed very painfully.
Sire, in the name of God the Creator,
If it pleases you, I will go with you
3048 Very willingly on this path.
I would be very useful to you
For procuring whatever you need."
The young man replied to her:
3052 "My dear, by your grace,
In no way can this be."
And so off she goes head bowed, she
Who was so wise and thoughtful.
3056 As a servant she dressed herself,
To the kitchen she went directly,
Well she knew how to succeed at her task there
And she went straight to the skinners
3060 Who were skinning stags and bears
And many other kinds of beasts.
She chooses two hides large and full
From two white bears and a serpent.
3064 So that no one notices anything
She returns directly to the chamber.
Well has she accomplished her affair.
My lord Guillaume calls her:
3068 "Alixandrine, sweet friend,
Do you have what we need?
— Yes, good sir, see it ready.
— Now, quickly, dear, make use of it,
3072 Think about how to prepare it without delay."
She took the smaller skin.
According to the desire of the young man
She stretched it out on Melior:
3076 Just as if she were dressed
In her best garments
Alixandrine sewed her into the bearskin.[39]

39. In the Middle Ages, women's dresses were typically loose-fitting *(continued on next page)*

When Melior was enclosed in the skin,
3080   She called to Alixandrine:
"Dear, how do I seem to you?
— My lady, in the name of God the sovereign King,
If I did not know that you were in that skin,
3084   For one hundred marks of gold I would not tarry,
You seem to have the body, limbs and head
Of a bear and a fierce beast."
Afterwards she took the other skin.
3088   According to the desire of the young man
With long and strong straps
She stretched it on top of his body;
On the robe that he was wearing
3092   She tightly sewed the skin for him.
When he was garbed in the skin
And was well laced and covered by it,
Then he called to his beloved sweetheart:
3096   "My love, says he, conceal nothing,
Tell me how I seem to you.
— In truth, sire, my heart is trembling
When I look at you, you seem so fierce.
3100   — My love, let us think about how to profit from it,"
Says Guillaume to the young noblewoman.
Tenderly Alixandrine weeps
For her lady and for the vassal,
3104   For she truly had a loyal heart.

When they were sewn into the skins,
Then both of them were unrecognizable:
There is no one to whom, as much as he might look at them,
3108   They would seem to be anything
Other than bears, vicious and fierce.
They do not want to delay any longer:
Of the young noblewoman they take leave
3112   And give her one hundred thanks from God
For what she had counseled them to do.
Their eyes are wet with tears
Out of pity for Alixandrine

tunics with long slits that could be closed by tightening laces to achieve a better fit. For further reading, see Newman, 113–114. Sewing Melior into the bearskin is a broad imitation of this procedure.

3116　Who because of them is tearing out her hair.
　　　　She is pulling out her hair and ripping her clothing,
　　　　Almost destroyed by her grief.
　　　　They set off on their way,
3120　But the maiden accompanies them
　　　　As far as the orchard gate below.
　　　　Often she sighs for the two of them
　　　　And weeps for them tenderly.
3124　And when it came time for their departure,
　　　　From grief three times she faints
　　　　Because of the pity she has for the lady.
　　　　And when she comes back from her swoon,
3128　To God she begins a prayer:
　　　　"Oh, true gentle Father Jesus Christ,
　　　　Most powerful of all kings,
　　　　True Father of men, omnipotent,
3132　Good Lord God, if truly
　　　　You formed heaven and earth and everything
　　　　And in the Virgin You became incarnate
　　　　And were made flesh,
3136　Lord, through Your holy annunciation,
　　　　And through the form of man and human flesh,
　　　　And if You protected in the whale
　　　　Jonah who had been swallowed,
3140　If all this is true, Lord, then through Your mercy
　　　　Protect and defend these two children
　　　　From distress, from evil and from torment
　　　　And return them to prosperity,
3144　Lord, through Your holy goodness."
　　　　Then she falls silent and they leave,
　　　　Whom God, the King of the world, advises.
　　　　They walk on all fours like hunting dogs
3148　And they watch each other.

　　　　A Greek had come to the woods;
　　　　When he saw the bears,
　　　　From death he believes he has no protection.
3152　As fast as he could he flees,
　　　　To the inn he arrived, pale and ashen,
　　　　As fast as possible, faster than ever before.
　　　　His companions say this to him:

3156 "Has something that is not good happened to
       you?
       —Yes. —What? —A very fearful thing.
       In this orchard, next to that tower,
       I had gone to see what was there,
3160 And two white bears, fierce and wild,
       Escaped, they went by there.
       They almost devoured me,
       Except they did not see me, I believe
3164 And I came away as I was able.
       To the vile devils I consign them,
       They are so very hideous and huge.

       Now I want to be silent about the Greeks,
3168 For later I have much to relate.
       So we will talk of the young people
       Who go off sewn into the skins.
       In the forest they have entered,
3172 Together the two have wandered so much
       That this night has passed,
       And morning has broken.
       The young man calls to his friend:
3176 "Melior, sweet damsel,
       See it is broad daylight and so bright:
       Counsel what we can do.
       From now on peasants will be about,
3180 Knights and men-at-arms,
       Those who are going to the wedding in Rome.
       God, who formed the first man,
       Lord, by Your commandment
3184 Defend us now from evil people.
       —Amen, Lord, she responds;
       May God the King of the world protect us from them.

       —My dear, says the young man,
3188 See here, the sun is already coming up.
       It is time to rest at present.
       Let us seek out either a ditch or bog
       Where we can hide ourselves now.
3192 —My lord, said she, as you please."
       In a marsh deep and broad

The two lovers[40] have hidden themselves
Beneath the branches, in the foliage.
3196   This life would have pleased them very much,
If they had not been so afraid.
They often appeal to the Savior
That He protect them now out of His pity.
3200   They were weary and fatigued,
And both of them were very hungry.
Very gladly, if they had had something,
They would have eaten, but they have nothing to eat
3204   And they do not dare look for anything.
Through the leaves the young woman looked
For nuts, acorns, and hay,
Wild apples and buds.
3208   "My dear, says the young man,
I do not know what will finally happen to me.
I will go toward the path
To see if I meet
3212   Anyone walking on the road
Who is carrying bread on his shoulders or on a beast of burden
And who is coming or going to Rome.
For if I find a man traveling alone,
3216   I will not wait for anything alive,
If he is carrying something which might merit eating.
You will have some of it, although it might not be pleasing,
For nothing worse can happen to us
3220   Than that we allow ourselves to die from hunger.

      — Sire, says the damsel,
Soon this news will be known
In Rome to the emperors.
3224   Those who have lost this day
Will have quickly carried the news to Rome:
The whole country will be in an uproar
And they will say all that you have done.
3228   If you steal, my lord, and if it pleases you
To believe me, it will not be thus.
— How then, my sister, my sweetheart?
— Thus, my lord, we will suffer,

---

40. Micha's edition, which reads "li sui amant," is faulty. My translation is based on Michelant's edition, which reads "li dui amant" and accurately reflects the manuscript.

3232   We will eat acorns and wild apples
And this other woodland fruit.
God who made us all in His image,
He is watching over us because of His kindness."

3236   They prayed a long time to the Creator
That He might watch over them and counsel them.
You have heard the astonishing event
And the adventure fierce and grand,

3240   How the wolf kidnapped the child
Because of the immense harm
And because of the brutal betrayal
That his uncle wanted to do to him,

3244   Just as you have heard told.
This wolf, the very same,
As soon as they were outside the chamber
And had set out on their way,

3248   Pursued them through the night
Until they were in their hiding place;
Then he left again quickly,
Right up to the main road he went.

3252   Well he knows what the two lovers need,
Who are weary and fatigued,
For they had traveled all night,
And both of them were very hungry.

3256   He watches on the road, sees a peasant
Who was carrying white bread and cooked meat:
Soon there will be, if possible, a battle between the two of them.
In a small sack he had enclosed the food,

3260   In that manner he was carrying it to his household.
The peasant comes and the wolf leaps out:
The man sees the beast and shrieks loudly:
"Help, sweet glorious Father!

3264   Protect me today, that this werewolf
Might have no power to kill me."
And the werewolf advances toward him,
With his teeth he seizes him and jumps to the side,

3268   He has a good hold on him because of the pleat in his garment;
He throws the peasant flat on the ground, all stretched out.
He seized the meat
That he was carrying to his household.

3272   But if the peasant's wife will be angry about it,

This will not matter very much to the beast.
In that place he does not stay any longer,
He leaves the peasant, then goes away.
3276 And the peasant does not at all linger
Who likewise very quickly flees from there.
He never believes he will see the night,
Many times he looks behind to see
3280 That the fierce beast is not going after him.
But he had already set out on his way,
To the two children he is bringing his prey.
A long way he goes through the woods;
3284 When they hear all the noise
They finally believe that they have been betrayed.
But when they see the beast coming
Who is bringing them the meat,
3288 Each one feels safe and is comforted
But they do not know what will happen.
The werewolf descends the knoll
All the way down to the bottom of the marsh;
3292 To the maiden and the vassal
In their hiding place he comes directly.
What he carries very humbly
The werewolf set before them,
3296 Then he retreated again
Into the forest at a rapid pace,
I know not where, to seek adventure.[41]
Guillaume takes the small sack
3300 And unties it quickly;
When they see the bread and the meat,
Know that they are truly joyful about it
And give thanks and express gratitude
3304 To the sovereign King of paradise.
Guillaume says to his sweetheart:
"My dear, you know, He does not forget us,
The King of all creatures.
3308 Sweetheart, now hear what an adventure!
Has such a miracle ever been seen,
When God by means of a transformed beast

41. The Guillaume poet thus establishes an unlikely parallel between the werewolf and Arthurian knights such as Erec, Yvain, and Calogrenant who go off on an adventure quest. In spite of his appearance, the werewolf behaves like a knight.

Sends us our sustenance?
3312   Truly He knows, beloved, that we are on this path,
For He certainly is proving it to us.
— My lord, says the noble Melior,
May it please Him that He knows it,
3316   May He want it and may it be agreeable to Him,
For I am greatly comforted by it."
Then they ended their conversation.

Then they eat, since they were hungry,
3320   From what they have they feed themselves well.
Each one pulled a naked hand
From the skin that it had been wearing,
For she who put them in the skins
3324   Stitched the covering in such a way
That each can free a hand
Whenever it pleases them, according to their desire.
By means of the mouth that is in the skin
3328   They feed each other morsels,
But they have neither sauce nor salt[42]
And they drink neither wine nor anything else.
But if the wolf can accomplish it,
3332   Before they leave the meal
They will have, if he succeeds, something to drink.
A cleric who was going to meet a priest
Was bringing to his house
3336   A small cask of very good wine;
But, I truly believe, the priest
Who ordered it will not taste it.

When the cleric sees the wolf coming
3340   He does not know what will happen in the end,
Everything that he was carrying he throws on the ground,
He turns in flight at such a speed
Like one who does not believe at all
3344   That he will be able to save his life.
And the werewolf picks up the cask,
For regarding the cleric he had no desire
To do him further harm.

---

42. Salt was an important commodity in the Middle Ages, not only as a flavoring, but also as an important nutrient and as a preservative for foodstuffs. For a discussion, see Newman, 5–6.

3348   To the maiden and to the vassal
He returned and tossed the cask down in front of them.
Afterward he kept on his way,
In that place he did not stay any longer.

3352   "Oh, said Guillaume, noble beast,
How you do me a great courtesy
When you help my beloved and me!
May He who sent you to us

3356   Receive our gratitude and our thanks
And may He protect you.
— Indeed, my lord, says Melior,
I am as greatly comforted

3360   As if peace had been sworn to us by
My father and the lord of the Greeks
And Lertenidon his son
Who was about to take me as his wife.

3364   But now he may well defer it,
And if it pleases God, he will do so."
Then they pick up the cask;
They have neither a drinking mug nor goblet,

3368   Instead they drink from the cask
As long as they want and as each is able.
When they have eaten as much as they please,
Then they fall asleep, for they are very tired,

3372   In the foliage, in each other's arms;
They have forgotten their great fear.
They slept so long in the branches
That just at the moment of vespers they awoke.[43]

3376   Again they marveled about this
That they have slept so long.
Thus they remained in the hiding place
Until night had arrived.

3380   Then the two lovers kept on
Their way through the forest;
May He now lead them, if it pleases Him,
The Savior of everyone.

3384   *At night they walk upright*[44]

---

43. Vespers is the sixth of the seven canonical hours of the day or approximately 6:00 P.M. in the summer and 4:15 P.M. in the winter. See Barber, 8.

44. Verse 3384 is missing from the manuscript. The verse provided here is not a translation but is based entirely on my conjecture.

And when they see that it is day,
Then they go on four feet like bears.
But know one thing to be true:
3388 That they are much more ugly to see
When they are walking upright on two feet
Than when they get down on all fours.
Thus they travel all that night;
3392 He follows their entire route well,
That wolf who does not forget them.
And when the dawn has brightened the sky
And it is broad daylight,
3396 ....
And he sees that they are hidden,
All that they needed the wolf
Generously provided for them.
3400 And when nightfall arrived,
Then they set out again on their way;
The beast always goes along
Behind, so that they will not see him.
3404 He follows immediately after them,
But they know not whether he is near or far,
And he helps them according to their needs
With absolutely all that they require,
3408 So that they experience no hardship.
In this manner they traverse the land
And distance themselves from their enemies.

Now I want to leave them here,
3412 Well will we know how to come back there
When the place is right, but now I want to talk
About the gathering that they brought about
In Rome that was so greatly attended.
3416 Very beautiful was the morning
And the weather fair and bright the day
And great the tumult and the noise of the drums
Which passed through the streets.
3420 All the people are excited:
On these upper floors are these maidens,
These ladies and these damsels
Who are there in order to watch the great wealth
3424 The enormous pride and the nobility

With which the streets were filled.
To each other they were all saying
That never had anyone seen such an awesome sight.
3428   The Greeks had come up
Along with all the Romans from the city,
Of which there were more than twenty thousand,
In addition to the other men of the country
3432   Whose companies are huge.
The Greek emperor had come up
And with him was his son
Dressed very richly,
3436   In such a way that no one can say how
Their garments were embroidered.
They were of such great nobility
That no man would be able to recount it,
3440   And because of this I will be silent.

Everyone mounted their horses
And issued forth from their lodgings
Where they await the news
3444   That the maiden has arrived at the church.
To the principal church, Saint Peter's,
Has come to officiate at the service
The pope who had been invested.[45]
3448   Never were such people seen
As those that he brought with him:
There are so many monks and abbots,
Cardinals, bishops and prelates
3452   And archbishops and legates,
All invested carrying crosiers,[46]
Who had come for the wedding.
No man has ever seen so many together.
3456   The whole city is shaking and trembling
From the sound of the bells and from the noise
That everyone is making throughout the city.
There the Greek is supposed to take his wife,
3460   But he will wait for her a long time,

45. An invested pope has undergone the ceremony of investiture, which confers upon him his authority and his symbols of power.
46. A crosier is a staff with a crook or cross at the end that is carried by an abbot, a bishop or an archbishop as a symbol of his office.

For I do not believe that he will ever see her
To receive any solace or joy from her;
Rather the one who will take comfort from her
3464   Is the one who is now holding her in his arms.

    In his most important residence
Is the emperor with his people,
His body so richly dressed
3468   In garments which are of such high quality
That they will never age
Nor will they worsen for wear.
I cannot describe everything to you
3472   Nor the construction recount, or tell
Who gave it to him, who had it made,
For there would be too much to relate:
Thus it suits me to be silent now,
3476   Since I still have much to do in the future.
Truly handsome for his age was
The Emperor Nathaniel.
He was more than eighty years old;
3480   His hair was hoary and white
And his beard as white as blooming fruit trees.
He had an exceptionally fierce appearance
And he was very valiant and wise.
3484   Around him were his vassals:
There were so many kings, dukes and counts,
Rich barons and lesser fief-holders
And young noblemen, not to mention the other army,
3488   That I can neither recount it or tell it to you.
And whoever might see the possessions and the wealth
Of the ladies of the different regions
Who were assembled there,
3492   The dignity and nobility
Of their costly and expensive garments,
And see the most valiant and most worthy
Maidens of the land
3496   Lined up in the palace,
Who had come to the wedding,
How richly they were dressed,
Would consider all this as nothing other than amazing.
3500   Never has anyone seen such wealth.

They are waiting until the damsel
Melior comes out.

The emperor especially
3504 Marvels greatly at
Why his daughter is tarrying so long,
For truly now it is the time and hour
That she ought to be up,
3508 Prepared and dressed
Just as she should be to go to the church,
For kings, counts, dukes and princes
And the high-ranking men were waiting for her.
3512 Nathaniel, the king of Rome,
Lets it be known how late she is
And messengers tell him
That in the chamber they did not at all find
3516 Any maiden who might tell
What might have become of her.
The emperor breaks out in beads of sweat
From anger and irritation, when he hears this.
3520 He enters the chamber full of rage,
He called Alixandrine,
Who was bent over in her bed
And thinking of the maiden;
3524 Because of her she often wept.
When she hears the emperor,
She fears his wrath so much
That she does not know what will become of her.
3528 If she is not able to protect herself now with a ruse
And defend herself with her intelligence,
Immediate death may she well expect.
Then she came out of a chamber
3532 And went before the king;
Her fear and her uneasiness
She covers with a joyful appearance,
And asks: "What pleases you, sire?"
3536 And he responds with great anger:
"Why has my daughter dawdled so
That she has not prepared herself?
For it is already terce; above all[47]

---

47. Terce is the third canonical hour of the day or approximately 8:00 A.M. See Barber, 8.

3540 I am having people search for her everywhere
      Yet no one can find her.
      I will be very angry and upset
      If I do not hear any news about her.
3544 — Sire, said the damsel,
      If it pleases you, do not get angry.
      They are not being courtly,
      Those who are making such a report about her,
3548 For over there within her chamber she is sleeping,
      Know this well with certainty.
      — Then go over there and tell her
      To get up immediately.
3552 — Sire, I believe that
      She would not want to speak to me.
      — Is that so? — Yes, upon my word.
      — Why? — I do not know, she responds.
3556 — In the name of the Lord who made the world,
      Says the emperor to the girl,
      I want to know the whole situation.
      — Indeed, sire, if I may be so bold,
3560 Very gladly will I tell you.
      — Yes. — I do not want to, I fear you too much
      And your daughter especially,
      That if I have misspoken about anything
3564 Either in words or in counsel,
      Please pardon me for it
      And in the name of God grant it to me for her.
      — I pardon you for it, but now tell me.
3368 — So be it, with your permission,"
      Replies the one who is no fool;
      She feigns her manner and her speech,
      Then she began her tale.
3572 Water rises from her heart to her eyes,
      Down her cheeks it flows.
      "Sire, says the damsel,
      I will not accept your sorrow,
3576 For I am of your lineage
      And you raised me from childhood,
      And so I have confidence in you.
      Your daughter hates me very much,
3580 But in error, as God knows.

I was present when she went to bed yesterday evening,
She had me sit before her such a long time
That it was well past midnight.
3584   The entire room was emptied
So that there did not remain, upon my oath of loyalty to you,
Man or woman except the two of us.
There she revealed to me her secret,
3588   Greatly did she complain to me about you.
— About me? — Indeed. — Do you know why?
— Upon my word, because of this gathering.
She did not want this marriage.
3592   For she has been well informed of the custom
Of the lords of Constantinople.
They will never have a wife, as noble as she might be,
None of such great value or so esteemed
3596   Or from such a high lineage
That she not be immediately locked up.[48]
She will hate very much, it is said, the land,
The wealth, the region
3600   Of which she has nothing but the name.
Except she will have the name of empress:
Worse cannot happen to her.
Thus she will live, but as a hog.
3604   Whoever loses his body for his possessions,
It is said that he makes a poor profit.
Whoever loses his body gains little;
It is better for her to love a duke or count
3608   Or the son of a poor fief-holder
Than to have such honor or such wealth
From which she will be forever in sadness.
Afterwards she said a word to me
3612   For which I reproved her and considered her a fool,
And for which she began so strongly to hate me."
Said the emperor, "Sister, my dear,
Say it then, I want to know it,
3616   Whether it might be folly or wisdom.
— Good sir, now do not look upon her badly:
She has given her heart to a vassal.

48. This is an intertextual allusion to the conclusion of Chrétien de Troyes' *Cligès* (vv. 6762–6783), which states that royal wives were locked up and guarded because Fenice had deceived her husband Alis.

       — Her heart? — Indeed. — Tell me how.
3620   — Sire, in the name of God the all powerful,
       She does not love anything as much as she loves him,
       Not even herself or anyone else;
       Truly there is nothing that she loves as much,
3624   It is this that she lamented most about.
       When I heard this, then I rebuked her for it,
       I reproved her and chastised her so much
       That she began to hate me for it
3628   And I parted from her on a bad note.
       — Go on, he says, do not conceal it from me:
       Who is the one who dared think
       About my daughter in such a dishonorable way?"
3632   She replied to the emperor:
       "Sire, it is the young man,
       The brave, the wise, and the fair.
       — Guillaume? — It is he without any doubt.[49]
3636   — Indeed? Thus he has caused me great offense.
       I had him raised and educated,
       I dubbed him knight and made him
       Seneschal of my empire.
3640   It is true what I have heard said
       That one might nurture one like him and do well
       But that it would come out better for him to raise a dog.
       He has behaved badly toward me,
3644   But in the name of the One in whom I believe,
       Who for us endured physical suffering,
       Absolutely all the gold that is in the world
       Would not save him, if I can capture him,
3648   From me having him burned or hung."
       Speaking quickly they went inside
       To the bed that was in the chamber;
       They raised the mosquito netting,
3652   They see the sheets and the pillow,
       But when they do not find the girl,

---

49. Notice how the emperor immediately guesses that Alixandrine is speaking of Guillaume, as if the adjectives "brave, wise, fair" could be applied to no one else. Melior reacted similarly (vv. 2474–2490) when the messenger told her about the battle with the duke of Saxony. Although "eighty sons of princes" were knighted with Guillaume (v. 1807), when the messenger identifies the vassal who saved all of them only as "the newly dubbed" she immediately asks if it was Guillaume. Now, with the emperor's recognition of his courtliness, Guillaume's courtly identity has been firmly established.

Alixandrine acts as if
She knows nothing of the affair.
3656 Out of fear she knows not what to do,
She is so afraid of the emperor.
"God, she says, for the sake of Your goodness,
Where has my lady gone,
3660 Since we did not find her here?
I believed her to be still sleeping,
Because last night she stayed up so late
That it was near daybreak
3664 When she, because of her intense irritation
Chased me out of her room.
But God knows well who is at fault;
For her own good I told her what I knew
3668 And for the sake of her honor and her profit,
But she never wanted to hear anything.
Whoever might have heard her argue with me
And mistreat me with her words,
3672 How they would consider me a foolish young girl!
She almost attacked me.
Sire, says she, she is not here any more now,
But think quickly about sending someone
3676 To the lodging of the knight.
If he is there, then your daughter has not
Left this city;
And if he is not there, they are together
3680 In the city or they are leaving it together.

The emperor is very distraught;
Water flows down his face
And falls off, drop by drop.
3684 He had the whole city searched
But he will not hear any news.
He believes he will finally die from rage,
His heart is almost breaking;
3688 Often water flows from his forehead
And drips down his face.
He does not know what to do with his shame,
He knows indeed that it cannot be concealed.
3692 Soon the affair was spread about:
Already everyone knows that with the vassal

The beauty left as well,
And when the thing was known,
3696   It was considered a most amazing event.
Quickly they abandoned the great feast
That had begun throughout the city,
The dances in round, the entertainments.
3700   The emperor of the Greeks
Furious with shame, humiliated and disturbed,
Came back to his lodging,
Along with his sons and his other barons;
3704   All the Greeks dismounted.
The king of Rome had mounted his horse,
With him were thirty of his closest friends;
To the king of the Greeks he comes and relates to him
3708   His great sorrow and his great shame.
To him he complains about the wrong
So great that his daughter has done
And about the valet that he had raised
3712   Who has treated him with such shame:
"So advise me, my lord,
In the name of God, about this dishonor."
Said the emperor: "Now it is thus.
3716   Have a cry go out everywhere
That everyone come from near, from far.
Whoever remains behind and does not respond to this affair,
Let him and his heirs fall into servitude.
3720   Make it be known by all your vassals
That there be no one who remains behind
Who does not do everything in his power to come.
Have the land surrounded,
3724   Have a search conducted everywhere and keep looking
Until Guillaume has been captured.[50]
And of this may each be certain,
Whoever finds him, you will give him so much
3728   That forever will he be recognized as rich.
And have the passes guarded,
The seaports and the riverbanks,
All the straits and the out-of-the-way places,
3732   Castles, towns, cities and villages;

---

50. This verse is not in the manuscript. The translation is based on a conjecture by Michelant.

Have the realm guarded so well,
That no man or woman passes
That their situation is not known
3736   Before they are allowed to proceed.
But I will stay
Either three weeks or one month
Until I know what will happen.
3740   But in the name of the One who caused me to be born,
If it were a certainty
That by chance someone might have done
This thing to me out of malevolence,
3744   Then it would be your misfortune to have confidence in me,
Because forever as long as you will live
This weight would not fall from your neck."
But Nathaniel, the king of Rome,
3748   Told him so much in conclusion
That the lord truly believed him.
Just as you have heard it said,
The people came from everywhere.
3752   Never was such a great army seen;
They separated into a thousand parties,
Encircled the entire land,
And took possession of the whole country.
3756   If the Savior of the whole world
Does not do it now because of His pity for them,
The two lovers will have no guarantee
That they will not be captured, for those who are hunting them
3760   Hate them very much and are threatening them
And assuring them of death:
If they are taken, it will be unfortunate if they die.
May God protect them now from this peril!
3764   I believe He will do it,
For the werewolf has not forgotten them,
Thus he often protects their lives,
For when the hunters would get close
3768   With their dogs to the place where
The two lovers were, the wolf would leap out;
He would put himself at risk[51]
In order to protect and defend them.

---

51. Literally, he would put himself in a hazardous situation, "en aventure."

3772 He would keep them all busy with him,
Until he had led them all away
And distanced them from the young people;
Afterward they had no more worries that day,
3776 Often they are afraid of death.

In this manner the beast leads them
With great fatigue and with great difficulty
And protects them from their enemies
3780 So that they are neither seen nor captured.
Many a perilous journey
Did he suffer and endure.
The Lombards, Romans and Greeks
3784 Never stopped the whole month.
They neglected neither woods nor plain,
Hedge, valley or mountain,
Castle, town, or city;
3788 They had searched and had been everywhere.
But they did not hear any news
Of the vassal and the maiden;
They considered it truly amazing.
3792 When the incident was known
About the two white bears who escaped,
Just as the Greeks related it,
Especially that same evening,
3796 Then everyone says with a common accord
That it was the girl and the vassal
Who left sewn into the skins.
And that is why they finally believed
3800 Then, when it had come to pass
About the vassal and the girl,
What the cooks in the kitchen are saying,
That someone had stolen from them two skins
3804 From two white bears tall and broad.

So when the affair is known
And the lords have heard it,
Once again they have the whole land
3808 Surrounded, searched and looked over,
Forests and plains and ravines,
And once again they make their proclamation:

He who is able to capture these bears for them
3812 Can expect such a reward
That never in his life will he be poor.
Thus it was decreed.
They encircled the country
3816 And searched and looked everywhere,
But they have all worked in vain,
For so far did the werewolf lead
The two lovers through his efforts
3820 That they have now escaped from the land.

When the emperors see
That they are working in vain each day,
Then they abandoned the foolishness.
3824 They dispersed all their people,
The Greeks take leave of the king of Rome,
And so they return to their lands.
But before leaving
3828 The emperor of the Greeks implored him
To have everything guarded well,
Straits, passes, seaports,
For as long as his power lasts.
3832 "And if by chance it happens
That the traitor is caught,
Please, do for me both
As compensation and as a feudal service
3836 That, after I leave, in order to do justice
You might send him to me in Greece;
With your daughter do
What you want; if I had him,
3840 Never would I ask you for anything again."
And the emperor grants it to him
And reassures him very much and pledges
That he will do everything he wants,
3844 If he can capture and detain them.
They kissed each other on the mouth and took leave of one
another,[52]
Good-byes are exchanged from all directions.
Nathaniel with his men

---

52. Men typically kissed each other on the mouth as part of the feudal ceremony of homage.

3848   Returned directly to Rome;
        And the other lords, because of their courtliness,
        With their company of Greeks
        They rode and traveled so long
3852   On mules that ambled smoothly along
        That they went straight back to Greece.
        Everyone marveled greatly
        All around the realm
3856   That their young lord did not bring back
        His wife to whom he had been betrothed.
        But the affair was related to them
        Exactly as it had happened.
3860   They considered it an amazing thing
        And spread the word everywhere.
        After a long time throughout the country
        They frequently took counsel
3864   As to how they would free themselves from this shame
        But Patrichidus the emperor would not agree
        To have anything more be done about the situation.
        Therefore he sets it aside at this time
3868   So that the Greeks will not do any more about it.

             Now I want to leave them;
        To Guillaume I want to return
        And to the werewolf who guides them
3872   With great difficulty, him and his sweetheart.
        Directly toward Apulia he leads them
        Because it was his domain.
        Often he suffers from great pain,
3876   Peril and malady and fear.
        They traveled so far both night and day,
        Still sewn into the two bear skins,
        That they crossed Lombardy[53]
3880   And entered the marches of Apulia.[54]
        One morning they looked,
        They see the towers of a city,
        The fortifications and the circles,[55]

---

53. During the 12th century, the Lombards were not established just in northern Italy; there were also the three Lombard principalities in southern Italy of Benevento, Capua, and Salerno.
    54. The marches of Apulia are the border lands of Apulia.
    55. According to Dunn, the circles referred to may be Trajan's *(continued on next page)*

3884   The eagles and the high enclosures,
The waters and the fisheries;
But there were no forests,
They see nothing but countryside.

3888   Benevento was the name of the city,
And it was loyal to the pope,
Except that the supreme authority over justice
Was the emperor.

3892   They are terrified and in fear
Because of the day that is for them so bright,
They do not know where to go for protection
Or where they might stay until night.

3896   They looked next to a large mound
And along the hill on the side
They see the white color of a quarry;
Both of them go off in that direction,

3900   But it is late for them to not already be there
Because it is broad daylight
And they are in the middle of level fields,
So they are fearful that someone might see them.

3904   Because of this they hastened on their way
Until they arrived at the quarry,
Which was truly huge and vast.
Within it there are many grottos

3908   That had been made by the people
Who had quarried the stone.
One of them was newly made,
And once again those from the city

3912   Would take from it stone for quarrels.
In an old grotto next to that one
The two lovers hid themselves;
But for all the gold that there ever was

3916   They would not have hurried there,
If they had known about the danger
That was already present for them at that instant.
If the King of the world does not do something,

3920   Never from that place will they leave.
They were tired and weary,
For that night they had traveled further
Than they had done any other night.

Triumphal Arch, or they may be the ruins of an ancient theatre (81).

3924 I will not speak to you at length about it.
The two young people fell asleep.
If He who saved the people of Israel
Does not save them because of His tenderness,
3928 They will never see prime[56]
And might be dead or wounded,
For the workers have come
From the city to quarry the stone;
3932 To do their work they entered
The old grotto where the two were sleeping,
Because they had put their equipment there.
They go in their direction, now they see the bears,
3936 And they are wondrously astonished;
Immediately they back out
And leave the quarry.
They called their companions over:
3940 "Good sirs, they say, you know very well
That our emperor, our lord,
Has made a decree throughout his empire
About two white bears, that whoever would find them
3944 Would never be poor,
He would give him so much money as a reward.
Now let us all be good companions
And be associated in good faith.
3948 In that grotto are both of
The bears that you heard me talking about.
They are lying down there next to a pillar,
And they are sleeping, so it seems to me.
3952 Now let us all guard them well together,
Except for one of us who will go to Benevento
For the provost and his men."
They remain and one leaves,
3956 He never stopped running,
Until he arrived in the town.
He asked for the provost
Until he told him the news,
3960 Which was very pleasing to him and good to hear.
"Are you telling me the truth, said the provost,
Then, that are hidden there the bears

---

56. Prime is the second canonical hour of the day, approximately 6:00 A.M. in the summer and 6:45 A.M. in the winter. See Barber, 8.

That the emperor has searched so much for
3964 Throughout the country and the land?
— Yes, sir, upon my word, it is true.
If the two of them are not in the grotto,
Then pierce both my eyes.
3968 My companions stayed there
To guard them. Come away,
And bring all your men,
So that they cannot escape from you."
3972 Then he had it proclaimed
That everyone come out armed or
Risk losing their possessions, their feet, or their life.

Then you would have seen the city giving the alarm,
3976 The men arming themselves with weapons and putting on their
          armor
And many of them leaving the city together,
Both those on foot and those on horseback.
The provost had one of his sons with him,
3980 Young and as fair as a fleur-de-lis,
And he loved him more than anything.
The young man was twelve years old.
He is taking him along with him;
3984 If he had known the mortal suffering
That immediately happened to him,
For all the wealth in Benevento
He would not have taken him along.
3988 They rode on their horses so much and traveled
Until they came to the quarry,
Everyone around dismounted.

The young lady had awakened,
3992 She was very weary and tormented
By a strange dream that she had dreamed
Because of which her courage has been completely modified and
          changed
And her body is trembling and quaking.
3996 She awakened Guillaume and told him:
"My lord, in the name of God, what will we do?
I have such a great worry from a dream
That my whole body is trembling and falling apart.

4000   — Fear not, my dear, he replies,
        And do not be so frightened.
        — But I am. — Why? — For misfortune
        I fear and dread, my fair and dear sweetheart,
4004   Because while sleeping it seemed to me now
        That there were coming to eat us here
        Bears and leopards and fierce boars
        And that they were being led by a lion
4008   That had only one cub.
        They were coming inside to capture us here,
        And we were unable to defend ourselves against them.
        When I looked to the right,
4012   It seemed to me that I saw
        Coming and heading this way
        Our beast that Jesus watches over.
        Right through the middle of the mêlée,
4016   He came cutting through, his mouth gaping open,
        Right to the lion cub without fail.
        In spite of all the other beasts
        He carried him away in his mouth;
4020   Then there was not a single beast
        That dared to catch up with him.
        And when he saw the people coming
        He quickened his step and forced himself to go faster."
4024   Now there is only violent grief:
        Melior and Guillaume hear the noises of the horses
        And see the armed vassals
        Who are readying themselves to enter the grotto.
4028   They almost lose their minds,
        Both of them are weeping greatly,
        For they are in great fear of death.

            Guillaume said: "My dear, sweetheart,
4032   Flower of beauty, rose in bloom,
        In such misfortune, in such grief
        Will we share today on this day!
        Oh, greed, evil thing,
4036   You do not stop nor do you rest,
        And you are merciful to no one!
        Oh, deceptive fate,
        How foolish are those who believe in you!

4040   For what reason or by what right
Do you hate our joy?
If I took my sweetheart away,
I did not do it out of my folly
4044   Nor to dishonor her,
But to take her as my wife,
To augment and elevate my honor.
To God I lament about it, I can do no more.
4048   But in the name of the One who made the earth,
The sea, the waters and the winds,
If I had my armor,
My horse, shield, sword and lance,
4052   Soon they would see my strength,
They would know at the beginning of the action
What beast this skin covers.[57]
Before I were dead or captured,
4056   I would have killed two hundred of them.
But so it is, it cannot be any different
Now it is necessary that everything be done
According to the will of our celestial King.
4060   My love, sweetheart, dearest,
Please take off the bearskin
And put nothing on your naked body
Or you will soon be killed, I believe:
4064   For me you will be quickly attacked.
If I die here, I have merited it well,
But you, beloved, please,
If they know it is you, you will not have to worry.
4068   — My love, may the evil flame burn me,
Should I want to survive without you.
How could my heart allow
Them to strike your naked flesh?"
4072   Then she fell down in a swoon.
He took her in his arms,
Tears flowing down his face.

During this time that they were thus,
4076   And while the provost's men who wanted to enter within

---

57. Unlike the narrator who boasts in the prologue about revealing his secret knowledge, Guillaume laments his own inability to reveal his secret: his prowess that is hidden by his disguise and his lack of knightly equipment.

Were being provoked to capture the two
By the judiciary lieutenant,
And greatly incited and goaded,
4080 At that moment appeared in the middle of the rocks
The werewolf with his gaping mouth.
Right through and beyond the army
He goes and seizes the provost's son,
4084 He would rather lose the soul from his body
Than not bring aid to the two lovers.
With the child lying in his mouth, he drags him away.
Quickly he goes off, he does not stop anymore,
4088 And when the provost sees the beast
Who is carrying off his son,
He cries out to his men anxiously:
"Sons of barons, mount up, mount up!
4092 Now we will truly see what you will do to it;
In the presence of all of you and in my presence
This wolf has kidnapped my son.
There is he over there, now help him!"
4096 Then they all leave to run after him.
Those on horseback had mounted
And those on foot have set off
After the beast who is fleeing.
4100 No one remains behind and everyone leaves.
Everyone has abandoned the quarry
To pursue the fierce beast
Who is carrying off the young boy
4104 Who from fear is losing courage
And screams and cries out very often;
And nevertheless he feels no pain
From anything that the beast does to him.
4108 The chase after the beast is enormous;
With the beast fleeing a little
And the men following after him.
When he is near them, then he distances himself from them,
4112 He knows well how to do his task,
And then come back toward those on foot,
But they do not want to throw their lances or shoot their
    arrows,
For they are afraid they will wound the child.
4116 Thus to distance the people from

The two lovers the beast does this,
Oftentimes in their direction he stops.

The two lovers have heard
4120   The uproar and the hue and cry.
They hear the noise and the shouting
About the wolf who kidnapped the child
And that all the people are following,
4124   They thank and praise God
Who is helping them in this matter.
Said Guillaume: "Dear, beloved,
Has anything like this ever been seen,
4128   When God by means of a transformed beast
Gives us help in such a situation?
Lord, wherever he might be, through Your tenderness,
Today, if it pleases You, protect him
4132   That he might experience neither pain nor injury,
For if it were not for him and, above all, God,
Never would we have any protection from death."
She responds: "That is no lie,
4136   Today because of us he is in such need,
In such a trap and in such a snare
That it will be a marvel if he escapes.
May God, for His own dear delight,
4140   Protect him from them and save him.
— Sweetheart, says he, now there is nothing more to be done.
The sovereign King above,
He is protecting us from them through His mercy.
4144   We can no longer stay here;
Let us leave." They went out,
They looked down, looked up,
They cannot make out a man or a woman,
4148   They see the countryside entirely empty and isolated,
For everyone, those from the city
And those from the realm, has gone after the child,
Who for their deliverance was being carried off
4152   By the noble beast in his mouth.

From far away they hear the clamor
That the people are making throughout the countryside,
The noise, the uproar and the pandemonium
4156   That they are causing as they pursue the beast;

Both of them pray that God will protect him.
Because of their counsel, because of their judgment
They removed the skins that had been sewn on them,
4160 So they remained in their tunics
That the skins had made unattractive and had stained.
Then they go off, they could not do so before,
But they did not forget their skins,
4164 Rather they carried them in their arms.
Quickly the two lovers
Set off on their way, very joyous
That they had escaped that way.
4168 Up on the right they looked,
A good two and a half leagues ahead
They spotted a great forest.
They go in that direction, but they greatly feared
4172 That they might be seen or captured;
They took care as best as they could.
They hurried and traveled
Until they arrived in the forest
4176 And did so in such a way that they were not seen.
They had traveled so long that day together
That it was past none.[58]
Very tired was the beauty;
4180 In the thickness of some foliage
The young people hid themselves,
For great need have they of rest.

They fell asleep in the foliage.
4184 Now it is truly right that I tell you
About the werewolf and the child,
About those who are following after them,
About the knights and the vassals
4188 Who are pursuing him on their horses.
They followed him so far and they chased him so much
That their horses are exhausted.
They dismount; they leave their horses,
4192 Together on foot they all surge ahead;
No one seems to hesitate through lack of courage.
They think they will get the beast,

---

58. None is the fifth canonical hour of the day or approximately 2:30 P.M. in the summer and 1:30 P.M. in the winter. See Barber, 8.

So they pursue him and follow closely,
4196   They believe he will not go much longer,
But still he is not out of breath.
The whole daylong he leads them thus
Until the sun is going to set
4200   And night is about to fall.
The beast sees the day failing,
He no longer wants to keep the boy,
On the ground he put him down so courteously
4204   That the child feels no discomfort;
And then he relies on his four feet
More so than do goats, stags, or doe;
From the men as fast as he can he distances himself.
4208   Well has he accomplished his task,
He does not appear to be tired at all,
In a little bit of time he went a great distance.

When they see him put the boy down on the ground,
4212   They came running in that direction.
The beast does not matter to them any more now,
To the child they run swiftly.
The father arrives there before anyone else,
4216   He stood him up in his arms,
He kisses his mouth and his face,
He believed him to be dead or mistreated,
That never would he have service from him,
4220   Not himself or anyone else.
He puts his hands all over his body,
But everything was both safe and sound.
When he sees neither wound nor blood
4224   On his arms, on his thighs and on his side,
He rejoices greatly about the adventure.
He kisses and comforts his child
Who still did not know
4228   If it was the beast who was holding him.
And when he recognized his father
And sees the men who were with him,
He holds his arms out to him and hugs him so
4232   And plays and laughs, and speaks to him.
And the provost is so joyful
That all his distress and pain,

All his discomfort and grief
4236 That he had had for his son that day
He has totally forgotten because of his joy.
They set off on their way back.
With great joy they are returning,
4240 But they are very weary and fatigued.
In the country they sheltered themselves,
As best as they could they rested.

That night they passed thus
4244 Until the next morning at the break of day
When they set off again;
Everyone went to their own lodging.
The provost did not forget it:
4248 Throughout the land he caused a proclamation to go out
That whoever would return the two bears to him[59]
Would never be poor,
So much wealth would be given to him by
4252 The emperor who wants to have them.
He summoned his men from all over the country
That everyone might come to search for these two bears.

About these men I want to be silent now,
4256 I want to return to the young people
Who are sleeping in the foliage
And to the werewolf who has not forgotten them.
That evening that he left the boy
4260 He did so much and searched and pursued
That to the two adolescents he returned,
Charged with wine and with meat,
Which he puts down in front of them, and then flees.
4264 Little remained of the day and it was almost night:
The young people woke up,
What they see is pleasing to them.
His hands joined together, Guillaume prays
4268 To the King of heaven who is Sovereign
That He save and protect his beast.
"Amen, my lord, may God hear you,
Said the daughter of the emperor,

---

59. Micha's edition, which reads "Qui les .II. cors li rendera," is faulty. My translation is based on Michelant's edition, which accurately reflects the manuscript and reads "Qui les deus ors li rendera."

4272   For we would not live a day without him."
Then they eat, since they were hungry;
They restore themselves well with what they have.
When they have eaten and drunk enough,
4276   Quickly they moved from that place
As if to go on their way;
But the beauty cannot tolerate it,
For she is so weary she cannot move.
4280   Whether she wants to or not, it is necessary that she remain.
Very softly she calls to Guillaume
And he responds: "What is wrong, my beloved?
— My lord, I cannot go now;
4284   Even if I were at risk of being killed,
I would not be able to go further, I am so weary.
— Sweetheart, do not be so troubled:
We will stay in the foliage
4288   Until you are feeling rested."
That night they remained thus,
In the forest they hid themselves again
Until it was the morning of the next day.
4292   Then arrived the peasants
Of the country and the fagot-makers[60]
Who came to the forest to labor
Just as they were always accustomed to do,
4296   For they lived off such products of the earth.
While they were making their bundles,
They began to speak among themselves
Of the thing that they had seen.
4300   Such a marvel had never been known
Like that of the wolf who had carried the child
And how those from the city
And the barons and the lords
4304   Had chased him all day,
And how at vespers he had put him down on the ground,
And how he had not hurt him or injured him.
Said one of them: "There is much more:
4308   Never such a marvel has anyone seen
Like that of the two white bears when everyone set off,
In the quarry they were found.

60. Fagots are bundles of twigs, sticks and branches tied together.

They have been saying for a while this news
4312 That it is our lady,
The daughter of the emperor himself,
And one of the knights, who took her away,
Who in these skins went off this way,
4316 For whom they are proclaiming and summoning
All the people of this land
That everyone come to seek out these two bears.
May it please God, through His grace,
4320 That they might be right here now both of them
In this marsh, beneath this foliage!
If it had cost me my harvest,
I would tell it to the magistrate:
4324 They would give us so much that we would be rich."
They reply: "Let us make our bundles,
We will not live from wishes,
If we want to earn a little,
4328 We have to do something other than wish.
Make it be so that God helps them and us,
For many more cruel threats
Have they endured and undergone,
4332 Since they left their country.
Let us leave, for we have been here too long."
They loaded and packed their chests
And set off on their way,
4336 And those who heard them well
Deliberated on the other hand about
By what means or by what artifice
They will be able to manage henceforth
4340 So that no one will notice their appearance.

Then behold there arose in the middle of the woods
A great uproar and a pandemonium
From which the two are taken with great fear,
4344 But they had no need to fear anything,
For it is the wolf who has not forgotten them
Who has attacked a beast,
A stag marvelous and grand.
4348 Up to them he is chasing it.
In front of the two lovers he caught it
And when he had killed it and slain it,

Then he leaves again very quickly.
4352 "See, dear, what an adventure,
Said Guillaume to the maiden,
See how our beast is hunting,
If we had yet another skin,
4356 We would leave our skins and we would take these,
Then we would be less recognizable."
The damsel responded:
"That is true, but I do not see
4360 How we can get them."

While they were talking thus,
There they see coming back the wolf
Who has caught a doe.
4364 By the nape of the back of its neck
He is holding it in his teeth and in this way is leading it;
In front of the ones for whom he is suffering so much
He was bringing it back in such a manner.
4368 In front of the stag he killed it,
Then he went away, he did not linger any longer there.
And Guillaume said: "Noble beast,
Have you therefore fear of me?
4372 I will never be safe without you.
If it were not for God and for you,
For a longtime I would have been killed and dead.
I know not if you are afraid of me,
4376 In you I place all my trust.
Well do I think and believe that you understand
And that you possess reasoning and intelligence.
I know not what you are,
4380 Except that in no way are you a wolf.

— So help me God, in my opinion,
I believe very much that you are telling the truth."
Then they spoke in diverse ways
4384 Until day passed to night,
Which from the sun takes away the light.
Then they set off on their way.
The maiden is completely healed,
4388 Well can she stay on her feet and hold to their path.
They embrace each other often;
No more will they fear anything.

Those from the country had come
4392   And they searched and sought everywhere.
They find the skinned animals
And the bearskins that they have abandoned:
By this they know the truth
4396   Finally about what they were.
Each one is sure and certain
That they left as deer in the two skins;
They do not dare search much further for them
4400   Because of the warriors and because of the war
That has ravaged the land,
Burned, destroyed and reduced it to rubble.
They turned back because of this fear.
4404   And they leave immediately on their way,
For this are they greatly comforted,
That they have crossed the whole country.
Burned are the cities and the hamlets,
4408   The fortresses and the towers,
They see the realm entirely devastated.
There remains there no man or woman
Who has not abandoned the land
4412   For fear of the war.
They do not know what land they are in
Nor from whence comes the one who is destroying it.
But now hear ye, do not worry,
4416   Who had devastated the land:
The king of Spain, himself,
And his son and their troops.
How did it happen, in the name of what cause?
4420   You have heard of King Embron
Who was of such great worth
And was a wealthy king of great power,
Who held Apulia and the kingdom.
4424   He died, may God have mercy on his soul!
The queen had a daughter,
Florence was the name of the girl,
Never was there ever such a beauty born.
4428   She had been asked for by the king
For his son, but in no manner,
In exchange for promises or prayers,
Nor by force nor by power

4432   Could he have the damsel.
    Because the king cannot have her daughter
    He is ravaging her realm.
    He has ravaged the entire country
4436   And he has pursued the queen
    Until he had her besieged in Palermo;
    He will not turn back until he has taken her,
    Just as he has said and sworn.
4440   Within the city there was
    The queen often lamenting;
    Often she complains and moans,
    For she sees her land destroyed,
4444   From nowhere does she expect help,
    Since she had sent to her father
    And to her brother seeking assistance
    That they might come to her aid;
4448   But they are about to wait too long now,
    For often those in the army shout:
    "You will not be saved, everyone surrender."
    Throughout the city they are talking about giving up,
4452   For if the king wanted to capture them,
    With their possessions and their lives secure,

    But they do not want the ones outside.
    Often they give their advice to their lady,
4456   Each one reprimands her greatly and blames her:
    Why does she not act according to the will of the king,
    Before he destroys the city,
    Before she is taken and they are captured?
4460   For he is too strong and powerful.
    They see their men weakening,
    Those of the enemy army are growing and strengthening;
    They need food and have very little.
4464   And the queen replies to them:
    "My lords, you are all my liegemen,
    And very loyal and valiant men;
    Indeed most of you truly know
4468   That I sent for the emperor,
    He is my parent, so that he might come to help me
    And that no excuses might keep him
    From helping me in this need.

4472   But well do you know that he is truly far away.
        He is my father; he must not fail me:
        Thus you must suffer still.
        So he must come, in time he will come
4476   Or he will send his army to me.
        I want to believe you; I must believe you.
        Go to the enemy army, tell the king,
        If I do not have aid within two weeks,
4480   The city will be his domain.
        Let me go away, my honor safe,
        To my father the emperor,
        And my daughter with me in the same manner.
4484   It will not be done otherwise.
        He will hold the land under his jurisdiction,
        He will not find anyone who will contradict it."
        They mounted up without any delay,
4488   They come to the king, and then they told him,
        But the king swears it will never be done,
        If he does not have her daughter, for any accord.
        The king was proud and arrogant,[61]
4492   To all the messengers he truly said:
        "My lords, tell this well to the queen,
        If next to me I do not have the girl,
        It will never be done otherwise.
4496   Do not conceal anything from her."

            They left; they took their leave,
        To the city they returned,
        To the queen they recounted
4500   Exactly what the king had said.
        When the queen hears the haughty and arrogant manner of
            speaking
        Of the king that the messengers pass on to her,
        She reentered her chamber,
4504   Suffering greatly and saddened.
        She implores God that He not forgot her,
        That He counsel her and help her.
        Often she weeps from the grief

---

61. Micha's edition, which reads "Li rois fu fiers er orgeillous," is faulty. My translation is based on Michelant's edition, which accurately reflects the manuscript and reads "Li rois fu fiers et orgeillous."

4508　That she has for the king, her dear lord,[62]
　　　And she laments and misses her dear son
　　　For whom she has now suffered so much;
　　　In no way does she know what to do.
4512　With a good heart she said a prayer:
　　　"God, true Father, if it is true
　　　How you through holy annunciation
　　　Became incarnate
4516　In the Virgin with humility,
　　　Who in her loins bore You so long
　　　Until at the proper time she was delivered of You,
　　　And You were born as a child,
4520　Just as we find when we read
　　　About the holy virgin maiden
　　　Who was both Your mother and Your servant,
　　　And You her Father and her Son,
4524　If it is true, fair Lord God,
　　　Then take care of my honor and protect me
　　　Against the might of my enemies.
　　　—Amen, my lady," said her daughter
4528　From whose eyes warm water is flowing.
　　　Both of them were weeping exceedingly,
　　　But if they knew now the comfort
　　　That God is transmitting and sending them,
4532　Never would such joy have been made
　　　As the daughter and the mother would make,
　　　The one for the son, the other for the brother,
　　　But they will not know it so soon.
4536　Here we will leave the account of this army
　　　Who often attacks the town
　　　And who strikes and hits at the walls,
　　　And the queen who worries about it.
4540　Now it is truly right that I tell you
　　　About the vassal and the maiden.
　　　They traveled so long, both him and her,
　　　With great fatigue and with great weariness
4544　Throughout the land that was ravaged
　　　From here to there, with some pain,
　　　Exactly as fortune leads them.

62. Queen Felise is weeping for her dead husband, King Embron.

Through the land that was devastated,
4548   They have crossed so many paths,
So many great rivers, fierce and wild,
Through the wisdom of their beast
And with the help of Jesus the King,
4552   That they arrived in Sicily.
But now hear how they crossed
The rivers, when they came to them:
They would go so far along the bank
4556   Until they would find a ship or small craft,
Then they would get in the boat.
The wolf in front with a rope
Pulled them forward and they rowed;
4560   In this way they crossed the water.

One morning they looked:
They see the land and the realm
And they see the town of Reggio
4564   That was situated on the Strait of Messina,
The seaport and the fleet
That is arriving beneath the city.
They hid themselves in a grotto
4568   Until night when you could not see a thing.
Then here comes the beast,
He appears to them, bows his head,
So that they might follow him, they do so:
4572   After the beast they set off on their way.
Down below Reggio, on the shore
They find at the Strait a great boat;
It was all prepared to cross,
4576   As soon as the moon had risen.
Those from the boat were sleeping,
Except the masters who were
In the city for their work.
4580   And so they got on the ship.
But they do it so stealthily
That they are seen by no one.
The weather and the night were black.
4584   On the ship there were empty barrels.
As best as they could they hid themselves in them.
Then the masters returned

For the moon was going to rise

4588   And they do not want to stay there any longer;

They have awakened their companions

And pulled up their sails.

They have embarked, they put out to sea,

4592   The sails inflate and fill with air

From the wind which blows there plentifully.

So far did they navigate, so long did they sail

Through the water of the salty sea

4596   That before dawn had broken

Beneath Messina they had made port;

But great fear do they have of death

Those who were in the barrels,

4600   For they do not know how they might

Get off the ship or in what manner

But the beast who had put himself

On the boat in order to deliver them

4604   Jumps into the water near the shore,

He begins to swim; he draws near the bank,

He pretends to be going to land.

All those on the ship jump out,

4608   They kick and attack the beast,

Often they make him dive into the sea,

They believe they will capture and drown him.

To save the two young people

4612   He is in great fear of dying,

In danger has he put his life[63]

In order to deliver them from the sea;

Thus he leads the sailors away.

4616   So far did they chase him on the sand

That a full half league

Were they above their barge,

And the two exit from the boat

4620   But they do one wise thing:

Of the meat that they have found

They have carried away enough

And one full cask of wine.

4624   Thereupon the two lovers abandon

The vessel and set off on their way.

---

63. The werewolf put his life in danger, "en aventure."

Each of the two of them sweetly prays
To Jesus, the glorious celestial King,
4628 That He be guardian of their beast,
But he was already out of the sea.
The sailors did not know what had
Become of him and so they returned;
4632 Promptly they leave.

So long did they travel through the land
That was ravaged by the war,
And very much was it cruel and evil,
4636 That Santa Maria della Scalla
In just a little time they crossed
And Cefalu, a city.
They are going on their way toward Palermo,
4640 Exactly as their beast is directing them.
They traveled so far that they saw the walls
And the crenellated towers that were turning green
The high church towers and the towers on wheels
4644 The rich halls of the bourgeois,
The crenellated towers and the castle keeps,
The banderoles and the pennons[64]
With which the walls are surrounded
4648 All around in the ancient part of the city.
It really seems to be a defendable town
And truly very charming.
They see the main palace,
4652 And on the principal royal tower,
Where the rich treasure is,
The eagle of fine gold that was gleaming;
And they see the army of the king of Spain
4656 That is covering the entire countryside.
There are so many tents and pavilions
And rich tents of barons
That no one can say how many there are.
4660 Never has anyone ever seen such a great military force,
It extends four leagues down the hill.
They see the principal royal tent
Next to an oak grove, on a hill,

---

64. A banderole is a narrow forked flag or streamer; a pennon is a long narrow streamer. Each may be attached to a lance.

4664   And the golden eagle that sits on its summit.
        Never was there such a rich tent,
        But I dare not attempt
        To depict or describe it,
4668   For there would be too much to say.
        They see the sea beneath the city,
        The rich port and the fleet;
        An orchard they see beneath the tower,
4672   Enclosed and fenced in with walls all around.
        This was the park of King Embron.
        There were many beasts there in abundance,
        But those in the enemy army had taken them
4676   And had hunted and killed many,
        Very few remained in the enclosure.
        That day they rested thus
        Until the hour that night fell.
4680   From their hiding place they came out,
        But now they do not know what to do,
        Neither where to go nor in what direction to go back,
        For they greatly fear the men in the army
4684   And that they will encounter them rather quickly.

            While they were thus,
        Then they see their beast coming.
        He looks back at the young people
4688   Encouraging them with a good expression to follow him,
        And they do so quickly without fear,
        For in him they have such great faith
        That they fear nothing, since they have him.
4692   Up to the orchard they came
        And they entered it through a breach
        That the men in the enemy army had made there.
        Very beautiful and pretty was the orchard,
4696   And when they had come within,
        They do not see their guide at all.
        There was not one of them who was not bothered
        And did not feel woeful and worried about it,
4700   But because he knew how to do this,
        They are not troubled about it so much.
        In a valley, a little further on,
        In the heather, beneath a pine tree,

4704   They rest until morning.
        The queen was in her chamber
        Sleeping in her bed,
        For that night she had thought very much
4708   And had prayed and appealed to God
        Because of those in the enemy army who were keeping her pris-
            oner
        And who were piercing and destroying her walls,
        That they might not have the strength or power
4712   To be able to take the city;
        But indeed they will have it; it will not be safe,
        If she does not get aid soon.
        The queen awakened,
4716   Very weary and anxious was she
        Because of a dream that she had had,
        Whence her color often changes
        And her blood is boiling and bubbling,
4720   For it signifies a great marvel,
        But she does not know what it can be.
        It seemed to her that on a hillock
        She had gone unaccompanied,
4724   She had only her daughter beside her,
        Around her there were one hundred thousand beasts,
        Bears and leopards and fierce lions
        And others of many kinds,
4728   Mouths gaping open, great and fierce,
        Who were all rushing forward to attack them;
        They would have died; there was no more to it,
        When a white wolf and two white bears
4732   Came to bring her aid,
        And when they had come near her,
        The bears resembled two deer.
        In front of their heads they have portraits,
4736   Each one the image of a child,
        And on their heads crowns of gold
        That were worth a great treasure.
        The image that the great stag was carrying
4740   Resembled her dear child
        Whom she had lost such a long time ago;
        And the one that was on the other
        Was in the semblance of a maiden,

4744   And it was very pleasing and beautiful.
      That one remained with the queen
      And the werewolf with the girl.
      The stag charged into the beasts,
4748   He did entirely as he liked to them.
      The most important and the strongest
      He took by force by himself;
      A fierce leopard and a lion
4752   He led into her house.
      Because these two had lost,
      Then the others despaired,
      And all turned in flight.
4756   Over the mountains and through the valleys
      They all flee like an arrow;
      She does not know where each one goes.

      When she was saved from these beasts
4760   And from the peril where she might have perished
      If it were not for the strength of the stag,
      Then there came to her a vision,
      A marvel excellent and grand,
4764   Such as no man living has ever heard:
      On the tower she had climbed
      To look out over the country;
      Both her arms grew so much
4768   And reached out so far
      That on the walls of Rome was her right hand
      And on Spain her left;
      Under her control was the realm,
4772   There was no man or woman against her.
      But from this vision
      The queen is in such a fright
      That she does not know what will become of her.
4776   With sobs, with tears, with sighs
      She appeals greatly to the Creator
      That He counsel her for the sake of His tenderness.
      Then the queen got up,
4780   Quickly she dressed herself,
      Then she entered the chapel.
      She calls a chaplain to her,
      Moysant was the name of the priest.

4784 He was a good cleric and wise master,
   Well indoctrinated in the arts,
   Master of the arts and of canon law,
   A very religious and virtuous man.
4788 The lady addressed him:
   "Good master, in the name of God what will I do?
   Advise me, I have need of it,
   About a marvel excellent and grand
4792 That came to me last night while I was sleeping,
   Whence I am truly in great fright."
   Then she recounts to him her vision
   Exactly as she had seen it.
4796 Well did the master hear her;
   To respond he is in no haste.
   Immediately he picked up a book
   And sees the external form of the dream
4800 And its entire significance.
   Then he looked at the queen:
   "My lady, says he, you were born at an auspicious moment,
   He has not forgotten you,
4804 The One who has established the world,
   Rather in time you will have help.
   My lady, now hear what it means:
   When you were on the mountain,
4808 Around you so many strange beasts
   Who wanted to devour your body,
   They are the besieging army outside
   Who night and day attack you inside
4812 And who for your daughter are employing all their efforts
   So that they will have her by force,
   But they will never have the power to do it.
   And when one wolf and two white bears
4816 Came to help you,
   And when they were nearer you,
   The bears resembled two deer
   And each one in front of his head
4820 Carried the image of a child,
   Each one a crown on his head
   Which was very beautiful and fine,
   My lady, they are two knights
4824 Powerful and courageous and fierce.

With them comes a maiden
Who is so very noble and beautiful.
The stag who before his head
4828   Was carrying the image of a child
Who resembled your dear son
And delivered you from the beasts
And led the leopard and the lion
4832   To you in your prison,
Well do I know his significance:
He is a vassal of great power
Who will save your land for you
4836   And will make peace from this war
And by force will take the king,
He will bring him to you in your prison,
The most important of the army with him;
4840   Both of them will be at your mercy.
I know not if he will have you as wife,
But he will be king of this entire realm.
The wolf that came with them,
4844   My lady, is one of the vassals;
He will be a knight without doubt
Who will put an end
To all this malevolence through his attention.
4848   And the lion and the leopard
He will deliver to you, so I believe,
And you will all be good friends,
And through him you will hear news
4852   Of your dear son that you have lost.
You will have very shortly your son
For whom you have wept so many tears,
But from Rome he will take such a wife
4856   From whom he will have a great part of the realm.
Under his jurisdiction will be all of Rome,
The poor people and the wealthy men.
Through him you will have great seigniorial authority
4860   In the land of Lombardy;
He will be both lord and master of it.
This is the meaning of your right arm
That you held over Rome.
4864   And the left that you had
Held and put over Spain,

My lady, it seems to me,
The son of the king will have your daughter.
4868 Know this to be true; it will not fail to happen,
By your son she will be given to him,
She will be lady of the entire country,
There your seigniorial authority will return.
4872 Now you have heard your vision,
Know this to be true, thus will it be."
When the queen hears the master say
That her son is returning,
4876 She is so joyous she does not know what to do,
But on the other hand she again has great fear
That he might perish as a result of misfortune.
She is both joyous and fearful all at once;
4880 She weeps from her joy, from her fear she trembles,
For she is without fail in very great fear
That by some fault he might be unsuccessful.
She had a mass said immediately
4884 And implores master Moysant
That for her he pray to the Creator
To watch over him out of His tenderness.
And when the mass was over
4888 And the queen had heard it,
She left the chapel.
To her chamber she went
And sat down near a window,
4892 Then she leans on her right hand,
Thinking about her adventure
And beseeching the Redeemer
That He might watch over her through His compassion.
4896 She looked down through the garden
And saw the young people
Who were sewn into the skins.
They were next to a wood of hazel trees,
4900 Together they were sleeping there
Under a bay tree, in a small meadow.
It was wondrously lovely there.
They came to that spot because it was so beautiful,
4904 For they did not go to bed the night before.
There they are lying head to head,
Showing great joy and great delight,

For nothing have they lacked
4908 That has not been brought or led to them.

   Guillaume is with his sweetheart
On the green grass, fresh and lush,
Together there they amuse themselves,
4912 They play and talk and laugh
And map out a plan about their situation,
How in the end they will be able to pull out of it,
And whether they will remain in the skins any longer.
4916 But finally they decided
That never will they remove the skins,
Never will they uncover their bodies,
If their beast has not given them leave to do so;
4920 About this they promised each other.
Guillaume oftentimes said:
"Glorious Lord, Father King,
My sweet dear beloved, what will we do?
4924 How it seems a long time
Since I have since your bright face!
— And I yours, my love,"
The damsel responded.
4928 "May it please God and His virtue,
Said Guillaume to the girl,
That the queen might be with us
And that she might bear good faith toward us,
4932 My sweet dear beloved, you and I,
And that she might want to give me arms and a warhorse
So that I might help her.
If I were sure about your safety,
4936 In the name of the Lord in whose semblance
We are made and shaped,
Such a man would she have encountered
That I would deliver her entirely
4940 Of the people who are waging war in this way against her,
But never will she know any news of me.
— I do not know what to say, said the maiden,
But I would truly like that it please
4944 The King of the world that it be thus."
The queen from her window
Looks down and sees their manner

And sees that together they are amusing themselves,
4948 But she does not know what they are saying.
If she knew it, then she would feel well,
But she knows nothing at all about it.
She puts all her effort into watching them,
4952 For it pleases her very much and is very agreeable to her
And about this she marveled greatly
That such an appearance of love she sees there.
Often she says to herself
4956 That never has she seen two beasts
Who loved one another as dearly
As do that stag and this doe.
"And they are not two transformed beasts
4960 Who are lying down there stretched out
Like they are doing, well can I say it.
God, says she, glorious Lord,
Counsel me through Your mercy
4964 About these beasts that I see here
Who are expressing their pleasure there.
It really seems and I believe it
That both of them have intelligence and reasoning."
4968 She remembers her vision,
Exactly as she had seen it the night before.
She is so attentive to the beasts
That never that day until evening
4972 Can one move her from that place,
And when the day is beginning to fail
So that she could not see the deer any longer,
She went back into her palace
4976 Among her people and her household.
The meal was ready,
Then she has the knights sit down,
Rank by rank, the length of the tables,
4980 The men-at-arms and the great squires
Who were defending the city.
They had enough in great quantity,
Like well-situated people in a castle;
4984 I do not want to mention it any further.
And when the tablecloths have been removed,
In several places the knights
Assembled throughout the palace.

4988   Among them has begun the discussion
        About the enemy army that is menacing them so
        And tormenting and threatening them so:
        Already the walls are split and smashed
4992   And the moat filled with debris,
        Since they have burned all their palisades,
        Fences and gates and posts.
        Thus they gathered each day
4996   And the enemy tormented them so
        That it is a wonder that they do not surrender.
        That if, under duress, the Spanish do not capture them,
        They will eventually do so; they will capture everyone.
5000   The others say no they will not,
        Never will they capture them in such a way,
        Previously there has not been so many of their people
        Dead and killed and slain
5004   Before the city is surrendered;
        And this will be nothing but astonishing.
        "Now we will well see, say the barons,
        Now we will see who are the good vassals
5008   And we will know the good from the bad;
        We will see who should be loved
        And who should be praised and who should be blamed.
        In great need, this is essential,
5012   One must be able to recognize the valiant man.
        Now there is nothing more to it than to do well."
        This discussion silenced those
        Who would make it more costly
5016   To defend the city and themselves.
        The queen heard the debate,
        She stood up in the paved hall,
        Noble was her body and face,
5020   She knew well how to speak, for she was very wise.
        She addressed the barons:
        "My lords, says she, it seems to me,
        As soon as people such as you are together
5024   Like you are among yourselves inside here,
        So young and so helpful,
        So bold and so able to defend himself,
        One should not hear any discussion there
5028   That might hold us to any evil.

Because of this I implore you, my lords,
Let each one of you watch over his honor;
Do not give me counsel for which I might have shame
5032 In a king's court or the court of a count.
You are truly a very noble household:
Be careful, for God's sake, that one does not say
That you have failed me unjustly
5036 Or that by default I have lost,
For you would have committed too great an offense.
You are my men and my barons,
Thus you must always help me.
5040 I am a woman; I do not know how to wage war,
Belt on a sword, put on a hauberk,
Sustain a mêlée or a war.
But you who are, dear lords,
5044 People raised on such labor,
Do it just as you must.
I will do all and whatever you advise,
Whether it might be to hold or to surrender.
5048 But whoever would do so much to resist
Until some help comes to us
In the name of the Lord who made the world,
So much would I give you generously
5052 Of lands, honor, gold and silver
That you would never be poor."
Everyone shouts throughout the palace:
"Noble and gentle queen,
5056 We would rather allow us all to be tortured,
Except herein, know this well,
So that you might not lose anything through us.
Now be totally reassured."
5060 Thereupon they ended their conversation.

They sleep until the next day
When those outside, the besieging army,
Came back in front of the city.
5064 There were more than thirteen thousand of them
Who are all shouting loudly:
"You will not be safe, wretched bourgeois,
It would be your misfortune to come out here.
5068 Come to the king, surrender yourselves,

Put yourselves all at his mercy
So that you will not be killed or slain;
Or if you will not, if he captures you,
5072   May he be considered a traitor if he does not hang you from a
        branch."
But those within put themselves in battle order on the walls,
What the others say is insulting to them.
Then begins the great attack
5076   From those outside against those within;
Stone-throwing machines and mangonels,[65]
Crossbows and quarrels
That they fire off and shoot in great quantity,
5080   And those within do not delay
In bravely defending themselves.
If they lose anything there, they sell it dearly to them.
In her chapel is the queen
5084   Who is beating her chest and her breasts
And imploring the Creator
To watch over His people through His gentleness,
To see that they do not die or perish.
5088   And when she had heard mass,
She went forth from her chapel.
To the window she came
That opened out above the garden
5092   And she looks down; she sees the beasts
Just as she had seen them the evening before.
Now the skins that they had put on
Had dried because of the heat
5096   And had shrunk and gotten smaller
So that toward the bottom by the stitches
Were protruding their garments,
Their precious crimson, violet and red fabric.
5100   The lady is so very astonished
When she sees the cloth sticking out from the skins,
And she invokes the Holy Spirit
That He might counsel her as to what this might be.
5104   She has the master come to her,
Then she showed him the situation.
When the master had looked at it

---

65. Mangonels are military siege engines that hurl stones.

And at the form of each one
5108   Very much did he rejoice about the adventure,
       For he knows well the deeds of these beasts;
       To the queen he reveals it:
       "My lady, says he, do not fear now.
5112   Now you can see your vision,
       Just as you told it to me the other day.
       My lady, a good while ago you heard
       A messenger relate in this tower
5116   About the emperor's daughter
       And about the Greek who wanted to take possession of her,
       Just as the messenger led us to understand;
       But she did not want the marriage,
5120   For elsewhere had she put her heart,
       In a vassal handsome and valiant
       And more pleasant than anyone has ever seen.[66]
       Thus he led her out of the country
5124   And caused her to leave her friends;
       But no one knew a man so brave
       In all the territory of Rome,
       Nor so handsome or so pleasant
5128   Nor with his arms so valiant
       As is the one with whom she went off.
       But very strangely did they do it,
       Since before they were out of Rome,
5132   In two bearskins they put their bodies.
       They put them on and laced them well,
       Just as the messengers tell us,
       So that they would not be recognized.
5136   Now it has befallen you well,
       That now you can see the knight
       Who has come to help you,
       And that is his sweetheart beside him.
5140   They are the ones in both those skins.
       You see there the stag and the bear
       Who were helping you
       In your vision of the battle:
5144   This is without a doubt the young man
       Who will deliver your land

---

66. Verses 5121–5122 are missing in the manuscript. The translation is based on Michelant's reconstitution, which he based on the prose text.

And put an end to this war.
But now they have abandoned the bearskins,
5148   I do not know why they have changed them
Nor where they were able to obtain these.
Now it is necessary that you listen,
Watch and determine
5152   How we might win the knight,
Both him and his sweetheart, over to us.
—May God remember it, if is pleases Him,"
Said the lady who rejoices greatly
5156   About what she heard the chaplain say.
....67

Then they arrange what they have to do
So that before it is day and before the sun appears
The queen will be dressed
5160   And well tied and well sewn
And laced in and dressed.
Through a small door she went down,
As far as the orchard came the queen.
5164   And along with her a girl.
No one knew anything more of her intentions
Except for master Moysant
Who had devised the whole plan.
5168   She ordered the maiden
To be there and stay until
The queen returned to her.
Then she goes off; she does not linger any longer;
5172   On all four feet like other beasts
She entered through the gate
Into the orchard; very softly
She came up to the small meadow
5176   Where the young people were lying.
Beside the wood she lay herself down.
But Melior had awakened.
She had seen a vision
5180   Which caused her entire body to be covered in perspiration.
Very softly she calls to Guillaume:
"My lord, said the damsel,

67. According to the prose text, Moysant then advises the queen to have herself sewn into the skin of a deer, so that she can go into the orchard and speak to Guillaume and Melior. She follows his advice and enters the garden at daybreak.

I am greatly afraid, comfort me.
5184   — My dear, do not be fearful.
— But I am. — Of what? — My dear beloved,
While sleeping it seemed to me
That a great and marvelous eagle
5188   Was carrying, my lord, both you and me
Up there to that great tower.
— If it pleases God, only good will come from it,"
Said Guillaume to the girl.
5192   Then they notice the queen
Who is lying beneath the bush;
Each one points her out to the other.
"My sweet love, said Melior,
5196   The beast that came here
Fell asleep beside that wood.
She is not frightened because of us."
Guillaume said: "Dear, she is right not to be,
5200   Because she does not believe us to be other than she sees us.
If she knew our situation,
She would not be our companion."

The queen responds briefly:
5204   "I know your entire circumstances well:
And because of you I will not flee at all
Far from your company,
Never because of me will you lose anything.
5208   And so I tell you that I know well
Your adventures and your situation."
They made the sign of the cross with their right hands,
When they hear the queen.
5212   The girl trembles with fear
Because she was not in safety.
Guillaume said: I beseech you,
Beast, in the name of the King of the world,
5216   If it is therefore through Him you speak,
Or if it is through other spirits,
What you are saying to me,
And if we will have difficulty because of you."
5220   The queen said to the vassal:
"Never will you have any trouble because of me
And I speak to you through God,

The King of the world who made us all.

5224   I am a beast just like you,
Of similar appearance, of similar nature.
Other beasts have chased me
From my pasture with their armed forces.

5228   Now I am coming to God and to you
For assistance and to seek help.
If you put them out of my land
And return my pasturage to me,

5232   You will be lord of all the grassland
Between you and your maiden
Who is my dear damsel,
Daughter of the emperor of Rome.

5236   I know about you all that is essential,
Everything as it happened to you.
You are both most welcome,
In a good port have you arrived.

5240   From me will you hear the truth:
The entire country is mine,
I am its crowned queen.
Now it is being very wrongly devastated

5244   By the king of Spain because of my daughter
Whom he wants to take by force through his arrogance;
But indeed, my lord, I do not want it,
And if it pleases God, he will never have her.

5248   He has menaced me so much here and there,
Burned and destroyed my land
And at the same time has stolen it from me,
He has left me only

5252   This city and a few people.
Now I have come to you here,
That you might aid me through your compassion.
In servitude and as recompense

5256   I will put everything at your disposal,
Land and possessions, gold and silver,
To carry out your will;
Thus you will help both yourself and me.

5260   You are the best and the most valiant,
Just as they say, that there is in all the world."
And Guillaume the warrior responded:
"In the name of God who governs everyone,

5264 Are you therefore the queen?
— So help me God, yes, good sir.
— And who could have related or told you
That we were here? — I know it well.
5268 — It astonishes me more than anything else,
My lady, how you might have known it
Or noticed our situation.
— I know it well: now it is thus.
5272 I ask you to have pity on me.
— You ask me? — Truly. — And why for you?
— For me and for all my land
That I have finally all lost
5276 If I do not get it back through your help.
But you are of such great valor
And I have such great faith in you
That I will get everything back, I do not doubt it at all,
5280 If I have help from you.

When Guillaume hears the lady,
He is taken with great pity for her.
He is so very distressed about her realm
5284 And how they are treating her wrongly.
But if he had known that she were his mother,
His loss would have been much more bitter.
They know nothing about it, neither she nor he,
5288 That he has a mother or that she has a son.
Nevertheless, he grants absolutely everything to her.
"My lady, says he, if God sees me,
I do not know what the future will be for us,
5292 And if I had faith in you,
You would not fail to help us."
The lady hears him, humbles herself so much
That she kneels down at his feet.
5296 He lifts the queen up,
Who takes his circumstances greatly to heart,
For nature makes her step back.
And she reassures both of them
5300 And promises and swears to them splendidly
That she will be faithful to them.
Then all three got up.

When each one was up on his feet,

5304   You would have been very astonished,

If you had seen them like that.

Guillaume put himself at the rear

And the queen goes to the head

5308   And then the maiden with her noble body.

They go directly to the postern gate,[68]

Where the maiden whom the queen

Had put there was still waiting.

5312   When she sees the three beasts

Coming toward her in such a manner,

She is about to flee from fear,

But the queen calls her back.

5316   "What's wrong, damsel, says she?

Do you fear me then?

— My lady, yes. — And why do you?

— Because along with you are coming two others,

5320   One of them is large and hideous,

I do not know what wondrous creatures they are."

And the queen replies to her:

"To see them I went out there.

5324   At the price of your limbs and your life,

I forbid you from telling anyone about it."

The damsel hears the menace

Of the queen, then stops,

5328   But she fears the great beast so much

That she does not dare approach him.

They entered a cellar,

Into a subterranean chamber:

5332   There the queen ordered

Two rich baths prepared.

First she herself

Was unstitched from her skin,

5336   And then to the young people she came.

With a knife she

Removed each one from their skin herself,

And when they had issued forth

5340   And the maiden saw the human beings

Who had come with her lady,

---

68. A postern gate is a small rear door or gate in a fortified wall.

She was so very astonished
That she does not know what it can be,
5344   When she sees the honest knight
And the maiden next to him,
And she sees that they are both so beautiful
In body, in limbs, and in face,
5348   But their faces had been
Discolored and dirtied from the skins.
Their baths were ready;
They removed their shoes and undressed,
5352   They got in and whatever is appropriate
For noble people was done for them.
Quickly were readied their garments,
Which the queen had brought to them;
5356   With the knight was the girl
And the queen was with Melior.
With a silken cloth all in gold,
Rich and beautiful and fashioned skillfully,
5360   Lined well with white ermine,
Was the maiden dressed.
When she had adorned her with everything
As best as she could, without trickery,
5364   Then she took her by the right hand.
From there she led her to the young man
Where the girl in turn was taking great pains
To bedeck him in such a manner
5368   That no one would be able to blame her for it.
No one will do it who will not be in the wrong,
For she dressed him richly
In opulent and beautiful garments.
5372   When the young man sees the beauty,
He goes toward her; he does not wait.
The queen returns his sweetheart to him
And says: "My lord, I return her to you
5376   To do your will.
— My lady, this merits being repaid.
And may God let me see the day
That this service might be returned."
5380   Together all three go up
All the steps of the arcade
Until they are in the main hall,

Which was very rich and beautiful.

5384 Guillaume and the maiden enter
With the lady who was very joyful.
On a stuffed feather bed
Of green silken cloth, edged in bands of orphrey,[69]

5388 That was thrown before her bed,
All three of them sat down.
And the queen with the bright face said
To the knight who was beside her:

5392 "My dear good sir, what kind of shield
Would you like me to ask have made for you?
— My lady, so that God might protect my body,
A shield of gold, but in the middle

5396 Let there be painted a portrait of a wolf
Great and corpulent with a fierce face.
Before the day had failed
The shield was ready

5400 And all his armor decorated
Just as he wants to have it.
They had absolutely everything that evening
The way they want it and as it pleases them;

5404 I do not want to make further comment about it.

The queen had a warhorse
Who belonged to the king, her dear lord.
Brunsaudebruel was his name;

5408 No man ever saw a better one than him.
But ever since King Embron had died,
He had not left the stable
Nor allowed any man to mount him,

5412 As bold or valiant he might be,
Nor had he shown any semblance of joy.
Now he jumps, now he leaps about, now he frolics,
Puffs out his nostrils, whinnies, puts his head down,

5416 Kicks out with his feet and expresses great joy,
For he smells and catches the scent of his lord.
Whoever might open the chain
With which the horse was tied,

5420 Directly to the young man he went.
They began to marvel greatly about it,

69. Orphrey is elaborate embroidery, especially in gold.

Those who were taking care of the destrier.
They go to tell the queen about it
5424 Up above, up in her chamber.
She is very happy and joyous about it,
For she truly believes that it signifies
The honor that will come to her soon.
5428 Guillaume heard everything
And all that was said to the queen;
A little bit toward her he bows down:
"My lady, said the knight,
5432 Is he then such a good warhorse?
— Yes. — From whence did he come? — He was the king's,
My good lord, who was so dear to me.
So I kept him because of his love,
5436 Never did a prince have a better warhorse.
— Was he the king's? — Yes, without a doubt,
There is no beast in the world that is worth him."
When Guillaume hears and understands
5440 That in the world there is no nobler destrier,
Nothing else does he desire as much.
To the queen he began to speak:
"My lady, in the name of the sovereign Lord,
5444 I will put on saddle and bit
By myself without any assistance
If you will lend him to me, with your permission:
Tomorrow those outside will see him.
5448 — My dear friend, silver and gold,
Land, honor and fiefs,
Horses and other equipment,
Take everything you like;
5452 Never will I have against you any possessions
That you might want, do not doubt it at all."
And the valet thanks her very much for it.
Thereupon they ended their conversation.
5456 With the night great misfortune had gone away;
They ask for wine, they go to bed
Until the next day when they get up;
But before the sun has risen
5460 The city was in a great upheaval
For those outside have already arrived.
They have run right up to their gates

And there are together a good three thousand of them.
5464   Those in the city are very frightened,
For all believe they will be captured.
Great is the noise and great are the screams
That the women and children are making.
5468   To the defenses run the men-at-arms,
The great squires and the bourgeois;
On the palisades and on the rolling towers
The archers have climbed with their crossbows
5472   To defend them and the city.
The knights had gone up,
Each one armed on his warhorse,
Through its streets, with very large troops.
5476   They have closed all the gates;
There is not one who dares leave
The city in the direction of the enemy army:
Thus they were in great fright.
5480   In the great palace that was the king's
Guillaume was with his sweetheart.
When he heard the word
That in front of the city had come
5484   Up to three thousand of the enemy army,
Then he had great joy in his heart
And as quickly as he could
The warrior equipped himself
5488   And put on his armor and his hauberk.
He asked for Brunsaudebruel,
And the queen ordered
That they do everything that he wants,
5492   Since she has no man that she knows,
As fierce or as brave he might behave,
Who dares put the saddle on the warhorse.
Guillaume hears her; he does not tarry any longer.
5496   By means of the steps of the arcade
He left the palace, came to the horse
And with him several vassals,
Men-at-arms, valets and knights
5500   To see him and the destrier.
When the horse sees his lord,
Never did a beast have greater joy.
He goes toward him bowing down humbly,

5504   Great love he shows him,
        Stamps his feet, stretches out his neck,
        And Guillaume picks up his tunic,
        Rubs his head and his ears.
5508   Very greatly amazed are those
        Who had come to watch;
        All of them were saying among themselves
        That he was about to eat him alive.
5512   Then he put the bit on the good warhorse.
        Afterward he put the saddle on him,
        Which was magnificent and very beautiful,
        And he laced on him the harness covering his chest.
5516   When he had completely equipped him,
        Out into the middle of the square he drew him;
        Just as he had armed his body,
        He jumped into his two stirrups,
5520   And the destrier, which was
        Marvelously powerful and fierce
        And full of great courage, plunged forward.
        He curled up his lips quite a bit,
5524   He had nostrils full and large
        And big eyes on his head;
        He resembles so much a fierce beast
        That is about to attack the people.
5528   And the valet who was on him
        Spurs him with such fury
        That he makes sparks jump from the stones;
        With small leaps he takes a run up,
5532   There was no longer any need in the world to search
        For a prince of more noble stature.
        He asks for his shield and they give it to him,
        He put it on the strap at his neck.
5536   The vassal picks up a strong pike
        That was cleaned, sharp and hard.
        Absolutely all the people who see him
        Looked at him with wonder.
5540   When they see him so beautifully armed
        And that he is holding the pike on the lance rest,
        Often one said to the other:
        "Oh, God, who all earthly things
5544   Made, who can this vassal be

Who is so very handsome and noble
And whose bearing is so fierce?
God, how he resembles a man of valor!
5548   If the entire empire of Rome
Belonged to such a lord,
Then would truly be safe the honor
And the crown and the kingdom."
5552   The ladies were at the windows
In the great hall of marble,
Both Melior and the queen
And Florence next to her mother
5556   Where she was watching her brother
Who she saw armed on a horse
With good eyes and a loyal heart,
And the queen her dear son.
5560   But they do not know who he is;
Neither the daughter nor the mother knows
That the latter has a son or that the former a brother.
They talked together so much about him,
5564   They describe his body and his beauty
And his noble bearing,
That Melior greatly fears
That the queen and the maiden
5568   Might have a new love for him.
She would rather still be in her skin
With the young man in the orchard
Than to have arrived where she was.
5572   But her fear arose from foolishness,
Since they did not intend her any harm.
The baron strikes the horse,
And he left galloping down the street.
5576   And the people are all moved
To ask who is this lord
But there is no one who knows.
To the knights he goes directly
5580   There where he sees the most together;
And when they see the baron,
They look all around at him.
They value and praise his great fierceness
5584   And they greatly rejoice about his arrival.
Everyone believes that they are to be helped

By him. They do not know who he is,
But they know well his warhorse.

5588   And he said to them: "My dear good lords,
I see that you are very well equipped
And wearing your armor and hauberk.
You seem very much to me well mannered,

5592   Very helpful people both noble and fierce,
Who all together must truly
Defend their rights well, and especially
Since I believe you are all from this land.

5596   So I am amazed about this war
That you have suffered so many days
And that you have consented to your defeat.
You can be greatly ashamed about it,

5600   You who are princes and counts,
The most valiant and the lords,
That in this way your honor is stolen from you
By people who never before were feared,

5604   And that they are holding you all in prison
And that you are not so valiant or bold
To go and prevent them

5608   From taking what is yours from you;
Thus they take it as they please.
May misfortune befall he who wants to allow
Them to mock you any more!

5612   These are you ancestors' lands,
If they want to draw near us now,
Never will a single one escape
And may they all be killed and slain and captured.

5616   Let us go against our enemies,
Let us confront them and show them
That they are in the wrong when they attack this land.
I know no more about suffering."

5620   Thereupon he had the gate opened,
Then he went out first
And with him some four hundred,
There is not one of them who does not have the desire

5624   To do as well as he is able to,
And they are all good esteemed vassals
And encouraged to do well.

When Guillaume sees the vassals

5628 Coming armed on their horses
And that they are hurriedly issuing forth behind him,
He is very happy about it and rightly so.
He stops and waits for them,

5632 Then he kindly said to them:
"Lord barons, see the men from Spain
Who cover the entire countryside.
If there are a lot more of them than us,

5636 Never fear them because of this.
They all believe they will capture you in their hands:
See how they are coming each trying to outdo the other,
They have neither battalions nor troop formations,

5640 They are all coming impetuously:
If this happens, all are destroyed.
Now keep yourselves all together,
Do not disperse yourselves, my good lords,

5644 Spur your horses on a little and attack.
Be careful that you do not lose any land because of them,
Thus you will finally see them conquered
Because they will never have any protection there.

5648 Here is one coming in front
Who is exceedingly well equipped
And richly mounted on his horse.
But know this well, little does he fear us,

5652 When he comes before his army this way.
I know not who will come out on top,
But I will go against this lord
And so I tell you that in fighting with him

5656 You will soon see him or me killed."
Thereupon he lets his horse charge
And goes to meet the vassal
With great rage, with such speed

5660 That goats or beasts of the wood
Would not be able to keep his pace.
As long as his horse could tolerate it,
The two barons, who were very powerful

5664 And good, come together.
The Spaniard was very valiant
And strong and fierce and courageous
And the seneschal of the king himself,

| 5668 | Prince and master of his realm: |

Prince and master of his realm:
The king and the entire army took action
According to his counsel and his advice.
About Guillaume he knows nothing at all.

5672 Thus it turns into great folly for him
When he dared to come to him;
Now he will be the one who will pay.
Because of that, Guillaume strikes him so hard

5676 On his shield that he totally splits it and
Breaks the wood of his lance on the hauberk.
Guillaume deals him such a blow
That he breaks the frame of his shield.

5680 On the hauberk falls the weight,
He completely breaks and tears apart the chain mail.
Right through his intestines
He puts steel and wood and banner,

5684 Sending him falling to the ground dead on the battlefield.
One thing he said to him:
"We will get all the land back,
Never will we have any difficulty because of you.

5688 It was for your misfortune that you came to this land:
For you the war is finished.
It was unfortunate that you abandoned your country
To attack our land."

5692 By its reins he takes the destrier,
Thus he leads him away through the heather
And so he returns to the rear.
The horse he sent to his sweetheart,

5696 Who was very joyous and happy about it.

The Spaniards grieve greatly
When they see their lord dead,
The seneschal who was so valiant

5700 And who was lord and master of all.
Then they arrive at the body:
There many fists were pounded and twisted
And many tears were wept there,

5704 Hair torn out, beards pulled,
For he was their entire support,
Their military governor and their leader,
Master of the army and counselor.

5708   They have him carried to the rear of the field,
     So that the horses will not trample him.
     Toward their enemies they rush,
     Their weapons lowered, they are going to strike them
5712   As hard as their destriers will allow.
     And Guillaume has his men
     Ride their horses tightly together.
     When they are armed, they allow their horses
5716   To race as fast as they can go.
     At their encounter they struck each other so hard
     That one hundred of their men fell to the ground
     Who would never again remount
5720   Or carry a shield or a lance.
     Guillaume broke his lance
     And drew out his naked blade.
     Inflamed with anger and full of pride,
5724   He lets Brunsaudebruel charge.
     Among the Spanish he thrusts himself.
     Then whoever would see him help a vassal,
     Slice through heads and brains,
5728   Spill entrails and bowels,
     Slash limbs and feet and hands,
     Unseat from their horses the bodies of vassals
     Dead and bloody falling to the ground,
5732   And make martyrs out of the Spanish
     Who have made peace from this war,[70]
     Whoever would see him, well could he say
     That in the world there is none his equal.
5736   The sword he carries and his arm and body are
     Totally tinted with the red blood
     Of those that he has mutilated and killed.
     The Palermitans[71] help each other admirably,
5740   They stab and slaughter and kill
     And bring a vassal to grief.
     They are so confident because of their lord
     That neither peril nor death do they fear,
5744   They put to flight the most valiant of their men,

---

70. That is, they have found the peace that comes after death.
71. The text reads "Li citoien," which means "the citizens" and is referring specifically to the citizens of Palermo. In each instance of "citoien," singular or plural, I have translated it as "Palermitan(s)."

Who search for their reins right and left,
Many a warhorse is without his lord
Who is suffering the agony of death on the battlefield.
5748 At that moment advanced through the troops
Carcant, a very noble vassal
Who was the nephew of the seneschal.
To avenge him the vassal comes
5752 With great leaps through the battle
And goes to strike Marcon of Reggio;
His entire lance he put
Right through his clavicle,
5756 Sending him falling out of his saddle to the ground dead.
Then he struck Casu of Cefalu,
He broke his shield below its rounded center section.
His hauberk was not strong enough
5760 And right through his body he thrust
The iron and the wood and the pennon,[72]
Sending him falling to the ground dead on the battlefield.
With this blow he broke his lance.
5764 Then he drew his sword, advanced on them
And struck Jasan, a Palermitan
On his helmet with all his force;
Neither his helmet nor his coif nor his armor[73]
5768 Saved him from his adventure
So that Carcant would not split his head in two
And spill out his brains.
He sends him falling off his horse to the ground dead.
5772 Afterward he said to them: "My lord vassals,
If I do you harm, I am not at all in the wrong,
Since you have killed my uncle.
You have paid for it and those who
5776 Have yet to die will pay for it."
Then he passes beyond very angrily.
He wounds and injures many Palermitans
And he kills and mutilates many of them.
5780 Those from Spain rally to him.
If the men from the city do not get help now,

72. Carcant's lance would have had an iron head and wooden shaft, as well as a pennon, a long narrow streamer, hanging from it.
73. A coif is a padded cap worn beneath a helmet as further protection and to keep the helmet in place.

Soon more than two thousand will die.

Now Guillaume the bold jumps
5784   On his warhorse who quickly runs to him.
With his blade of steel he disperses the crowd.
He sees the vassal, rushes toward him
And the vassal comes to meet him.
5788   Both of them strike each other so hard
That sparks fly from their blades.
Guillaume was both strong and fierce,
Such a blow he gives him with his sword
5792   That he will never be protected from any weapon.
He cuts the ear off the head.
The blow falls marvelously
On the shoulder with such force
5796   That he causes it to separate completely from the trunk
And the side, so that the entrails
All spill out over the battlefield.
The body from which the soul departs
5800   Falls dead to the ground on the other side
So that the helmet flies into the sand.
"Pass beyond, vassal, said Guillaume,
If you have harmed us,
5804   You will not repeat it to your men.
Never will the king your lord know it,
If someone other than you does not go tell him."
Then he thrusts forward among the Spanish,
5808   But now they have turned their back to him
So that there are none paying attention to the combat.
Thereupon they flee toward the camp;
Those who are able to flee escape,
5812   Those who stay must die
Or be captured and detained.
They were destroyed; there were no more.

The citizens of Palermo returned
5816   With their booty and their plunder
Happy and joyous to the city.
About Guillaume they spoke considerably,
About his virtue, about his strength.
5820   Because of him they forget all the dead,

They show great joy and talk a great deal.
The queen embraces him vigorously
And welcomes him and is so very joyful;
5824 She puts everything in his control,
Her realm and her land and her army
To do as he commands:
So that he might be guardian and commandant
5828 And seneschal and governor.
Then they disarmed the vassal,
They have the horse taken care of
So that he will have all he needs.
5832 Then they go into the chamber to sit
By the windows, overlooking the orchard.
There they sat and rested,
The three ladies and the vassal.
5836 Beautiful was the day and great the heat.
Thus as they were talking there,
They look down, in the orchard they see
That the werewolf had come there.
5840 But such a marvel has no one ever seen:
He had his front paws joined together and on his head
The fierce beast had placed them,
So he is standing up on his rear paws.
5844 With an affable visage, with a gentle face
He bows in greeting toward the chamber and the tower
And the ladies and the lord,
Then he hurries away back into the wood.
5848 The queen is greatly amazed
By what she sees the beast do.
To the knight she could not be silent
For she had immediately said to him:
5852 "My lord, in the name of the Holy Spirit,
Did you see down there
The marvelous spectacle of that transformed beast,
How he imitated us in this action?
5856 — Yes, my lady, if it pleases you,
Said Guillaume to the queen.
I believe that the beast announces to us
The honor and the good, in my opinion,
5860 Which will come to us very soon.
And God the Lord will grant it to us.

— Indeed, if I dared to say it,
Says the lady, my lord, he is the one
5864   Who stole my dear son
Whom I lost a very long time ago,
For whom my heart is still grieving
And will be as long as I live.
5868   — How so, my lady? — I will tell it to you,
My dear sweet friend, says the queen.
Know that this was the whole truth.

      In that orchard we were one day,
5872   Myself and the king my dear lord,
Knights, ladies and barons
And other people in great abundance.
That day was very beautiful and warm.
5876   Thereupon leapt out from the woods
A wolf with an appearance
In body, in fur and just as big
As the one that we saw just now.
5880   In the presence of the king himself,
Right through the entire gathering
He came rushing, mouth gaping open.
My son that I had at that time,
5884   Whom I loved more than anyone,
Was not any more than four years old.
Now in this world no one alive
Has seen such a beautiful creature
5888   In body, in face or in form.
His name was Guillaume, the one kidnapped.
Never since, good sir, have I seen him.
— Was he not pursued then?
5892   — Yes he was, good sir, know this.[74]
— So he was not captured? — No. — How is that?
— He never had any fear of our men.
So they followed him each one faster than the other
5896   And in front of everyone first
The king himself
And his barons and his troops,
Many of the people together,

---

74. My translation is based on Michelant's edition. Micha does not indicate a change of speaker for this verse.

5900 Those on foot and those on horseback.
They pursued and followed him so far
That in spite of themselves they pushed him to the Strait of
    Messina.
To the depths he went, then they did not see him.
5904 Thus through such a calamity
And because of such great misfortune
I lost my young child."
When Guillaume heard the wondrous account,
5908 A small part of him refuses to believe it,
For well does he remember about the cowherd
Who raised him and was so dear to him,
And about what he told the emperor
5912 That in rich clothing, in noble finery
He had found him in the woods when he was little
And that he had raised him sixty months,
That never did he find anyone who asked for him.
5916 He truly would believe himself to be her son,
If the queen had not said
That her son had drowned in the sea.
Therefore he stops thinking about it.
5920 About those in the besieging army we ought to speak
Who have enough of both grief and wrath.
They make much noise and suffer greatly
For their relatives, for their friends
5924 Whom those within the city have killed.
They grieve exceedingly,
For that day they have lost many
Of their friends and their relatives.
5928 The king is so very distressed about it,
That he almost becomes totally enraged
Because of his loss and because of his damages.
He often asks who did this
5932 And the ones that fled who came back
Told it to him and related it
Exactly as it had happened.

"Sire, they say, now listen to us.
5936 The whole truth we will tell you,
For never will we lie at all to you about
How you lost your men.

From their army such people came
5940   That never has their equal been seen,
As fierce or as hardened,
As valiant or as well equipped.
There is one knight above all
5944   Who is so very valiant and worthy
That he has no equal in the world.
He kills and destroys everyone,
Against the blows of his steel blade
5948   Nothing can be of any use.
Whomever he is able to strike without hindrance
Cannot be protected by any weapon
From being split or cut in half.
5952   The knight that I am telling you about
Who is so very powerful
Has a wolf painted on his shield.
He killed our seneschal
5956   And his nephew, the good vassal
Who had taken the day so well
And injured their men
So that all would have been finally vanquished,
5960   If the baron had lived a little longer.
But he could not escape his fate,
For the lion who devours everyone,
Who killed your people today,
5964   The knight who is carrying the wolf,
When he saw the young man
Who was making carnage out of his men,
He rushed over to him as fast as he could.
5968   Neither a throng nor a crowd could hold him back
And he passed beyond forcefully.
His naked sword he drew out,
So hard did he strike Carcant
5972   That never did his helmet
Or the coif of his white hauberk
Protect the noble vassal from being killed.
He cut the ear from the head,
5976   The shoulder and the left side
He severed from the body with his blade.
He passed beyond and fell dead.
Thus died the good vassal

5980 And his uncle the seneschal.
It was not possible for us to bring back one of them,
For it was too dangerous to remain there.
On the battlefield they are lying grievously
5984 Among our men and theirs
Of which there is a great number.
The one who is carrying the wolf on his shield
Did all this damage to you
5988 And destroyed all your warriors.
Take counsel as to what you will do
And how you will make amends for this shame."

Thereupon entered the son of the king,
5992 Counts and princes with him.
Well has he heard and understood
How his men were vanquished,
How they died and were captured,
5996 And he heard the noise and the shouts
That those from the army are making
For their friends whom they have lost.
He has a very great anger in his heart about it.
6000 He calls to the king and says: "Good sir,
Now it is thus, we have lost
Some of our vassals, some of our barons,
But we still have knights
6004 As many as sixty thousand,
That is everyone without counting the other lesser men.
In this way the thing happened,
There is nothing to worry about,
6008 Except to be careful and to avenge
This shame and this insult
That they have brought on us and done to us,
So that they will not be able to continue their mockery.
6012 Never may I have any land to hold
Nor honor any day of my life
If it is not sold very dearly to them.
If they dare to issue forth tomorrow,
6016 They can be assured about their lives:[75]
If outside the gate I can find

75. According to Micha, this verse should be read ironically: they will not escape alive. See note
to verse in his edition, p. 217.

The one who they say is carrying the wolf
Who has done this wrong to you,
6020 I will return his head to you.
When they have lost that one,
The others will never be saved.
If they want to keep the city,
6024 We will think about attacking it;
By great force they will be captured
And they will all be put in your prison.
When you hold them here outside
6028 Then take vengeance on their bodies,
May what they merit be rendered to them
For your damages and your loss.
When you have taken your vengeance,
6032 From within let the lady and her daughter
Be dragged out so that no one remains inside.
Send both of them to Spain,
There you will do your pleasure with the ladies.
6036 Then the realm, the crown and seigniorial authority
Will be yours free from all claims.
There will be no man in the world that will deny it,
As much as he might still have power.
6040 — Good son, just as you have ordered,
Said the king, will it be done."
Then they set aside the entire discussion
Until the night was over
6044 And dawn had broken.
Those who must get on their way wake up,
They arm and equip themselves
In the best and most beautiful manner they can.
6048 They do not linger or tarry.
Mounted on their destriers were
Up to twenty-two thousand
Good men fierce and bold,
6052 The best of knighthood.
In front of everyone the son of the king
Divides his squadrons,
He made and separated out ten horse troops,
6056 In each one there are two thousand men-at-arms;
There is a good commander for each one.
After him come, one by one,

His own troop first, three thousand of them,
6060 They ride their horses toward the city.

When the sun and the day came
Great brilliance flashes off the weapons;
The helmets and the shields gleam
6064 And the hauberks formed with small mail,
The banners and the pennons
That flutter in the wind across the sand.
They see the field; they grieve exceedingly
6068 For their friends that they see lying there.
They see so many helmets of gold gleaming
And so many vassals lying on their backs
And so many shields and so many lances
6072 And so many beautiful figures painted on the shields,
So many lances, so many blades of steel
And across the field so many good warhorses,
So many hauberks with bloody mail,
6076 So many intestines and so many entrails
Lying all over the meadow,
So many heads severed from trunks,
So many feet sliced, so many chests
6080 And so many ribs and so many spines.
And you would see so many young men
Lying on the field dead and bloody;
They weep and have pity for the pain
6084 Of their men whom they see across the field.
When the seneschal was found,
Above all he was pitied and his loss was deplored,
For they loved the baron very much.
6088 They look around for Carcant;
They found him in turn on the battlefield,
Next to him were lying his entrails.
They recognized him by his arms
6092 And have him carried on a shield.
Back to the camp on two pack horses
The knights have him brought.
Another had his friend carried back
6096 Who would never see him buried,
For before nightfall he would have to die.
The Spaniards are very eager

To avenge themselves and their friends.

6100   There upon they abandoned the bodies;

Further on they stopped in a valley

That was between them and the city.

In that place they left

6104   Some of their knights

And in their trap have

Put four thousand of their men.[76]

If it is necessary to use them,

6108   They will jump out from their ambush

To help them. Then they leave,

Near the city they have come.

But those within were already outside,

6112   Their bodies very nobly armed.

They are very richly adorned

And mounted on their horses.

Six troop formations have been established,

6116   All of them ready and equipped

As if to fight their enemies.

Knights made up four of the formations

And the fifth formation

6120   Was made up of men-at-arms and bourgeois,

The sixth was of foot soldiers,

In front of the palisades they lined up.

Guillaume was in the first line;

6124   The others take counsel from him.

He arranges well his battalions,

To each one he designates a good prince,

Very beautifully he instructs them and sets out a plan

6128   And incites them to do well.

Then he looks around and sees the enemy

And says to his men: "See, my lords,

See their men coming, now it is time to do well!

6132   We have shamed and vexed them,

They want to avenge themselves; I see it well.

See how they are coming in troop formation.

They have no desire to be in disarray now;

6136   They want to do it wisely

76. The manuscript actually reads "Mis .IIII. et .IIII. de lor gent" ("Put four and four of their men"). My translation is based on Michelant's reading of the verse: "Mis quatre mil de lor gent." The prose version also reads "quatre mille hommes."

Like honest and brave men. And let everyone know
That they will all be dead and destroyed,
Never against us will they have any protection.
6140 There I see one of them coming in front,
Who has armed his body very well.
He is holding a war banner unfurled and suspended from his
    lance.
How rich his horse seems
6144 And how fierce and noble the vassal!
God, how splendid is his armor!
Is he then the lord of these men?
— Yes. — Who is he? — The son of the king,
6148 A knight of great nobility,
For no man is worth what he is.
— He is truly about to have difficulty,
Since he rushes today into such a place.
6152 If there were twenty-four like him
As you say that he believes himself to be,
Now I want to make his acquaintance,"
Said Guillaume, who desires it so.
6156 He picks up his shield very angrily
And kicks Brunsaudebruel forward.
His eyes become totally red
From the blood that rises to his face.
6160 His bravery increases and he gathers his courage.
In front of his men he gallops
With his lance with its sharp blade;
Like a small pennon for his weapons
6164 He picked up his shield by its straps.
The son of the king on the other hand
Takes note of Guillaume,
By the wolf that he bears on his shield
6168 The baron has recognized him well.
Of his men he asks: "Is he then the one
Who caused us such losses?
— Yes, sire, he is the one,
6172 This is the vassal whom we saw, to our own misfortune.
See how brave and vigorous he acts,
He is fiercer than a leopard.
His destrier was King Embron's,
6176 In this land I know of no better one

Than the one that is prancing in that place.
Cursed be his might
That he has put us in such dread!"

6180 About this the son of the king is not worried,
So he lets his horse charge toward him
As fast as he can go,
For he hates him excessively.

6184 Guillaume, who does not grant him safety
When he sees him, does not stop;
Faster than thunder or a tempest
He rushes to meet him.

6188 Then both of them struck each other
So that they pierce and break their shields
And smash and shatter their lances.
The warhorses collide with each other

6192 And both of the knights
So hard that both of them stagger;
They almost spill out each other's brains.
Guillaume had a stronger warhorse.

6196 He sent the king's son falling,
And along with him his horse,
Down to the ground;
He almost broke his spine.

6200 Above him Guillaume kept his sword drawn,
"Palermo" he shouts, and those
Who neither desire nor expect anything else charge.
Then you would see their men coming

6204 In hordes, by the hundreds and thousands
Of those within against those outside
On piebald and sorrel horses,
The blades of their lances lowered.

6208 Since the world has begun
Never has such a mêlée been seen,
So well attacked or better sustained,
Nor so perilous or so cruel,

6212 Nor with such a loss of vassals.

Those from Spain go into the mêlée,
They strike and thrust vigorously.
To rescue their young lord

6216 They cause many bowels to be spilled there,

Many brains, many entrails.
The Palermitans in the battle are
Confident and fierce because of their lord.
6220 They send falling to the ground among those in the enemy army
Many a high baron and many a vassal,
Like a wild boar they join battle with them.
For Guillaume the powerful, the valiant
6224 The valorous and the proud
Strikes forcefully and enthusiastically.
He massacres many of the enemy,
So hard does he strike down, so much does he thrust up.
6228 He breaks through the press around him,
Neither because of danger nor because of worry
Does the baron distance himself from the son of the king.
On the contrary, he holds on to him by the vent in his helmet.[77]
6232 He yanks and pulls him from the battle
Forcefully and powerfully.
Out of the mêlée the baron leads him,
To the citizens he delivered him,
6236 They have him taken to the city
And have him surrender to the queen.
Those outside almost fly into a rage
When they see their young lord captured.
6240 They put their horns to their mouths
To call for those in the ambush,
Who rush back at top speed,
When they have heard they are needed.
6244 The troops are coming very dense and strong,
Great is the dust from the horses
And great the throng of vassals,
Just as they are coming in disarray
6248 To help the son of the king.

Guillaume sees their men coming,
From the field he has his men leave.
Back to the city he leads them
6252 With great difficulty and great effort,
For many a lance has already been broken there
And many a naked sword has been drawn,

---

77. His helmet had a *ventaille*, an opening that allowed him to breathe.

Many a blow given and many returned,
6256 Many a helmet smashed and many a shield
And many a breastplate has lost its gold band,
Many a head severed from its trunk,
Many a vassal killed and many a baron.
6260 Then at high speed arrive those
Who had left the ambush,
But they have come too late,
For all the Palermitans
6264 Have entered inside the city.
Around up on the walls climb
Both the men-at-arms and the foot soldiers
And into the cellars and the fortifications.
6268 Those who shoot crossbows
Establish themselves among the battalions,
So that those outside will not attack them.
But they have drawn back,
6272 At this time nothing more was done
And they leave for their lodging,
There they dismount from their horses.
At the royal palace Guillaume
6276 Dismounted from his horse,
The one who took care of his destrier was first-rate.
There the knight was disarmed by
Thirty young noblemen in front of the hall.
6280 The lady descends to meet him,
Along with her were the two maidens
Who were very gracious and beautiful.
Up to Guillaume they came
6284 And when the baron saw them,
He leaps up to them and is very happy to see them.
The maidens express great joy.
For her prisoner the queen
6288 Ardently thanks the baron.
Then they take hold of each other by their fingers,
All the steps of hard white limestone
They climb to the hall above.
6292 Into the great chamber they came,
They sit again at the windows
That are made of black marble.
There all four of them sat down

6296   To amuse and entertain themselves,
And to profit from the air and the coolness,
For it was immoderately warm.

Just as they are talking there
6300   And speaking about this and that with their good-natured
        remarks,
The lady examines the young nobleman
Whom she sees is so courtly and beautiful
And more than anything he resembles
6304   King Embron, or so it seems to me,
In body, in limbs, in face,
In nose, in mouth and in chin,
With a sincere visage and appearance.
6308   Her heart becomes tender,
When she remembers her son;
From her eyes flow
Down hot tears.
6312   Guillaume said: "You are behaving very badly,
My lady. Why are you so anguished?
Now you should play and laugh
And cheer up your household
6316   Who are very weary and fatigued,
Make promises to one, give to the other
And comfort the wounded,
Since you have someone now, my lady,
6320   By whom you will get back your kingdom
And your fief, know this well;
Never for any reason will you fail.
— My lord, it is true. May the One who is
6324   Above all powerful and strong protect you.
I know well, my lord, that with your help
I will get back all my seigniorial authority
And my entire fief without any doubt:
6328   Of this I am truly confident.
One of my greatest enemies
You have captured and given to me today.
May our Lord be grateful to you for it.
6332   I no longer value them or their threat
To be worth one leaf from this branch,
Because I see you so safe and sound.

But now hear, good and dear sweet lord,
6336 Why I weep and why I am in such anguish:
More do you resemble my lord,
The king who maintained this fief,
May God have pity today on his soul,
6340 Than anyone else, said the lady,
In body, in limbs, in face.
If you were of the same age
As the king, never did I see a person
6344 Who resembled another so well.

    When I looked at your appearance,
I remembered my dear son
Who would have been your age now.
6348 My lord, if God might give me honor,
When I remembered my son again,
I had to weep, so it happened to me.
I am a woman of feeble courage,
6352 Well do I know that I was not at all wise,
And that I ought to have been more wary of my conduct.
 Whoever might hold his naked sword
On my neck would not possess me,
6356 My lord, if God protects me.
  — My lady, says he, it often happens:
That someone clearly resembles the other
But it never amounts to anything for him.
6360 And nevertheless, know this well,
I would really like to resemble him,
For truly valiant and noble was
King Embron, just as they relate.
6364 But what is it worth and what does it matter?
Since he is dead, it is worth nothing,
There is no remedy now."

    The queen is not at all pleased
6368 About what she had said to the young nobleman,
Since she considered her son dead,
For she believes that Guillaume is her son.
Her heart advises her and tells her all this
6372 And her soul makes her believe it.
Thus as they were speaking there,

They look down, in the orchard they see
That the werewolf had come back there.
6376 On the ground he had put his two knees
Before Guillaume and the queen
And the maidens, the beast bows down to them
Two times very simply,
6380 Then goes on his way, he does not linger.
The queen sees the marvelous spectacle
That the beast has prepared for her.
She begins to wonder a great deal.
6384 "My lord, says she to the knight
Who is sitting beside her at the window,
For the love of God the celestial King,
What is wrong with this beast and what does he want,
6388 This beast who is asking something of us? From what is he
      suffering?
Yesterday he bowed down to us thus
Just one time very simply
And now twice. There is no doubt
6392 That this is significant.

⋯⋯⋯⋯⋯⋯⋯⋯⋯⋯⋯⋯⋯⋯⋯⋯⋯⋯⋯⋯⋯⋯⋯⋯⋯

— But it is entirely true, He who gives and shares
All that is good protects him
Because of His compassion, because of His grace,
6396 Never such a noble beast have I seen.
Thus I am confident that he is a sign of
The honor and joy and seigniorial authority
That will come to us soon, I believe.
6400 All your enemy that is outside
Will finally be destroyed.
— Amen, each of the women reply,
Good sir, may God hear you."
6404 Now, if it pleases you, I would tell you
Of those who left discouraged.
They related and told the king everything
Exactly as it had happened to them
6408 And how they had lost his son,
How those within hold him captive.
The king almost flew into a rage,
When he heard their news.
6412 Angrily he moans and sighs,

Full of wrath he looks at them.
"Ah! Evil men, says he, cowards,
How greatly shamed are all of you,
6416   And you have killed and destroyed me!
You have killed me and dishonored yourself.
How did it happen? How was he taken?
For what reason, by what presumption
6420   Have you caused me such a great loss?
You have deprived me of
What I had in my hands.
How did you allow him to be captured?
6424   You should all be hung from a branch,
Because he has remained there without you."
Thus the king is infuriated with them,
He had already insulted them greatly
6428   When the barons told him about it.

Afterward he said angrily:
"Who captured my son? — The one who captures everyone,
Who takes away and carries off everyone.
6432   — Who is it then? — It is the one who they say
Carries the wolf on his shield.
— Thus is he of such very great strength?
— Indeed. — What? — Yes he is without a doubt.
6436   — Then the entire army is lost
And we will all be captured, if he is like that.
But cursed be anyone who believes you
That one single man might have such power;
6440   He has truly dishonored all of you.
— Dishonored? No, he has not. — Yes, he has. — How?
— Five hundred men would not do
What you say a single man did.
6444   — You are wrong to say we are shamed and dishonored.
He killed our seneschal
Whom you considered such a great vassal
And his nephew and the barons
6448   Who are still lying in the sand,
Who rode wildly,
For they were not at all being careful.
— Because they did not know that in the city
6452   There was anyone other than its people,

So they perished because of their disarray.
But in the name of the One in whom I believe,
Tomorrow I will show them my body
6456 And my power and my strength.
And the vassal who carries the wolf,
If I can find him outside the gate
And I can get my hands on him or capture him,
6460 In their presence I will have him hung;
Of this they may be assured.
Never will the walls be strong enough,
The towers or the earthen ramparts tall enough
6464 That I will not make them fall to the ground
And that I will not pull them down by force.
Too long have I tolerated their protection,
Now I will make them pay dearly for it."
6468 He has his decree proclaimed everywhere
That the next day, before daybreak,
The army must be lined up well,
And that a single man must not remain there
6472 Who is not bearing arms or has not donned a sword.
The next day, before the crack of dawn,
They were armed together
And all issued forth from the tents,
6476 Their bodies very well equipped.
They spread out down the plains,
Well armed are the troops.
Twenty horse troops were established;
6480 Never has one seen any better equipped
In splendid arms or in horses.
The good vassals had mounted,
The king divided them properly
6484 And encouraged them to do well.
"Barons, says he, let us avenge the injustice,
The grief, the loss and the harm
Done to us by those
6488 Who captured and killed our friends.
I would rather be captured and killed.
They are harming my son,
I cannot reward them or pay them back in any better way
6492 Than to seek and take vengeance from them."
Then he orders them to ride out.

Very loud and great is the noise
Of the voices, of the bodies and of the tumult
6496   That they are making as they set off.
Those horns are blowing and those bronze trumpets;
From a full distance of four great leagues[78]
One can hear the noise:
6500   It makes the whole earth tremble.
Those in the city hear them,
All of them immediately pick up their weapons.
They armed themselves and put on their armor
6504   And issued forth from the city.
The brave Guillaume is in front
Of his barons, leading them.
He has separated them into ten horse troops,
6508   In each one there are seven hundred men-at-arms,
As many knights as other men.
To all he said reasonably:
"Barons, be careful that there is no misfortune
6512   And that nothing vile is done contrary to justice.
Of this war you see the conclusion.
Now all of you conduct yourselves like valorous men.
Today this very day this war is coming to an end.
6516   Know it to be true; it is the whole truth.
The king and the entire army are coming to us,
But do not be afraid because of this:
If there are more of them, they will lose more,
6520   Never against us will they be safe.
We have seen many of their men
Held in check by our men.
Against one of ours have been twenty,
6524   But in spite of this it came to pass
That we vanquished them and captured them,
Chased them from the field and defeated them.
Thus within we have of their vassals
6528   The most valiant and the most important,
Even the son of the king.
By that loyalty that I owe all of you,
Good can still happen today.
6532   If God wants to grant it to us,

---

78. A league is equal is 3.0 statute miles or 4.8 kilometers.

By caprice we will have the father.
The son we have, that is certain truth.
But keep yourself together
6536 And ride tightly."
With short steps they ride close together,
But they have scarcely gone forward,
When they see the lance banderoles of the enemy
6540 That appear over the plains,
The banners, the war standards hanging from their lances
And the great troops of warriors
One coming right after the other,
6544 Each one with his lance on his lance rest.
In this way the horse troops are riding,
One after the other, without disarray.
The earth shines because of their arms.
6548 It would not be necessary to seek out more handsome men.

When the two sides notice each other,
They do not wait for anything more
But hang their shields at their necks,
6552 Charge and spur their horses on and rush forward,
They make the whole earth shake.
There you would see what was happening to them,
So many wooden lances breaking and so many shields,
6556 And so many hauberks with small chain mail,
So many helmets of gold shattering and breaking,
And so many vassals being thrown violently to the ground,
The noise increasing and swords being drawn,
6560 And men killing and slaughtering each other,
Heads and fists and feet flying,
One dead on top of another crushing him
And the earth covered with blood
6564 And warhorses fleeing across the field,
Their reins broken, their saddles bloody,
Whose young men lie dead,
Their bodies being trampled by their horses
6568 Who had brought them there,
Through the throngs, to great grief.
The king of Spain was in the mêlée
With his men, with his assembly of warriors.
6572 To those in the city he causes great injury,

He goes to great trouble to destroy them
And to slaughter them and kill them;
For he truly detests them with a great hatred.
6576　He has punished them severely
So that he almost slaughters them all.
The king shouts out and said:
"Where is, where is the knight,
6580　The arrogant, the strong, the fierce,
The one who carries the wolf on his shield
Who has slaughtered and killed my men?
Where is the wolf, since he has not come back?
6584　Now he dreads so much, perhaps, and fears
These dogs who are guarding this prey,
He is not so bold that he might be seen here now.
Such a very daring beast he will be
6588　If he lingers in front of dogs the likes of
Such as I have unleashed down here."
Then he charges and spurs on his horse
And goes off to strike a knight,
6592　A young nobleman, the son of a prince:
Poonciax of Bisterne was his name,
He was a relative of the king of Palermo.
He makes a hole beneath the shield's bulging center section
6596　And he tears his hauberk and breaks its rings,
Right through his chest the king thrusts his banderole,
He fells him to the ground dead on the battlefield.
Geraume of Melant sees him,
6600　For the youth he grieves sorely,
Angrily he attacks the king.
He completely shattered his lance,
On his shield such a blow he gives him
6604　That the king quickly becomes inflamed in anger and bends
　　　back
From the great blow that he received.
He draws his sword forcefully,
With such fury he strikes Geraume in turn
6608　Through the top of his helmet
That he completely splits and puts him in pieces
And right through and beyond his brain
He thrusts the sword down to his chin.
6612　From his saddle pommel he sends him falling dead.

Then he strikes Aquilant of Candis.
Neither his brilliant green helmet
Nor his coif of iron decorated with precious stones
6616   Against the sharpness of the sword
Were worth a marsh bulrush to him
And he pierces him down through his face,
Thus he brings him down dead and without life.
6620   He sees his men; he shouts his rallying cry:
"Strike, barons, avenge the injustice
That they caused us with our warriors."
Then the king charges through the ranks.
6624   Soon those from the city are about to perish
If they are not quickly helped.
But nevertheless if they have lost,
They are making them pay very dearly,
6628   For the best of them they send falling to the ground.

        Guillaume is in the great crowd
Where he does not stop nor does he cease,
He tortures those from Spain.
6632   So many does he kill, so many does he mutilate,
So many does he fell, so many does he slaughter,
That all the ground is bloody from it.
There is no knight thus armed,
6636   If he touches him with his blade of steel,
Who will ever see any protection from it.
Everyone turns away from his path.
The baron looks up to the right
6640   And sees coming down a knoll
Some of his men
Who were proceeding very poorly,
For they were coming away in total retreat,
6644   All of them were fleeing as best as they were able.
He sees the king who was chasing them
And was causing them great injury.
If they do not get any help, they went there for their misfor-
        tune.
6648   Now the men from the city see them.
They shout loudly to Guillaume:
"Sire, what are you doing? Help your men,
Those are your men who are fleeing there,

6652 Hear how the Spanish are booing at them.
   What are you waiting for, baron? Please look at yourself,
   Help your men, why do you tarry?
   That is the king on that sorrel charger.
6656 He has no equipment that is not made of gold."
   Guillaume heard it well,
   Well did he recognize the king.
   He is extraordinarily troubled
6660 When he sees his army put to flight.
   Then he looks among the heights
   And sees the men fleeing.
   And when he sees them, in order to bring them aid,
6664 He spurs his destrier and lets him run.
   "Palermo" he shouts, "knights!"
   Afterward some three thousand charge,
   There is no one who fails to be there
6668 In the mêlée or in the battle.

    The courageous Guillaume, the valiant,
   Sees and goes to meet those who are fleeing,
   With a loud voice the baron shouts to them:
6672 "Hey, barons, do not flee!
   For God's sake, do not be afraid,
   But let each of you have a confident heart.
   Abandon this, turn toward me."
6676 Thereupon he charges at the king's men.
   With his blade of steel that slices and cuts
   He breaks through and disperses the throng.
   Through the largest troops he passes.
6680 Now many a helmet he breaks and smashes,
   And many a vassal and many a baron
   He brought down dead on the sand.
   He causes those who were fleeing to turn back
6684 And those who were chasing to retreat.
   When the Spaniards recognize him,
   They do not hasten to pursue him any further.
   And when they are all so very much in the mêlée
6688 And they are mixed in with those from the city,
   Then you would see on all sides
   The striking of lances and javelins,
   Naked swords and maces,

6692 Bodies covering the sites,
   A painful battle, difficult and cruel,
   One of them killing and the other slaughtering,
   Tinting the earth with red blood,
6696 Some dying, the others lamenting,
   Warhorses fleeing down the plain.
   There is not a single person who looks after them:
   They all have enough to do,
6700 Since all those who could be attentive,
   Who had been born then, without fail
   Had not seen such a cruel battle,
   Nor one so wicked or so deadly.
6704 With the king there was a vassal
   Marvelous and strong and helpful
   Whose son was his constable,
   And his name was Meliadon.
6708 The other day he had come to the camp
   And he had brought knights
   All from his land and born there
   And some of them of his lineage.
6712 When he sees the loss and the injury
   That those from the city are doing to their men,
   He almost dies from grief.
   Above all he sees Guillaume helping,
6716 Slaughtering his people and wounding them.
   He looks and sees the king beside him:
   "See, sire, how that vassal is wreaking havoc
   There on your men as he is doing.
6720 In faith, if we do not help them quickly,
   Soon they will all be killed and captured."
   The king responds: "Good gentle friend,
   You speak the truth; it is unfortunate that he was born.
6724 He is the devil, the demon
   Who has caused me so much shame and grief.
   I hate nothing as much as I do him.
   Whoever is able to capture him dead or alive
6728 And deliver him and give him to me,
   All the days that I still live
   I would do whatever he desires and pleases."
   Meliadon hears the king,
6732 He shouts his battle cry loudly

And those who are with him hear it,
Spur their horses and charge and rush in.
Their shields joined in front of their chests,
6736   They go off in search of their enemies.
Into the battle they came,
Against those from the city they raise their cry.
They intend to destroy many of them,
6740   But they retreat and defend themselves
Like good and valiant men.
Many sword blows were struck there,
So many shields shattered and so many breastplates
6744   And so many people felled to the ground,
Many a helmet of gold broken and smashed
And many a baron led to death.
Meliadon goes through the mêlée
6748   Urging his men on against theirs.
The baron struck so many blows there
That he caused many of their men to be felled.
Because of his arrogance, because of his excess
6752   He is asking for his own great harm,
For he is seeking Guillaume.
But I tell you well, in my opinion,
It would be better for him to distance himself
6756   Than see or approach him,
Just as you will shortly hear it told.
Those from the city become so very angry
Because he has killed one of their barons,
6760   A native of Brindisi, the lord of the port;
From the port he received the income.
His youth caused them to lament greatly,
For he was very valiant and courageous
6764   And handsome and noble and likeable;
Tardant was the baron's name.
Then at that moment came charging up
His brother who saw him fall,
6768   And who believes he will die from grief.
Dolant was his name, I think,
Newly dubbed was he,
He was not any more than twenty years old,
6772   Very valiant and renowned was he.
He sees his brother in the middle of that place;

Near him he gets down and then he takes him in his arms.
He runs his hands all over his body,
6776   But he feels neither pulse nor breath there.
He sees the blood that is flowing from the body,
The hauberk torn apart and the great wound
Cruel and evil in the middle of the hollow chest,
6780   His beautiful eyes closed and his face pale
And his soul departed from his body.
He curses himself and he hates his life,
His life he hates and he blames himself,
6784   On his brother he often swoons.
He cannot stay there long,
For he wants to take him away from the throng.
In front of him on the pommel of the saddle,
6788   Kissing his eyes and his cheek,
He carries him out of the mêlée.
Beneath a tree, far from the enemy,
There he put his brother on the ground.
6792   There was no need to seek greater grief
Than what he expressed and demonstrated.
To God he commended his soul
That he might take charge of it through His mercy.
6796   The young nobleman took leave of the body.
Thereupon he leaves, mounts his destrier,
And at top speed, to avenge him,
He charged back into the battle.
6800   It does not matter to him any more what direction he goes,
Nor does he consider any moderation,
For his life he no longer has any concern.
He is entirely disposed to come to blows
6804   And out of anger he charges and spurs his horse on;
Toward those from Spain he is arrogant.
He encounters Maron of Alidos[79]
With his blade of steel he struck him so hard
6808   That he sliced completely through him down to his teeth.
He fells him to the ground dead, passes beyond,

79. My translation is based on Michelant's transcription of the verse, "Maron encontre d'Ali-dos." Since Dolant is still the subject in verse 6819, it is likely that Dolant is also the subject in verse 6806, as well as in vv. 6807–6818. Micha's transcription of the verse, "Maron encontre Dali-dos," would be translated as "Dalidos encounters Maron" and Micha suggests that Maron is one of Guillaume's knights and that Dalidos is a Spanish warrior. I would suggest instead that Maron of Alidos is a Spanish warrior.

In the middle of the crowd he shoves them together.
He strikes great blows there; he does not hesitate through lack
    of courage,
6812   He sends many of the enemy falling dead to the ground,
Many of them he unhorsed,
The healthiest of them is so injured
That he will never again have one more day of good health.
6816   He sees Meliadon in the mêlée
Who is menacing so badly those from the city,
Whence the most valiant are overwhelmed.
Dolant sees him, he knows him well.
6820   As much as he is able he moved toward him,
For his hatred for him is lethal and pitiless,
Because he had killed his brother.
There is nothing in the world that he desires as much
6824   As to be able to kill the vassal.

      When Meliadon sees him coming,
He does not want to flee because of him,
Rather he charges toward him.
6828   Thus the two of them strike each other
With their blades of steel with such vigor
On top of their helmets painted with flowers
That they crush and smash both of them,
6832   And break their coifs and unlace them.
There is no blade that is not wet with blood
Nor is either one not in pain from it.
Meliadon recovers first
6836   Before Dolant is able to move,
With his blade of steel he slices and cuts
His head near the collar of his hauberk
And sends it flying more than six feet.
6840   Guillaume sees him; he grieves sorely
For the two brothers, for the two friends
That Meliadon had killed.
He considers himself dead if he does not avenge them now.
6844   Right through the throng he advances toward him,
There is no one in the enemy army who gets in his way
Who triumphs over him.
They make way for him and he leaves.
6848   With his drawn and naked blade of steel

He makes his way toward Meliadon,
Who looks at the baron.
From his shield he knows him well,
6852   By the wolf that they said it bore.
He sees the vassal and the warhorse
That is so very powerful and fierce:
He would not have waited for him for any fortune,
6856   If he had been able to escape;
But since he must do it,
Toward him he charges as fast as he can
Like a vassal filled with valor.
6860   He fears shame more than injury.
His naked sword in his right hand,
Forcefully and powerfully
The baron spurs his horse as fast as it will go.
6864   The two barons come together.
Meliadon quickly strikes Guillaume
Entirely on his helmet in such a way
That he completely splits and slices and cuts it
6868   And breaks the links in the chain mail of his iron coif.
On his head he gives him a great wound
So that red blood flows from it.
If the blow had not been deflected as it was
6872   I believe he would have been killed.
Guillaume sees his blood flowing
And looks at the knight
Who had struck him, because of whom he is troubled.
6876   He extends his blade, aims his sword
And remembers the great injuries
That he had done to his warriors,
For which he sought him and is grieving so much.
6880   He leans on his spurs and raises himself,
And gives him such an enormous blow
On top of his helmet, brilliant with a greenish cast,
That he totally slices through it and puts it in pieces.
6884   He smashes the coif and breaks the rings of the hauberk,
He completely slices his head in two.
The blow descends downward,
Which was struck very rapidly,
6888   His chest and his entire upper body
He cuts through down to the waist.

The body, which no longer lives nor endures,
Falls dead in the middle of the plain.
6892 When those from Spain see it
And they see Meliadon die,
Then they do not know what will become of them,
They no longer know where to seek protection.
6896 Each one would like to be in his own domain,
For there is no one in the entire army
Who dares to boast about avenging him,
They fear the baron so very much.
6900 And he spurs his horse toward them,
His sword drawn, with his company.
The entire army of Spain is trembling because of him,
They fear him so much and dread him so much
6904 That in front of him everyone flees.
The noise begins and the shouts,
The chase and the carnage.

Well does the king see them coming then,
6908 He does not know where he can protect himself.
He sees his companies of troops retreating,
His men fleeing and not charging back:
They are defeated and are not rallying to get assistance,
6912 He becomes furious and desires some common sense.
He sees Guillaume, who is coming toward him,
It is not astonishing if he fears him,
It is because of him that he sees his men lost,
6916 His army vanquished and crushed.
If he is afraid, it is not amazing,
To his barons the king counsels:
"My lords, says he, I know not what to do,
6920 We have no place where we can retreat.
We see our men overwhelmed,
Now there is no recovery,
And yet here they come.
6924 We will not save ourselves by fleeing,
Never by running away will we find any protection
And we will all be captured while trying to escape.
And since we are about to fall into their hands,
6928 Then it would be better for us to defend ourselves.
It is preferable to die honorably

Than to be captured dishonorably.
If the one who were leading them were dead,
6932 Then we would still be safe, I believe.
Cursed be the one who allows himself to be captured,
As long as he is able to defend himself.
Let us put ourselves in peril,
6936 I do not see any other deliverance.
If we wanted to flee from here,
I would not know what direction to go.
Here is the sea that is surrounding us
6940 And they are coming very rapidly.
Now let us ready ourselves to come to blows,
May God act according to His pleasure."
Then they took up their shields in their arms
6944 And they drew out their good clean blades.
As fast as the horses are able to go,
The vassals charge and spur them on.
They are entirely disposed to come to blows.
6948 When Guillaume sees them coming,
He points them out to his men and says: "My lords,
Here is the king and all of their men.
They have regained their courage, now it is time to do well,
6952 Take care that their great arrogance becomes apparent to them."
Thereupon they headed for each other,
But the Spanish army did not gain very much,
For those from within the city
6956 Bring down dead and bleeding
Sixty and more of their company,
Among the most valiant of those from Spain.
The others they attacked in such a manner
6960 That they have killed and captured all of them
And destroyed them.
Guillaume was a great man of valor,
He spotted the king who was fleeing
6964 Through a valley with great haste.
As fast as he can he rushes toward him,
"Palermo" he shouts loudly.
He reaches the king, takes his horse by its bridle,
6968 Two blows he gives him immediately
With his armored fist, with his entire blade,
On top of his gleaming helmet.

He pulls and turns the king toward him,
6972   Then he shouts at him: "You no longer have the strength now,
King, you no longer have the strength now, you are dead!
It was for your misfortune that you arrived at our ports.
Now you will rectify the injury
6976   That because of your great excess you have
Done to us in this land.
Today draws to an end your war
That you have sustained for so many days.
6980   Now it will cost you very dearly."

Of death the king has great fear,
Thus he shouts loudly to him:
"Sire, have pity, in the name of the Lord
6984   Who had compassion for the sinner.
I surrender myself to your mercy
To do what you command,
Whether it is to live or to die.
6988   Here are your men coming toward me:
They all hate me and they are not all wrong,
I have maltreated them, to my very great error.
Because of this I say to you, if they have the opportunity now,
6992   They will kill me dishonorably."
Thereupon he surrendered his sword,
The baron took it and received it.
Afterward he said to him: "You will not die,
6996   Since you put yourself in my power,
Except that I will lead you to my lady
And to the prison I will take you
To do with you as she desires."
7000   Thus the king surrenders to him.
Then he makes his men draw back,
For he does not want in any manner
That in his capture they might harm him more,
7004   Although he might be their enemy.
Then there was no one who approached him
Who looked at him with an evil intent.
In this manner they maintain a delicate peace for him.
7008   Up above inside the main palace
They have already told the lady
That the enemy army has been vanquished:

"My lady, they have been defeated.

7012   The king of Spain, their lord,
        Is being brought to your prison
        By the man who is the most valiant, the most valorous
        That indeed exists in the entire world.

7016   — In the name of God, friend, are you telling me the truth?
        Said the queen to the messenger.
        — My lady, this is the whole truth,
        May I lose my head, if I am lying.

7020   — For God's sake, friend, tell me how it happened.
        Was the king captured? — Truly he was, without a doubt,
        And his troops defeated
        And those in the army dead and vanquished."

7024   Never before was the queen so joyous,
        Than when he told her.
        Then she asks him who the lord is.
        "My fair good friend, what is his name?

7028   — Who, my lady, if not Guillaume,
        The courageous, the bold and the noble,
        The courteous, the valiant,
        The best of all the others and their master?

7032   It could not be anyone else."
        Then other messengers arrive,
        Men-at-arms, bourgeois and knights
        Who go up into the palace

7036   And in turn gave her a similar account.

        When the queen hears the news,
        She is so happy that her heart immediately jumps for joy
        And she makes the sign of the cross above her chest

7040   For those in the enemy army who have been defeated
        And the king who has been captured whom they are bringing to
            her.
        Without more ado she makes a sign to Melior:
        "My damsel, come here.

7044   Of your friend you are about to hear
        Some news, that he has captured the king
        And defeated those from Spain,
        Putting all their men out of action.

7048   My dear, it is fortunate that you were ever born!
        May goodness come to the land from which you issued,

From whence both of you came to me here."
Thereupon entered within
7052   In great throngs into the city
All those who are returning from the battle.
Never did anyone see greater joy
Than that which they express and show in the city
7056   About those in the enemy army who have been vanquished.
Then they ride to their lodging,
There they descend from their horses
Between Guillaume and the barons.
7060   The king of Spain and the prisoners
Descend in front of the main tower
And the valet takes the horses
And then leads them away to rest.
7064   On the square there are many knights,
Barons and princes and marquis;
Each one has removed the armor from his face.
From the principal stone hall
7068   The queen has come down,
With her are many damsels.
And there were Florence and the maiden
Who were beautiful and pink.
7072   Their color is marvelously fresh,
Their faces sincere, their visages pink.
Never would you see two more noble women,
With their gentle appearance, amiable and merry,
7076   And their delicate and honest souls.
In consideration of their heads and their hair that was undone,
They had covered themselves very well
In richly embroidered silken cloth.
7080   They held each other by their fingertips,
And with them many a maiden
And many a wealthy damsel
Who came with them
7084   And who are proud of their attire.
They truly thank the Creator
For the great joy and the honor
That He has done to them for His pleasure.
7088   When Guillaume sees them coming,
He goes to meet them in truth
To greet the queen

And both maidens.
7092 "My lady, says he, welcome to you
And to your entire entourage.
— Good sir, may He bless you
Who is more powerful and stronger than everyone,
7096 May He watch over you and protect you
Just as I would truly like Him to."
By their opulent silk garments
And by their hands the baron takes hold of them,
7100 For he was not at all a peasant.
Up to the barons he led them,
But there were so many people assembled there
That the crowd was immense;
7104 Each one is anxious to see the king.
Guillaume makes the people disperse
And has the ladies come forward.

In front of all his men, the baron
7108 Delivers the king of Spain and his prisoners
Into the total discretion of the queen
To do as she commands:
She can do with all of them as she pleases.
7112 The gentle noble lady
Thanks my lord Guillaume for them,
Joins her hands together; humbles herself so much
That she might have thrown herself at his feet,
7116 If the baron had allowed it,
But he lifts her up and reprimands and blames her
And says: "Oh no, do not do this, my lady!
It is not right. — Sire, why not?
7120 — You are queen, and the wife of a king
You were and the heir of an emperor
And a lady of very great merit.
You must not abase yourself
7124 In front of a poor soldier.
— Indeed, my dear good sir, but I must
In the name of the Lord in whom I believe,
I do not consider you a soldier,
7128 But rather a lord and a prince,
And you may do whatever you desire
With my entire realm and my land,

Just as you have merited it.
7132   I had no man so bold
Who dared set foot outside of here,
When God wanted to send you to me.
Before, we were about to surrender each day,
7136   When you came to defend us.
You conducted the affair in such a way
That you have ended my war,
Captured this king and restored my realm
7140   That I had finally totally lost,
And rescued our bodies from prison,
From which we might never have left.
So no one should marvel,
7144   If I want to humble myself
Toward God and toward you, dear friend;
From the hands of my enemies
You have delivered me and vanquished them.
7148   The compensation will be well worth it,
If God wants to grant it to me."
In the middle of the square they leisurely
Disarmed the king and the princes.
7152   They led them up to the hall
Which was very grand and beautiful and large.
They have the entire assembly of warriors sit down,
They have the king sit down first,
7156   Then the barons and the princes;
The poor they have removed from the hall.
Next to the king is seated the queen,
Between Florence and Melior
7160   The baron Guillaume sits down then.
When the noise had calmed down,
The king fervently requests and beseeches
The queen, if it pleases her,
7164   Saying he would gladly like to see his son.
The queen grants his request,
To the king she has his son come.
The king has him sit beside him:
7168   "Good son, says he, in what difficulty,
In what shame and in what harm
We have fallen because of your presumption!
— Father, it is true. It is ill advised to take something

7172 When one must make such reparation for it!
We have made ourselves a gift to her,
So she can do everything she wants with us.
Cursed be he who takes a wife
7176 Against her will.
When one takes her in accord with her desire
And by the approval of the other people
And he treats her as best as he can,
7180 Then has he not done all that is necessary?
I believed I could have her by force.
Now she can do as she likes
With us and with all our land;
7184 There is nothing to be done except ask for mercy.
In the name of God, may she have pity on us!
See the barons together here,
See Guillaume their lord there.
7188 Beseech the lady; implore them.
Find out what they want to do with us
And to which leader we will present ourselves.

The king commences his discourse,
7192 The barons hear him very well:
"My lady, said he, if it pleases you;
And if your counsel suggested it,
I would very gladly make an agreement
7196 To make reparations for the wrong
That I did. If you want to accept it,
I am entirely ready to repair the offense,
In such a manner that it will be appreciated by
7200 Clerics and bourgeois and knights,
Who have come because of the war.
And so I will hold my land from you
That I never before held from any lord
7204 Except only from the Creator."
While they were talking thus
And they were offering to make such an accord,
At that moment came the werewolf
7208 Right through the hall, in the presence of everyone,
Near the king he kneels before him,
He wets his feet with his tears.
With his two paws he picks up his foot,

7212   And he tightly embraces it.
Moreover, he seems to be asking
That he grant him something.
Then he gets up to leave and bows down to him
7216   And then to Guillaume and the queen
And to the maidens as well.
From all directions the men leap out.
They run to their lances and to their javelins,
7220   They pick up their halberds and their falchions.[80]
The shouts following the wolf are great.
He would already have been killed from all directions,
When Guillaume the baron jumps up
7224   And swears to God and His miracles,
If there is anyone who harms him,
Never will there be a such a man, know this very well,
That he will not take vengeance on him.
7228   Everyone let him go out of fear.
The wolf flees and kept on his way
And Guillaume sends envoys after him.
Throughout the city he had a decree proclaimed
7232   Preventing and forbidding everyone,
If they valued their head,
From doing any harm to the beast,
And that they must let him come and go in safety
7236   And that everyone must keep the peace with him.
As soon as the proclamation was heard,
It was faithfully followed and obeyed.
Now the beast can go entirely
7240   In safety wherever he desires,
He comes and goes safely,
And does not find anyone who stands in his way.

    Throughout the country everyone is filled with wonder,
7244   Everyone talks about him and offers their opinion.
All the people are excited
About the amazing spectacle that they have seen,
But the king marvels more
7248   Than any of the others,
For he remembers something

---

80. A halberd is a long spear with a wide axe-like head and a spike; a falchion is a large single-sided sword with a curved cutting edge.

That he never wanted to hear from anyone:
About his dear son he remembered
7252   That his men said he was a werewolf
Transformed by the magic spell of his wife,
Afterward they had to pay dearly for saying it.
He never wanted to believe any man, no matter who he might be.
7256   Now he repents for it, if it might be possible.
Now he believes those men and hates the woman
Who had mistreated his son like that.
Guillaume, when he sees the familiarity
7260   That the wolf demonstrated with
The king of Spain, as well as his manner,
Will not let the matter drop and asks him about it.
He has the noise quiet down,
7264   Then he calls the king and implores him
That because of the loyalty he owes to the Creator
And if in the future he ever wants
To make an accord with the queen
7268   And if he wants her to have pity on him,
If he truly knows, let him tell him
What this beast signifies,
His entire thoughts, whatever he believes about it,
7272   What he thinks he might be,
If he knows him or ever saw him before.
The king responds and said thus:
"Sire, in the name of all the saints
7276   And in the name of the King who made the world,
I like you and value and fear and believe you.
I do not know what will happen to me,
But because of a threat or because of a fear
7280   I will not allow myself to not tell you the whole
Truth and what I think,
Exactly as I believe it happened.
Some time ago, since I was of high nobility,
7284   I took a wife of high noble birth,
Gracious and noble and charitable.
I loved her so very much in a grand manner.
From Gascogne she was, the daughter of the king.
7288   It happened that she was pregnant by me,[81]

81. My translation is based on Michelant's correction of verse from *(continued on next page)*

And when it was her time
That the queen should give birth,
She died during the delivery.
7292 God saved her offspring:
A son I had by her, I believe,[82]
No man has ever seen a nobler infant
Or one more guileless or better formed;
7296 He was of a wondrously great beauty.
In accordance with my desires my name was given to him
By those who made the child a Christian.
They called him by his name Alphonse
7300 When they sprinkled him with cold water.
I had him nursed well near a year.
In that time and in that year
About which I am telling you, I took another spouse,
7304 A lady of great merit,
Marvelously wise and well educated
And born of a royal lineage.
God gave me this young man
7308 Whom you see before your eyes.
When my wife saw her son born,
She did not have great charity for mine:
She saw, if my eldest son lived,
7312 That hers would not hold the realm.
So much did she work her spells and her potions,
Her magic and conjuring
That my son became a werewolf.
7316 Never again did I know what became of him.
This is what my liegemen told me,
The most valiant and most worthy men,
But I never wanted to believe a single one,
7320 For my wife made me believe
That they were saying it out of envy
As men would do who did not like her at all.
So she said he was drowned in the sea.[83]
7324 No man was ever able to find him.

"Ains que ençainte fust de moi" ("Before she was pregnant by me") to "Avint que ençainte fust de moi." As Micha points out, there is possibly a lacuna in the manuscript here.

82. The king's uncertainty here reflects medieval concerns regarding the uncertainty of paternity.

83. Notice the parallel between Alphonse's supposed fate and Guillaume's.

Many days I had them search for him
And I grieved most exceedingly,
Because everyone deceived and betrayed me.
7328   Thus as you have heard,
I lost my son because of my wife.
In the name of all the saints to whom one must pray,
That wolf that was here with us just now,
7332   That made such an appearance to me and to you
In the presence of all our people,
No man who has his reason can see him without thinking,
Nor would anyone be able to take the idea away from me,
7336   That this beast is none other
Than my lost son Alphonse.
Now he has come back to me
To seek mercy and to plead
7340   That I take vengeance against my wife for him."
Guillaume, who rejoiced greatly
About what he had to say to the king, said:
"Good sir, in the name of the celestial King,
7344   It is the truth, thus it can be;
He has as much wisdom and good sense
As I have, or more, and still more.
Thus he proved it to me in many places,
7348   For he delivered me from many perils
Where I would have been killed and dead in the end,
If it were not for God and for him.
I must love him as long as I live,
7352   And I do so in good faith:
He will not lack anything that he wants,
Whoever might complain or grumble about it.
I will not fail him any more than my brother.
7356   If it is true that you are his father,
You have not received a great loss,
Rather a great joy has been revealed to you,
If he returns to the form of a man.
7360   And know it well, he must do it,
For you will never leave prison,
If you are not delivered from it by him;
He holds the key to your freedom.
7364   Now quickly, without any delay
Send for the lady that she might come,

Let no excuses keep her there,
And do not let anything prevent her from coming quickly,
7368   Or if not, with my entire army,
In the name of all the saints who are in Rome,
I will go take the lady by force
And I will destroy the entire kingdom.
7372   Whether she likes it or not, I will bring her back."
The king who is pleased to send for her
Said to him: "Good sir, gladly.
It pleases and satisfies me very much
7376   That the queen will be sent for,
So that if the wolf my son comes back,
She might be able to undo her spell.
So help me God, never such joy would I have
7380   Than if I had my dear child.
But by the loyalty that I owe you
I cannot see whom I might send there,
If you do not allow my men
7384   To go to my land for the lady.
It would be good to send them there,
Because they would be more readily believed.
The queen will believe them well,
7388   If they tell her the situation,
Just as it happened to us,
How we have been captured and held."
Guillaume answered the king:
7392   "In the name of God, sire, I grant it.
I truly want you to send such men there
That she will believe and that you trust."
Thus was this counsel endorsed.
7396   The king hurries, no more can he do.
Now he has his letters written
And sealed and put in wax.
He selects his men and his messengers,
7400   From the most valiant and the most wise
And the ones he considers his closest friends.
He gives them his letters and his writings,
And he appeals to them softly:
7404   "Barons, in the name of God the Omnipotent,
You must go to my land
To seek our freedom.

Be sure to say to my wife Brande
7408 That if she ever wants to see me
Or her dear son again both safe and sound,
She should pay no heed to either difficulty or peril,
But should come quickly to set us free.
7412 And if she tries to refuse
To come here, tell her well
That it will not be of any use to her.
The man who is holding us would go in search of her
7416 And would devastate all her land;
He would force her in the end
And it would finish badly for us.
Be sure to tell her; do not conceal it from her:
7420 In Palermo my son has been found
Who she made me believe
Had drowned in the seaport.
She must come prepared to heal,
7424 So that she might make him become a man."
And they say that they will indeed do it.
Weeping at their separation they go off,
They mount on ambling mules from Spain.[84]
7428 Fifty are in their company,
High-ranking princes of great properties.
They lead an entourage of knights in armor and many people,
But I cannot recount for you
7432 Their voyage or their journey,
Or the cities where they lodged.
So far did they go, so far did they ride,
That on the tenth day they came to the place
7436 Where Queen Brande was.
A city very well situated,
Rich and fertile, beautiful and grand,
It sits on a hill near the sea.
7440 Carmant was the name of the city.
The messengers entered within,
They ride through the city;
Many people are there who recognize them.
7444 They run after them and are anxious

---

84. An ambling mule, or horse, would have a smooth easy gait because it lifted at the same time both legs on one side and then those on the other side.

To hear the news that they might tell them,
But they do not delay or linger;
They hear neither man nor woman.
7448 Up to the palace they allow no interruption.
On the square they dismounted,
All the steps of the vaulted arch
They climb up into the palace
7452 Where the queen and the people are.
Among her men they found her,
On behalf of the king they greeted her
And did the same on behalf of her son.
7456 There are so many people that have come near
To ask about their friends
That the palace is completely filled.
The queen saw the barons,
7460 She knew them well and knew their names.
The lady made her way toward them;
Very joyfully and happily she received them.
She has them sit down in front of her,
7464 And had everyone be quiet.
Something urges her to do this because of their appearance,
Which causes her to become very upset.
She gathers them together around her,
7468 Very softly she addresses them:
"Barons, for God's sake, what is my lord doing?
What is my son doing who holds the empire?
What is the army doing? What are our men doing?
7472 What did my lord do with the lady?
Has he conquered her by force?
Has my son taken the maiden?
Does he hold the realm? Is he king?"
7476 And they reply immediately:
"My lady, nothing is concealed,
The matter worked out differently:
Everything that we wanted to do to them
7480 Has turned to the contrary for us.
We had quickly captured towns and villages,
Castles, cities, keeps and towers
And conquered the entire land
7484 And besieged the lady in Palermo.
She never had a way to defend herself,

Thus she wanted to surrender each day,
Except for her daughter and herself.
7488   She did not exclude anything else
And was abandoning her entire kingdom,
When assistance came to the lady:
A knight of such valor
7492   And there is no man who is as wise as he.
He vanquished our men
And demoralized and destroyed the army.
Thus he killed our seneschal
7496   And his nephew the good vassal;
And he killed in turn the constable
And many other barons who could have helped us.
He captured the king and your son,
7500   Never will they escape from peril,
If you do not go there. — My lord, why?
— We saw come before the king
A marvelous wolf.
7504   In the middle of the hall in the presence of everyone
He knelt before him,
Kissed his foot and his leg,
Then bowed very humbly
7508   Upon his departure from the other people.
From his appearance it truly seemed
That he was asking for something.
They implored the king
7512   To tell the truth about him,
And he told them that he was Alphonse,
His eldest son that he had lost.
You caused him to become a wolf;
7516   Because of this you must go there.
If you do not go, you will be captured.
They will do with you as you deserve,
And so that you might better believe us,
7520   Here are letters that he sent to you."
She takes them and breaks the wax seal.
Well did she find out what the letter said,
From one end to the other she examined it.
7524   Just as they had told her
She sees the loss and the grief
Endured by her son and his lord

And the barons and the entire army.
7528 These news were very quickly known
By the people of the land.
There were therefore many palms beaten,
Beards torn out, hair pulled;
7532 Great was the mourning that was made about it.
The queen does not tarry,
She prepares and arranges for her voyage,
Well has she obtained her necessities:
7536 Whatever she might need
She has brought to her, and then she mounted up;
All her people set off on their way.
They do not go unaccompanied,
7540 But with a great quantity of people,
With maidens, with knights,
And with men-at-arms and with squires.
They took leave of those in the realm,
7544 Thereupon the queen herself left.
Each day they ride without interruption.
I cannot tell you everything
As they did it or accomplished it
7548 Nor the inns where they lodged;
The voyages that they made
Will not be recounted to you by me.
They kept to the right road so much
7552 That in Palermo they arrived.
The lady entered the city,
By the people she was closely examined
And her entourage greatly esteemed,
7556 For she comes very well prepared.
The knights carefully observe her
As do the barons and the princes,
The ladies, the maidens and the bourgeois.
7560 They make the palfreys keep ambling until
They have arrived in front of the hall.
Many people go down to meet her,
The king, his son and the prisoners
7564 And the queen and the barons.
In front of the others Guillaume
Came to her and helped her dismount.
The baron very honorably

7568   Received her and the other people,
And the king of Spain and his son,
Their eyes all wet with tears,
Gave her a warm welcome
7572   And all her people and her entourage
And the barons of the country.
And many tears were wept there
By the queen for the grief
7576   Of her son and her lord
And the princes and fief holders
That she sees chained in irons.
Then they led the queen
7580   Into the great marbled hall.
Guillaume kept her to one side;
All the people came after her,
So that the entire hall is filled.
7584   Guillaume has the barons of the queen
Withdraw from one part of the palace,
In order to put an end to the war between the two sides;
Afterwards he has their men sit down
7588   Row by row throughout the palace.
He had the king and his son and his wife
Seated in the better places.
On a rich silken cloth from Bisterne
7592   The queen of Palermo is seated;
She and her daughter and Melior
Are also seated at that time.
Guillaume was in the middle of the hall;
7596   His countenance was not at all pale,
But candid and well formed,
His face was young and full of color,
His body robust, well made and handsome,
7600   Well do his garments suit him,
Because of his body they were unfastened.
He was scrutinized by many people,
For he really looked like a nobleman.
7604   Those who saw King Embron
While he was alive
Say that he truly resembled him;
Many of the people were saying that.
7608   But now hear of the behavior

Of the wolf who found out
That the queen had arrived,
His stepmother whom he hated so much.
7612 In a chamber he was lying down,
For after the messengers had left
Until they returned
To the city with the queen
7616 He had not been outside of the palace;
Thus he was in such a manner and in the same way
Imprisoned among the people
As if he had been raised among them.
7620 His bed was in front of Guillaume's
In the chamber with the baron.
So they are both peers and companions.
They do not go far from each other night and day
7624 And his brother and his lord
He has totally abandoned for his friend.
When he hears the uproar in the palace
And the tumult of the people,
7628 He immediately leaves that chamber
And comes into the chamber which was large
Where he sees the assembly of barons seated,
The dukes, the counts, the marquis,
7632 The king and those from his country,
His stepmother and his father together.
His heart trembles from rage
When he thoroughly recognized her.
7636 He saw her and his eyes roll;
He does not delay any longer,
At top speed, his mouth gaping open,
He runs as fast as he can to seize her.
7640 Already the lady would truly have perished,
If they had presented her to him at the beginning of the meet-
  ing;[85]
But she sees the wolf coming,
As loudly as she can she shouts:
7644 "Help, help, holy Mary
Or I will soon die in dishonor.
Protect me today on this day."

85. My translation is based on Micha's suggested reading of the verse.

The king jumps to her, I do not know how far,
7648 The baron Guillaume who holds him back
Right in front of her, tightly hugs him,
And very gently tells him:
"My friend, said the baron,
7652 You can trust me in absolutely everything,
You can trust me as if I were your brother
And as a son must trust his father.
Whether it might be foolish or wise,
7656 I will not fail you for anything;
But now listen to me, if you please.
I sent for this lady here;
I sent for her so that she might heal you.
7660 For this reason I made her come here,
So I will tell you by what action.
Well does the lady know it, as does everyone:
If she does not cure you,
7664 She will be burned in fire and in coal
And her ashes thrown to the wind.
The king and his son as well
And their barons and all their men
7668 Whom we have captured because of the war
I will have confined in such a prison
Where light might never be seen.
They will die there in great anguish.
7672 The wolf looks at the lord;
For what he says he manifests great joy,
By signs and by his appearance he gives him his consent
So that he kisses both his feet.
7676 Now the queen was relieved,
When she sees the beast humble himself.
So she began to address him
Very humbly, as she is very wise,
7680 In the hearing of the king and his men.

"Good sir Alphonse, says the queen,
"With me I have the remedy
By which you will be completely cured.
7684 My lord, sire, dear friend,
I know indeed without a doubt that it is you,
Well did I recognize you completely.

I have come here to heal you
7688   And to throw you out of this prison
That has covered you such a long time.
But now we will see everything out in the open,
Before I have finished my work,
7692   And what beast this skin is hiding.
It is true; I do not want to conceal it any longer,
That in order that my son might inherit
And to steal your seigniorial rights from you,
7696   I made you flee like a wild wolf.
God did not want to let you perish,
You came back because it pleased Him.
For this offense I beg mercy of you
7700   Here before your father the king;
And I beseech these ladies, these barons,
That I might reconcile with you, good sir Alphonse.
I will love you faithfully
7704   And I will serve you as my lord.
Never, as long as I live,
In any way will I harm you.
For this offense I implore your pardon,
7708   And also I entreat this baron
Who is restraining you so very gently,
And ask that you forgive me because of his love.
For him you would do more, it seems to me,
7712   Than for all these others together.
Now do with me as you like,
I surrender myself entirely to your mercy."
Then she threw herself at his feet.
7716   God, she wept so many tears
Of love, of tenderness, of pity!
Guillaume was implored greatly
By the king and the other valiant men
7720   And by the maiden and the lady
To totally pardon the queen
For her malicious intentions and hatred
And he gladly granted it to everyone.
7724   Then the length of the hall there was
Abundant and marvelous and great joy;
And the queen, my lady Brande,
Does not want to linger there any longer.

| 7728 | In a chamber painted with flowers |

7728   In a chamber painted with flowers
        She led the wolf.[86]
        There the queen and the werewolf were all alone.
        Then she drew out a golden ring
7732   That was worth more than a great treasure,
        Whose stone was so exceptional,
        Whoever had the ring on him
        Would never be bewitched
7736   Or deceived or tricked,
        And by venom or poison
        No man could ever harm him,
        Cause him to miss his objective or lead him astray
7740   Or turn him away from his wife,
        And whoever sees him, on that day
        Cannot diminish his honor.
        The ring that was so powerful
7744   The lady hung from his neck
        On a thread of red silk.
        The wolf displays great joy
        At what the lady is doing to him.
7748   Then the lady pulled out a book;
        She read it entirely and conjured until
        She changed the form of the vassal
        And totally restored his appearance.
7752   He who sensed his deliverance,
        When he shook himself, became,
        Although he was completely naked, the most handsome man
        Who ever was, to my knowledge,
7756   With the exception of only Guillaume;
        I do not know anyone else I can exclude.
        He sees his appearance and his body
        That was totally without clothing and naked
7760   And he sees the lady before him.
        He is so ashamed that he becomes violently agitated.
        The lady is quite distraught because of this,
        She calls to him and tells him:
7764   "My lord, in the name of God who made us all,
        Do not be ashamed because of me,

86. Verse 7729 is missing from the manuscript. The verse provided here is not a translation but is my conjecture based on the prose text.

If I see you naked, without clothing:
There is no one here but the two of us.
7768   I see in you nothing that is not good
Nor anything that is not as it should be.
See beneath that silken cloth there is
A temperate bath, pleasant and very soothing.
7772   Well do I know, good sir, if I may say so,
That you were never dubbed a knight
Nor did you ever have any arms or armor.
Today you will receive them with such honor
7776   As befits a lord like you."
Then she took off her mantle
And put it around the neck of the young nobleman.
Up to the tub she led him.
7780   The bath he finds warm and moderate,
He enters it, and the queen
Was his chambermaid and servant.
She takes the mantle and then asks:
7784   "Sir, says Queen Brande,
From whom do you want to take your arms?
— My lady, by the loyalty that I owe you,
From the greatest man within here
7788   I want to receive my armor:
By no other do I want to be dubbed:
Go get him and bring him to me.
— Is this the king, your dear father?
7792   — No, my lady, rather the knight
Who protected you from me today.
— Is he therefore the one? — Yes, upon my word.
Thus there is within here no man as great,
7796   My lady, not even as far as Rome;
I do not know a single man greater than he,
Neither myself nor my father nor anyone else,
In parentage or lineage."
7800   The lady was intelligent and wise.
From the chamber she issued forth,
Straight to the baron she came.
She gets his attention and asks him thus:
7804   "Sire, says Queen Brande,
He wants garments and is asking for ones
That are splendid and attractive,

Such as would be suitable for the son of a king,

7808   And the werewolf also asked me to

Tell you to come to him

Entirely without the company of anyone,

Other than Melior and Florence,

7812   Please: he truly wants to see them,

But do not bring any other people there."

Guillaume threw his arms around her neck,

When he hears what she says.

7816   From joy he hugs and kisses her.

Said the baron: "Sister, gentle friend,

By God, do not conceal anything from me,

Is it true that he is asking for clothing?

7820   — Yes, good sir, now he is.

Here, upon my word I swear it to you.

— God, said the baron, I am healed now,

Since I will have my companion again;

7824   I wanted nothing but him."

He displayed his very great joy.

"My lady, says he, it is fortunate you were born,

And it is fortunate that you came to this land,

7828   For this war will end because of you."

The queen of Apulia shows

Her great joy as do the other people from the city.

They do not speak very long:

7832   The garments are prepared,

Marvelously rich and fine and beautiful,

A long silk surcoat, bright and new,[87]

Green and flecked with gold crosses,

7836   Entirely lined in white ermine fur,

And whatever a knight needs

To equip himself beautifully

They have a valet carry to him,

7840   And all four go after him.

The others are very eager

To see the young man.

Thereupon they came into the chamber

7844   That was painted and covered in paneling

87. A surcoat was a long, loose-fitting sleeveless tunic worn over another tunic. Some were used for additional warmth, others for ceremonial purposes. For a discussion, see Newman, 110.

With rich stone and with enameling.
The maidens and the vassal
See the curtained bath.
7848 They look in the other direction,
On the bed they observe the young man.
Never have they seen anyone more handsome,
As it seems to them and so they thought,
7852 But they did not recognize him
And nevertheless they greeted him.
And the young nobleman replies to them:
"Good sir, may God bless you
7856 And this beautiful company
That you have brought with you.
Well do I know that you do not recognize me,
Sir Guillaume, said Alphonse,
7860 Now I am here in your home.
You should bring me honor,
For I have served you many a day,
For you I have endured many pains,
7864 Perils and difficulties and great fears.
From many a peril I have extracted you
Where you might have been captured and killed,
If it had not been for me and above all God.
7868 Now you do a little bit of the same for me,
But you do not know who I might be,
For now I have greatly changed my situation
And my appearance and my entire nature,
7872 Since you never saw me before."
Sir Guillaume responded:
"It is true that never before have I seen you.
— Oh yes, you have, I know it well.
7876 — I cannot recall at all
That I have ever seen you.
Now, may God protect you,
Tell us therefore who you are.
7880 — Indeed, good sir, the werewolf
Who for you has many voyages
And many tribulations endured."

When Guillaume hears what he says,
7884 He approaches him and hugs him so

With such love, with such a manner
As a mother would her son;
He kisses his eyes and his chin.

7888   Never has one seen joy the likes of
Which they demonstrate because of the vassal,
For Melior exactly in the same way
Put both her arms around his neck.

7892   And the maiden with the bright face,
Florence, who had drawn back,
Marveled greatly
About the joyous greeting that they gave him.

7896   Out of modesty she hides her eyes
Beneath her cloak, but the queen
Sees her embarrassment and her manner.
Very gently she calls to her:

7900   "Florence, sweet lady,
For what you see do not be shocked,
Do not withdraw, nor distance yourself,
They are honoring him, as they must.

7904   Know that they are not deceived about him.
Let us go to him, both you and I,
And let us honor the son of the king."
Thereupon they came to the bed

7908   And the queen said to them:
"Friend Guillaume, you are right
If you are happy because of him,
For he was very useful to you,

7912   As I have learned and understood.
If it is to your liking now,
It is time to clothe him,
To adorn him and get him prepared,

7916   For very eager are
The people who are waiting outside for him,
The king his father and the other men.
Here are his garments; they are ready.

7920   — My lady, Guillaume answers her,
You say it well, now let it be done so.
See that your handsomest finery is evident
And that he is attired in such a manner,

7924   With such an appearance and such quality
That we will not be blamed for anything."

Thereupon they picked up his garments.
They dressed him in his shift[88]

7928   And his fine breeches and put on his hose.
His hose are of a luxurious silken cloth
That is well suited for a knight.
Then they clothe him in a long silk surcoat;

7932   No man ever saw one more splendid.
With delicate cords the maidens
Laced up both of his beautiful arms,
Then he stood himself up.

7936   Noble was his body and his face,
His hair was blond and finely curled,
His limbs straight and well made.
From a trunk the queen removes a belt

7940   Spectacularly decorated in rich gold
And offers it to him.
The baron buckles it on and then closes his garments
With a fastener of gold that is wondrously beautiful.

7944   Around his neck they put a cloak
That is beautiful and noble and suits him very well.
Then they put on all his other equipment.
When they have adorned him well with everything

7948   And fitted him out richly,
So that one would find nothing to improve,
They have the door opened by the valet
Who was there in the chamber to serve him,

7952   And he does everything that they ask.
Without delay he immediately opened the door,
Then they take each other by their fingers,
From the chamber they issued forth,

7956   They all stayed together hand in hand,
And when they entered the palace,
All the people got up to meet them.
The king recognizes his son Alphonse.

7960   Such great joy has never been shown by man
As that displayed because of him by
His brother and all those who had come from other lands
And by the others throughout the palace.

7964   Never has there been such great joy

---

88. A shift or chemise was a long-sleeved undergarment, worn by both men and women.

As the delight that they express about
The arrival of the baron.

The lady of Apulia was very happy,
7968 For God had instructed her very well,
And she marveled greatly
About the person that she saw.
Afterward she had the people be seated
7972 To bring the uproar to an end.
Then the knights sat down
Along with the barons and the princes.
On a luxurious silken cloth from Bisterne[89]
7976 The queen of Palermo seated herself,
Beside her Florence and the Roman maiden,[90]
With the queen of Spain.
Next to Alphonse sat Guillaume,
7980 Who gave him many hugs and rejoiced with him.
Both his father and his brother
Were seated near him on the other side.

When the household was seated
7984 And the noise had subsided,
The king spoke first
Before the princes and the people.
Very gently he calls to his son
7988 And he kisses him on his cheek:
"My sweet son Alphonse, said the king,
May God from His holy cross
Be adored and thanked,
7992 Son, because you have returned to me.
Never have I had in my heart such joy
As I have had on this voyage.
May God be adored first of all
7996 And then all His angels and all His saints
That I came to this country.
See the barons of our country:
All of us were captured and are being held in prison
8000 By the queen of this land.
Never would we have issued forth from it,

89. Bisterne is a Saracen town that is mentioned in *chansons de geste* and is known for its silk cloth.
90. The Roman maiden would be Melior.

If it were not for God and if it were not for you.⁹¹
But just as it was said and spoken,
8004   By you we will be delivered.
Thus I thank God and His goodness
Because he has returned you to me.
You have come back, may God
8008   The glorious, our Lord, be praised for this.
Now, son, I have need of your help.
— Father, says he, you will lack nothing.
Do not trouble yourself, but now tell me
8012   How and why you came here.
What were you seeking in this land?
Why did you provoke this war?
What were you asking of this lady?
8016   What were you seeking in this realm?
Why did you treat her so badly
And burn and devastate her land?
— Son, upon my word, because of our presumption
8020   We came to seek a marriage
That I desired to make with her daughter,
Whom I wanted to have for your brother:
She completely refused us.
8024   I summoned my men and advanced on her,
We seized all her land,
Here within we laid siege to her by force.
There was no knight so valiant,
8028   So bold or so willing to do battle
Who dared issue forth from here.
We did what we wanted with all of them.
Each day they were about to surrender
8032   And abandon all their possessions,
This city and this kingdom,
Except that the maiden and the lady
Would be allowed safe conduct
8036   With a few possessions, with a few men,

91. The manuscript actually says "li tiens cors" ("your body") instead of "ti" (picard for "toi"; "you"), a common substitute in Old French. Variations of this particular verse recur throughout the romance. Use of this phrase becomes more significant here if one keeps in mind that Alphonse has just been returned to his human form: he has just recovered his human body. This significance is strengthened with repetition and variation in verse 8006, which literally translates: "Because he has returned your body to me."

To go to the king her father in Romania.[92]
But I did not want to grant it to her,
For I wanted to have together
8040   Both the girl and all her possessions.
Good son, thus we might have succeeded,
When this valet next to you
Came from I know not where to help them.
8044   But no one has ever seen such a knight,
As bold or as enterprising,
As valorous or as powerful,
Who would be able to endure without fail
8048   A deadly mêlée or intense battle as much
As this one can, son, and as he has done.
Why should I give you a long discourse?
He has truly ruined and harmed me
8052   And he has put my great army to flight
And killed and slaughtered my barons
And because of his great strength he has captured us.
— In the name of God, father, said Alphonse,
8056   Very great was the offense
When by force you wanted to have
The maiden against her will.
If you have lost, it is no wonder to me,
8060   You did not have good counsel.
But now the affair has proceeded in such a way
That this loss will truly be recuperated;
It is not worth a French parchment.[93]
8064   Then he appeals to the queen about it:
"My dear lady, now hear me
And this assembly of barons on all sides,
And especially you, my companions, pay attention,
8068   I beg of you, above all others."
So he makes the people calm down and be quiet:
"I want to tell you something here
That will make each of you joyous."
8072   Thus the court was calm and silent,
No one talked there and no word was heard
And no one spoke to anyone else.

---

92. Romania was another name for the Greek empire.
93. According to Micha, in this verse "froncine" ("French parchment") signifies something of little value.

Everyone fell silent and he begins,

8076 Publicly before the court:

"My lady, it is true, it is well known

That you had finally lost,

Never would the castle have remained yours,

8080 Nor villages nor towns nor cities

Would you and your daughter have had

Without the aid of some man,

When this vassal came to help you,

8084 But no one knows where he came from

Nor who he is or from what land.

So he kept your war going,

Defeated the enemy and captured the king.

8088 I will tell you in good faith

That no one should be amazed about it:

The son really ought to help his mother,

Protect her and her land,

8092 And defend from all men.

If he protected the kingdom,

By nature it came to him.

He must truly do it. —And how must he?

8096 —My lady, know this with certainty

That the land is his and that you are his mother.

King Embron was his father,

His father was the valiant king.

8100 My lady, you carried him nine months,

You bore him, from you was he born.

I am the wolf who kidnapped him,

I kidnapped him and I was not wrong to do so,

8104 For he had received a death sentence.

The women who were watching him

Had both sworn to his death

For a brother of King Embron

8108 Who because of his evil treachery

Had promised the nursemaids so much,

Possessions and lands and marquis,

That they were about to do what he wanted,

8112 Such as causing the child to die

And the king as well.

They would never have lived long

And would have died in dishonor

8116   For the profit of the traitor,
                 Because he would have the entire kingdom,
                 If his brother had died without an heir.
                 When I discovered the whole plot,
8120   I could not allow this evil deed
                 Nor the very great betrayal:
                 So I carried him away to safety.
                 I was chased very far; I was followed very far,
8124   But they could not catch me.
                 The king and all his men were there,
                 Very great was the throng that came after me.
                 So far did I go that now I return him to you:
8128   See him totally in the open here."[94]
                 When the queen hears about her son
                 And that he was Guillaume,
                 Just as she had heard it told,
8132   She is so full of joy she does not know what to do.
                 And when Guillaume sees his mother
                 And learns that the king was his father,
                 Whom he had never seen,
8136   Know that never had he been so joyous.
                 He never knew who bore him
                 Nor did he know who fathered him.
                 Now he knows that he was the son of King Embron.
8140   Never has one seen joy as great
                 As that expressed by the son and by the mother,
                 And as great as that expressed by the sister for her brother.
                 All three take hold of each other by the waist
8144   And on their eyes and nose and mouth and face
                 They kiss each other one hundred times or more.
                 No one has ever seen such great joy
                 As that lavished on him by both mother and sister.
8148   So many tears from a joyous heart
                 And from pity and tenderness
                 Because they see their lord
                 Flow down their faces.
8152   When the virtuous and wise Melior
                 Hears and understands that her sweetheart

---

94. "Tot apertement" ("Totally in the open") reinforces the theme of revelation and reminds the listener/reader that the narrator promised in the prologue that he would openly reveal his hidden knowledge.

Is the son of the king of this country
And that King Embron was his father
8156 And that the queen was his mother
And that he would be lord and king of the realm,
The joy that she feels is such
That no maiden ever felt a greater joy.
8160 Afterward the baron calls to Guillaume:
"My friend, hear me:
Here in front of my father the king,
In the presence of my mother and the barons
8164 And other people, said Alphonse,
I want to show you openly
What I did and suffered for you.
It is true, when you were kidnapped,
8168 That after me were great the shouts;
The noise and the tumult were loud,
And the commotion of the people was tremendous.
Everyone jumped out to follow me.
8172 The king himself was
In front of them spurring them on,
For his heart was grieving sorely,
Friend, because I was carrying you off.
8176 I could not avoid fields or paths
Or get into the woods or distance myself from them
And they pushed me into the sea.
If I had not gone into the sea,
8180 Very quickly would the king have killed me.
Through the Strait of Messina in high seas
I had to cross with very great difficulty,
Through the sea I passed by swimming.
8184 There I had a very painful crossing,
Greatly did my body suffer from the effort,
For I never had a ship or barge,
And yet you never suffered any harm to your body.
8188 When I arrived on the other side and got out,
Never had I been so happy about anything.
Together with you I kept on my way
So that I carried you straight to Ardaine,
8192 A forest full of beasts
That is one league from Rome.
Never has a beast done this for man

As I have, sire, for you."
8196 After all this he told him
How he traveled at night with him
And how during the day he obtained what Guillaume needed
In the villages and from the people;
8200 He felt the teeth of many watchdogs
And many a cry, and many a shout
He heard from the people of the country.
And then he tells about the cowherd
8204 Who raised him and valued him so dearly,
How the emperor carried him off,
How he presented him to his daughter,
How the two of them loved each other,
8208 How he loved her and she loved him,
How the Greeks came from their land
To Rome to seek the maiden
And how she was given to them
8212 And was to be married the next day,
When they sewed themselves into the bearskins
And left the land,
And how the people throughout the realm
8216 Were assembled to search for them;
And how if someone approached them,
He would jump out in front
To lead the searchers astray;
8220 The great trials and the fears
And the difficult and long journeys
And the quests for their food
Which he provided for them in abundance,
8224 When they were lodged:
Everything that he had suffered for them
 He related very openly to them.
Afterward he told them
8228 What happened to them in Benevento,
In the quarry, surrounded
By the citizens of the city
Whom the provost sent to that place,
8232 How he had diverted them
By kidnapping his son there,
Just as you have previously heard;
And how for their deliverance

8236   He put himself at risk of death
        And how he made them leave their skins,
        Take the stags in exchange for the bears,
        And how they crossed the water,
8240   Thus everything about how they traveled,
        And what he had done for them
        Lord Alphonse recounted to them.
        Guillaume hears the young nobleman,
8244   It is marvelously pleasing to him,
        That they now know everything; it is the complete truth,
        That he is the son of the king and the queen,
        And that his nursemaids had betrayed him,
8248   Those traitors, those wicked women.
        Between his arms he embraced him closely.
        "Good sir Alphonse, my good dear friend,
        Said Guillaume to the son of the king,
8252   It is true, so much have you for me
        Suffered and endured and done,
        Just as you have related here,
        To save me and my sweetheart
8256   That I will not be able, perhaps, to compensate you for it.
        But there is nothing so dangerous
        Nor such trials or such great suffering
        ···
        And about this I inform you well
8260   And thus I really want people to know it,
        Whoever might find joy or grief in it,
        You will not want anything that I do not want,
        Nor love another; know this to be true.
8264   I love you and I will serve you to the best of my ability.
        Very happy ought to be the one
        Who can be sure of your love.
        May our realms be entirely one,
8268   And may our will be common.
        I want to do all that you want,
        I put absolutely everything at your disposal:
        My land and fief, life and possessions,
8272   You can take them and do as you please with them.
        — Lord Guillaume, I thank you.
        Exactly as you have heard
        And I have said here and recounted,

8276 And these barons have listened to my tale,
I suffered and acted on your behalf.
Of this reward I make myself a gift.
— Indeed, my friend, never have I had such joy
8280 Like the joy I would experience if I had anything
Which would please you. — Yes, good sir.
— My friend, may it now please you to say it.
— Will I have it then? — Yes, without a doubt.
8284 If it were my entire land,
Nothing would ever be excluded
Except only for my sweetheart Melior.
— Sire, I do not want your land
8288 Nor do I want to wrong you with your beloved,
But since you have made me this gift,
Now I ask this, if it pleases you,
That you might give me your sister
8292 To have as my wife and spouse.
— Oh! Dear friend, are you telling me the truth
That you want to have my sister?
— Yes indeed, my dear good sir,
8296 If it pleases you, I would very gladly.
— If it pleases me? But she was born at an auspicious moment,
Since she pleases you and satisfies you so much
That you want to take her as your wife.
8300 And may God compensate you and return
The honor that you are showing me with her.
Now we will truly be perfect friends,
Perfect friends and brothers-in-law.
8304 Happily and joyfully I grant her to you,
And half of my wealth
Will be given to you with my sister
In marriage." And he responds:
8308 "May it not please the King of all the world
If I ever take any of your possessions.
We have enough land in Spain,
We have enough towns and villages,
8312 Castles, cities, keeps, and towers,
And land wondrously fertile and beautiful.
I want nothing but the damsel;
I do not want castle, city, keep,
8316 I only want the beauty."

Thus she was given to him.
He swore an oath to her and was betrothed to her
In the presence of the court and the assembly of barons.
8320 They are very pleased about the marriage.
Very happy was the young lady,
So was her mother the queen,
The king of Spain and the barons
8324 Both rich and poor from all around.
Thus Alphonse became engaged to Florence on the spot.
When the news had gone out
Across the land, through the country,
8328 There remained no prince or marquis
Or valiant man of any territory
Who did not come to see the lords.
So many from the realm came there
8332 That the city was filled with them,
So that many had to be lodged outside.
To their tents had returned
The Spanish knights who had fled in defeat.
8336 Never has there been such great joy,
As when their lords were reconciled to them
And all their men liberated.

Now hear next
8340 About Gloriande and Acelone.
When they have heard the news,
Of their death they are certain and confident.
Their plot has been discovered
8344 And their great treachery exposed:
Both of them are sure they will die;
If they are afraid, they are not at all wrong.
From their chamber they issued forth,
8348 Barefoot, dressed in shifts of horsehair.
They are wearing no other garment
Except each one only
Has on her head a black veil.
8352 This signifies that they are greeting
Death, whence their hearts are filled with anguish.
Their heads bowed, their faces sad
And ashen with fear, and limp and pale,
8356 One after the other down the hall

They come straight before Guillaume.
And when the baron sees the women,
Very well did he recognize them,
8360 Because he had recently seen them within the palace.
They kneeled down;
In speaking they are well instructed
And all the people turned back.
8364 The first to speak was Acelone:
"My lord and sire, please hear me.
We have come before you
To receive your judgment:
8368 Deal with us as we deserve.
If you deliver us to death,
We have merited it for our crime, you are not at all wrong.
But we have passed so many days
8372 It will not be a great honor
Nor a great vengeance on such ladies,
Even if we had just now killed three men,
To take away our lives.
8376 We are such old women, abandoned
And feeble and decrepit,
And totally destroyed,
That you will not find a nobleman or a peasant
8380 Who would ever deign to lay a hand on us.
But if you wanted to take pity on us,
Allow the two of us to go
To an abbey or hermitage
8384 Or within some other place in the woods.
There we would always lie down in horsehair shifts
In order to do our penitence
And we would serve our Lord
8388 And we would pray to the Creator,
As long as we would live, my lord, for you
And for your mother and for the king
That God might truly pardon him."
8392 The barons agree to this idea.
Guillaume hears this advice,
He does not want to go against his people.
In the hermitage they were put,
8396 There they ended their days and died.
Now I must stop talking about the women,

To the story I want to return.

Guillaume selects his messengers,
8400   Valiant and courtly and well-spoken
And high-ranking barons of great merit;
He gives them his letters and his writings,
Thus he sends them to the emperor:
8404   That, if it pleases him, he might come for the day
When his daughter will become the wife of
The king of Apulia and of Sicily,
And if a young woman is still alive
8408   Whose name is Alixandrine,
That he bring her with him, for his daughter heartily
Beseeches him to do so and she would be very pleased.
The men respond that they will accomplish the task.
8412   Thereupon they depart, so they leave,
The messengers do not wait any longer,
But are prepared to ride.
That night they sleep until morning
8416   When they set off on their way.
With them they take a great troop of armed knights and many
    men,
Horses and other equipment.
The equipment that the barons were wearing
8420   Must be discussed:
Everything was of gold with bands of orphrey.
Without delay they made their palfreys amble
Until they came to the city of Rome.
8424   They found the emperor,
They greeted him and his entourage
On behalf of King Alphonse of Spain,
Who was formerly his comrade,
8428   And then on behalf of the son of Embron
Who is king of Apulia and all Sicily
And on behalf of Melior his daughter.
When the emperor heard
8432   The greeting from his daughter,
He marvels and then responds:
"My lord, may God give you great goodness
And may He watch over you. But tell me,
8436   I heard you speak of my daughter,

Baron, do you know anything about her?
Yes, I have news. — In the name of God, what?
— She is in Palermo with the king,
8440 Thus she has sent us to you here.
The king is going to take her as his wife;
Through us he is inviting you to the wedding ceremony.
Come there, good sir, to the court,
8444 Let nothing deter you from it.
You will see great joy there.
Here are his people whom he has sent to you."
Then he gives him the sealed letters
8448 And Emperor Nathaniel
Received them and broke the wax
And had a clerk read the letters.
The clerk spread open the parchment,
8452 He read the letters with very great joy:
He told how the lords,
Together with his daughter,
Have sent for the emperor,
8456 In the presence of the princes and the people,
Just as the messengers have said:
In the name of God, if Alixandrine lives,
He must have her brought with him, please.
8460 Thus the clerk recounted everything to him.
The emperor does not tarry,
He had summoned from the entire assembly of warriors
Of his princes and of his men,
8464 The most valiant and the most valorous,
For he does not want to remain any longer.
He had many great men at his command.
Alixandrine was sent for,
8468 Who must not be forgotten,
She was adorned richly;
Very costly were her garments.
Damsels to serve her
8472 Are brought entirely according to her pleasure.
The beasts of burden were prepared,
The men-at-arms and the knights
And the bishops and the abbots
8476 Who were in abundance in the entourage.
While riding the emperor

Spoke to the messengers from Apulia.
He constantly asks them for news
8480 Of his daughter who preoccupies his thoughts:
How she was, what happened to her,
How she came to Palermo
And where the king will marry her
8484 And where she was, and how he knew her.
And they tell him the adventure,
Everything word for word without concealment,
Exactly as it had happened
8488 And as you have heard it:
About Guillaume who was kidnapped,
When he was so young and small
How the werewolf carried him off,
8492 How he crossed the sea with him,
How he was found by the cowherd
Who then loved him very much and cared dearly for him,
How he protected him, how he raised him,
8496 How the emperor himself then carried him off,
How the two young people loved each other
With a good love, with a loyal faith
And how they left the realm
8500 Never again to return,
Both sewn into bearskins.
The perils, the misfortunes and the fears
That each one suffered and experienced,
8504 Everything was recounted by the messengers.
Then they tell the emperor
About the great prowess of the lord,
How courageous he is, noble and powerful,
8508 Strong and bold and valiant;
How Palermo was besieged
And how it would have been captured now
If he had not come so quickly
8512 And immediately vanquished the enemy,
How he pursued them and conquered them
And how he captured the king and his son.

"My lord, said the emperor,
8516 In the name of God, our Lord and Father,
How do you know that he was saved?

— From the werewolf that kidnapped him.
— From the werewolf? — Indeed. — How is that?
8520   — I will tell you plainly:
He was not a beast by birth,
Thus he was fathered by a king,
The son of a king he was, the king of Spain.
8524   — This marvel is very strange:
How can one believe it then?
— Sire, you will quickly hear the truth of it.
At the time of his delivery
8528   The queen died giving birth to him.
The king took another wife
Who, so that her son would inherit,
Cast such a spell on the child
8532   That she caused him to flee from the kingdom;
In order to steal from him his seigniorial rights
She made him flee like a savage wolf. 95

Through the throng, in the sight of everyone,
8536   The werewolf came into the hall,
Toward him he humbled himself so much,
He was seeking mercy from him, or so it seemed to us.
The king knew him immediately.
8540   He told all of us who were close enough to hear
That it was his son. Then the queen
Was sent for from his country.
When she arrived, then
8544   She removed her spells and her curses.
The young nobleman became a man again.
Now there is no one in the world more handsome,
Except for my lord, so well made,
8548   When he regained his strength,
His human form and his intelligence.
In the hearing of the court, in the presence of the people
He recounted this entire affair to us,
8552   Just as you have heard it told."
When the emperor hears the adventure,

95. Although there is a considerable lacuna in the manuscript between verses 8534 and 8535 (covering the flight of the werewolf from Spain until his recognition by his father in Palermo), since the messengers are recapitulating events that have already been narrated at least once, it does not hinder our comprehension of the romance.

He is entirely confident about it,
He knows that it is true; he has no doubt about it.
8556   He summons his barons along the road,
And he recounts it to them with very great joy.
So much did they keep to the right path
That they soon drew near Palermo.
8560   With a marvelous troop of men on horseback,
Dukes and princes and barons,
Guillaume and Alphonse issued forth.
They rode their horses and traveled until
8564   The lords encountered each other.
Guillaume sees the emperor,
Never has a man displayed greater joy
Than did the baron and all his men.
8568   He comes to him in the middle of the road,
Jumps to the ground beside his destrier,
And runs to embrace the emperor's leg.
The emperor stops,
8572   He sees Guillaume, recognizes him easily,
And dismounts from his horse to greet him.
They embraced each other very much
And were very courteous and hugged each other.
8576   The barons rode their horses and traveled
Until they met up,
Everyone greeted each other.
Then the king of Spain arrived
8580   With his two sons and their entourage;
The emperor knew the king,
So he kissed him and embraced him,
For they were comrades in the past
8584   And they were very good friends.
The emperor who was very kind
Did not recognize the young noblemen.
He asks the king who they are.
8588   "My sons, sire, the king replies.
— Your sons? — Indeed, my good dear sir."
Then he began to tell him
What had happened to Alphonse,
8592   How he had lost him for a long time,
How God had returned him.
The emperor said, when he heard him:

"Sir, then it's true, in just the same manner
8596   Did I hear it from your men."
So much joy was expressed there
That it would not be possible to describe it to you.
Now Alixandrine rode up;
8600   When Guillaume sees the young woman,
He is very joyful about her arrival.
He runs to meet her, his arm extended.
He takes her down from her palfrey
8604   And greets her more than one hundred times.
Then he asks her how she is:
"Please, in the name of God, sir,
I am doing very well, said the maiden.
8608   For God's sake, what is my lady doing?
Are you both safe and sound?
— Yes, fair sister, on my word,
Thanks to the Son of holy Mary
8612   And thanks to you, sweet friend and sister,
Who worked so hard and suffered for us.
Before this week has passed,
We will complete our love,
8616   The perils, the unhappiness and the suffering
That we experienced so often."
Then they put an end to their conversation,
Because the barons are about to mount up
8620   And do not want to tarry there any longer.
Then mount up on their palfreys
The emperor and the king
And Guillaume, the noble, the wise,
8624   And the maidens and the entire entourage;
Toward Palermo they make their way.
In the city they find such joy
And such wealth and such decorations
8628   That no man has ever seen greater
Nor will he ever, I believe.
The palaces, which were decorated,
Were very beautiful and pretty,
8632   For the paved halls were entirely
In white limestone, in grayish-brown marble,
Everything inset with gold.
Hung all around were curtains

8636   Of silken fabric worked in gold,
       With works of gold and with paintings,
       With many different figures
       Of birds, of beasts, and of people.
8640   The interior of the chambers were
       Painted and well illuminated.
       No one ever saw any better ornamented,
       So pleasant or as charming,
8644   As beautiful or so suitable;
       There were the lords received.
       Never has anyone seen greater joy
       Than that expressed by Melior for her father
8648   And that shown by the emperor for her.
       Guillaume's mother and his sister
       Express joy for her in turn with good hearts.
       Guillaume does not linger
8652   In the middle of the great hall.
       Right in front of the entire assembly
       He led Alixandrine
       To Melior's chamber.
8656   And when that beauty saw her, then
       Melior displayed great joy because of the maiden
       And Alixandrine for her damsel.
       They rejoiced greatly with each other
8660   For they were very good friends.
       Alixandrine asks her,
       And she is very concerned to know it,
       That she tell her about her situation,
8664   How it happened, how it can be,
       When they left the country,
       That they were not found or captured.
       And she related everything to her
8668   Just as they had done previously
       And everything that had happened to them.
       Well was it heard and understood
       By the barons and the king of Spain
8672   And the emperor of Germany[96]
       Who had entered inside the chamber.
       With great amazement did they speak of it

---

96. The emperor of Germany is Nathaniel, the emperor of Rome.

When they heard such a thing,
8676 How a penance of that sort was made
By such young people, since they did not die,
And nevertheless they are very joyous about it.
About the adventure they display great joy.
8680 Why should I tell you about their meal?
There was such abundance for everyone
That each had all he wanted.
And when the time for dinner was past,
8684 Messengers entered the hall.
From the land of Greece they came,
Men of valor and very wealthy were they,
Of high rank and of great merit.
8688 They were sent to the queen,
They greeted her on behalf of her father
And on behalf of Lertenidon her brother.
"My lady, they say, be happy:
8692 Your father has not forgotten you,
Thus he is sending you such a military force
That there is no man who could tell its number.
Across the sea are coming the assembly of warriors
8696 In ships, in barges, and in small boats.
Your brother is bringing them to you,
Each day he does his utmost to get here.
Such an army he is bringing to you
8700 That you will not find a prince or king
Who has harmed you while waiting for the army
Who will not be forced to surrender to your mercy.
In an unfortunate hour were born your enemies,
8704 If they do not come seeking your grace."
When the queen hears the news,
You can know that it was very pleasing to her.
To the messengers she responded:
8708 "My lords, you are welcome here
And may God protect my dear father
And Lertenidon my brother.
For their health may God be thanked.
8712 Is my brother far away or nearby,
And the army of Greece, where can it be?
— My lady, in the name of God the celestial King,
On the third day, know this to be true,

8716   You will see your brother here
        With a marvelous company
        Of his barons from Romania.
        The army is sailing beautifully after him,
8720   For there is such an abundance of men,
        Of ships, of barges, and of boats,
        Warhorses and mules and palfreys,
        They cannot come so quickly
8724   And they do not want to disperse the army."
        The queen is overjoyed
        About the news that she has heard.
        She honored the barons greatly
8728   And welcomed and celebrated with them;
        She has them lodged richly
        And served honorably;
        Then they wait until the third day
8732   When the son of the emperor will come
        And with him the Romanian people,
        The greatest barons from his kingdom.
        When the Greeks had arrived,
8736   Never has one seen such great joy
        As the queen of Sicily
        Lavished on her brother, by her and her daughter,
        And by the noble and courtly Guillaume,
8740   On his dear uncle and on the Greeks.
        He does his utmost to honor him,
        To make his acquaintance and to love him;
        And so does the valiant Alphonse,
8744   The king's son who was a werewolf
        And his father the king of Spain
        And the emperor of Germany
        And all the barons together.
8748   They rejoice greatly that night,
        Greatly did they honor the Greek,
        And then they quickly recounted to him
        The whole affair about his nephew,
8752   Just as you have heard it told,
        How he left the land
        With the emperor's daughter
        Who as wife was betrothed to the Greek,
8756   How they escaped from the country

By sewing themselves into bear skins
And the great difficulties that they suffered,
How the werewolf had served them
8760 And protected and defended them,
And how he came back to his land
And how he brought his war to an end.
Of the marriages in turn they spoke,
8764 How they were made and brought together,
And how Guillaume is taking for his wife his sweetheart
Whom he has won at a high price,
And who was the daughter of the emperor,
8768 And how his sister is to be taken by
Alphonse, the son of the king of Spain
As equal, as wife and as companion,
And how he will make her his queen.
8772 Then they spoke of Alixandrine.
They continued the conversation until
She was promised in marriage to Brandin,
The brother of Alphonse, the younger,
8776 And he took her gladly
Because of the command of his brother
And with the consent of his father the king.
Afterward they told the Greek in turn
8780 The whole truth about Alphonse,
How he was a beast and werewolf
And now he is valiant and courageous
And a knight. Then they pointed him out;
8784 With great wonder the Greeks who heard
All of this looked at him.
About the knight they expressed great joy,
But the one who marveled so very greatly was
8788 The Greek, that it was his nephew
Who had stolen his wife.[97]
If the army from Greece had arrived,
He would rejoice no more about it, if it were possible,
8792 But would rather take her by force.
But this cannot be,

97. Lertenidon is the unnamed Greek prince in verse 3434 and 3459 who came to Rome to marry Melior. Verses 8788–8789 are an intertextual allusion to Cligès, in which both Cligès and his uncle Alis love the same woman, Fenice, and to the legend of Tristan and Iseut, in which Tristan falls in love with his uncle Marc's wife, Iseut.

Like it or not, he must remain.
That night they left him thus.

8796 The beds were prepared,
Marvelously beautiful and noble,
As were suitable for such people.
The lords went to bed,

8800 They slept through the night until the next day.
The next morning at daybreak,
The city was awakened by
The bronze trumpets and the drums

8804 And the bugles and the horns,
The musical instruments and the hurdy-gurdies,
The ladies and the damsels
And the valets who had grown to more

8808 Than three thousand throughout the city,
Who were hurrying through the streets
Bumping into one another,
For they have heard the news

8812 That their lord will be crowned
And that he is about to marry his sweetheart.
Alphonse who was the son of the king
In turn was about to marry their lord's sister,

8816 Florence with the bright coloring.
The third damsel will have
Brandin and so she will marry him,
Thus they will have one wedding after the other.

8820 It is because of this that they are making such a great clamor.
The knights got up
And the marquis and the princes.
The damsels had arisen,

8824 And were dressed and adorned
In fabric of such noble fashioning
That it was nothing but marvelous.
Of the garments I do not want to make any discourse,

8828 For there would be too much to tell:
Royal was the clothing
As were the maidens
Who were very well ornamented,

8832 Then they mounted up on their palfreys.
Afterward the queens mounted up
And the ladies and the young noble women

Who had come to the feast.
8836   All of them were richly attired.
The emperor of Germany
Is leading the beautiful Florence
By the reins with the golden bit,
8840   The king of Spain Melior,
And Lertenidon Alixandrine.
On the Saracen mule
Next to Melior at her reins was
8844   The noble lady of Palermo
Who arranges and adjusts her very much;
And beside her daughter Florence
Was the lady Queen Brande
8848   Who was very anxious to serve her,
And to adorn her in such a manner
That she could not be blamed for it.
Thereupon they issued forth from the palace,
8852   But there were so many people in the streets
To watch the maidens
That they can scarcely pass.
But the men who were carrying sticks
8856   Were dispersing the crowd ahead of them.
To separate the people they take great pains;
They arrive at the church, and then they dismount,
Afterward they entered the church.
8860   They were accompanied by barons
Up to the main chancel
Where the clergy were garbed in their vestments,
The patriarch of the city
8864   And the bishop of Sicily.
The young noblemen had mounted their horses,
Lombards and Apulians together;
And when they are outside the palace,
8868   So loud is the noise made by the horns,
By the brass trumpets and by the bugles,
By the musical instruments and by other kinds of trumpets
That the whole city resounds from it.
8872   In order to observe, everyone had
Gone to the upper rooms and to the galleries of the upper floors
And to the attics and to the windows,
Ladies, maidens and bourgeois,

8876   In order to observe the new kings,
The queen and her nobility
And the other nobles in her entourage.
The clergy had already issued forth
8880   And had come to meet the men at arms,
As is right and fitting,
With crucifixes in procession,
With the book of the Gospel in gold, and with reliquaries
8884   Which were of high quality and were very valuable.
They were wearing chancel cloaks
Of silken cloth, edged with gold.
When Guillaume sees the priest,
8888   He immediately dismounts
And across from him makes the sign of the cross,
As was right and fitting,
As does his brother-in-law and his barons.
8892   When each has said his prayer,
They make the sign of the cross over their body and their face,
Then everyone goes into the sanctuary;
There each one touches devoutly
8896   Both his eyes and his mouth,
Then they enter the church
Where there were people of many sorts.
They go straight to the main chancel
8900   Where the priest was waiting for them.
The patriarch Alexis
Consecrated and blessed them
And crowned them very richly
8904   As well as the queens;
Then he unites them in marriage
According to the custom and the usage
That was practiced in that country.
8908   Brandin married his wife,
My lady Alixandrine,
But he is not king nor she queen,
And yet nevertheless they have enough
8912   Castles and towns and cities
And land marvelous and fertile.[98]

---

98. This is an echo of Alphonse's refusal to take anything other than Florence (verse 8314), as well as a reminder of Brande's greed. Even though her plot failed, Brandin has enough to be satisfied with, without having to be king.

And then the service is begun by
The patriarch and the priest
8916 Who were already prepared.
Grand are the songs, high the voices
For the consecration ceremony of the new kings.
I do not know what the offering might be worth,
8920 Marvelous it was and rich and grand.
And when the mass was said
They all returned to the palace,
The dukes, the princes, the counts,
8924 The kings and the emperor
And the barons and the queens
And the ladies and the maidens.
The celebration that begins there is so great
8928 That I do not know how to describe to you
The wines, the beverages, the meals,
The ladies and the knights,
The maidens and the barons,
8932 The presents and the beautiful gifts
That the lords gave to each other.
About the preparations or the decorations
I would not be able to describe
8936 Nor relate or speak about half of them.
The affair lasted an entire month,
Never was there one so magnificent.
The kings had from their wives
8940 All they wanted and everything they desired,
And the ladies with their lords
Brought their love to completion.

When the barons observed
8944 That the wedding feast had lasted long enough,
Each one wants to return to his land,
And so they come to the king to seek permission to leave.
Lertenidon first of all
8948 Bids his sister farewell.
The queen kissed her brother
And sent greetings to her father,
The emperor of Romania:
8952 May God keep him in a good life
And watch over and protect him;

And the Greek took leave
Of Queen Melior
8956   And then he commended her to God,
Next he said goodbye to the emperor
And next the king and his sister,
Alphonse the newly crowned,
8960   Who had been a werewolf.
He commended the king of Spain to God
And the lady Queen Brande,
Alixandrine and her baron,
8964   And the group of barons nearby.
Thereupon he mounted his palfrey.
He had a great escort of barons;
The king his nephew accompanied him.
8968   And when it came time to take leave,
Guillaume sent one hundred greetings to his grandfather
Saying that he would like to see him.
At their parting they kissed each other;
8972   The king remains behind and the others leave;
The Greeks rode their palfreys rapidly
Until they saw their army.
When the men in the army see their lord
8976   And the troops on horseback that they were waiting for,
The best are all joyous about it,
And they do not want to stay there long.
They have readied the ships.
8980   It is a fair day and the weather is beautiful,
Happy are they about their return.
They board their ships on the spot,
Pull up their anchors, raise their sails,
8984   And sail with the wind and by the stars;
Thus they returned to Romania.
When the news was heard,
Just as it had happened,
8988   They considered it to be a great marvel.
The emperor learned the truth
About who the knight had been
Who had taken the maiden given to his son
8992   And from what land he was born.
He is greatly astonished about it,
But of this he is joyous and happy

That his grandson was of such valor,[99]
8996 Of such renown, of such might,
Such a knight and so bold,
And so he had killed his enemies
And restored peace to his realm,
9000 And that in this way the quarrel ended
And he was lord and king of all.
Here we will leave the Greeks,
So we will tell about the emperor
9004 Who does not want to stay long.
He has made all the preparations for his voyage,
Because he wants to return to Rome.
His knights have already mounted up
9008 And he has assembled all his beasts of burden in order to set off.
He comes to his daughter, bids her farewell,
And she very pitifully
Weeps tears from the beautiful eyes of her face
9012 Because he has bid her farewell
And because he wants to go back to his country
Where he was born and where he was from.
That beauty is right if she weeps,
9016 For she will never see him again after that hour
When he parts from her.[100]
The emperor kissed her.
"Daughter, says he, I do not need to,
9020 But one thing I do want to implore you:
That you think greatly about doing well
And that you be noble and good,
Wise and virtuous and honest,
9024 Just as you ought to be because of your lineage;
And thus you will hold very great authority,
Just as our ancestors did,
The queen, that good lady
9028 And the noble men of the realm;

99. My translation of verses 8989–8995 does not adhere to the original, as the passage contains scribal errors and makes no sense as it is. I therefore made modifications as necessary. My translation of the original is as follows: "The emperor learned the truth / About who the maiden had been / Who had been given to his son / And from what land she was born. / He is greatly astonished about it, / But of this he is joyous and happy / That his nephew was of such valor...."

100. Here the narrator reminds us of his superior knowledge. He is telling the story and is therefore in control, although his omniscience and omnipotence are artificial; he knows the end because he is telling a story that happened in the past.

Do not agree to rob or
Suppress the poor people,
For they will pray for you
9032 And for your dear lord the king;
Have no desire to be proud,
But above all creatures
Honor God and His holy church
9036 And glorify His kindness."
She replies: "Dear sweet father,
So help me God, most gladly,
You will never hear anything but good about me."
9040 He kisses her on her chin,
Thereupon he parted from his daughter;
To the queen of Sicily,
May God maintain her joy,
9044 He took leave and he beseeched her
That she honor his daughter and that she chastise her
If she did anything wrong.
And the queen replied to him:
9048 "Sire, in the name of all the saints who are,
And for the sake of the One who caused me to be born,
I do not love as much any woman who could exist,
Whether she were my daughter or niece or sister.
9052 She will be treated with great honor,
All who serve her will be happy
To do absolutely everything that pleases her,
As she commands and as she wants;
9056 And if there is anything she wants to have
That one might have, she will not lack it."
And the emperor thanks her for it.
Then their farewell was said;
9060 From the queen he departed.
Afterward he said goodbye to the queens
And to the ladies and the maidens
Who were there in the hall
9064 And they commended him to God.
He did not forget Alixandrine,
To her he came, and he embraced her.
"My dear, said he, listen to me.
9068 You have married very highly:
God has not forgotten you,

Since you have the son of a king for your husband.
From me keep one thing
9072 That will be very useful to you, I believe.
Honor all things
That you know might please your lord.
For this you will be honored more
9076 And better served and better loved."
She responds: "My dear lord,
I will do so, may God acknowledge you for it.
About me you will hear no bad report,
9080 Unless it is said through great error
Or because of envy or because of sin."
Then he bowed to her and bid her farewell.
He took leave of the king of Spain
9084 And of all the barons as well
And of both his children.
"My lords, says he, know this,
In me you can have confidence.
9088 If any difficulty arises for you
With the Saracens or your neighboring countries,
Inform me about it,
For know this well, you will not lack
9092 My help or my aid."
And they thanked him very much for it.
To God they commended each other,
And they bowed to one another.
9096 Nathaniel left and they returned.
To Palermo they came back,
But they did not have a long conversation there,
Because the king and his entire company
9100 Want to leave for Spain.
The army had already left:
They had returned to their fleet
Where they were readying the ships
9104 And waiting for their lords.
King Guillaume sees very well
That they will not remain for any reason.
When he sees that he cannot keep them any longer,
9108 He has his entire treasury opened to them
And he offers them
Gold and silver in abundance,

Magnificent gemstones, jewels,

9112   Rich and beautiful silken cloth;

But they do not want to take anything.

The king was not lacking in manners:

To all the barons, against their will,

9116   He gave magnificent jewels,

For the king of Spain and the queen,

His sister, and for Alixandrine

He had their chests filled

9120   With jewels to give as gifts and distribute,

When they arrive in their land.[101]

All together they go to seek permission to leave

From the queen of Sicily.

9124   The queen kisses her daughter

Gently, with hot tears running down her face.

And she does the same to her mother.

It is no wonder if they weep,

9128   Since they must be so distant from one another.

They commend one another to God.

The lady Queen Brande and her lord

Are implored by Queen Felise

9132   To honor her daughter.

They respond: "Do not speak at all about it,

Never has a lady been better served

Than she will be or with such magnificence,

9136   As much as if she were a queen or duchess."

And the lady thanks them for it.

All together the company

Bid farewell to Melior.

9140   They bow to her and give her thanks

For the honor that she has shown them;

And Melior rose to acknowledge them,

For she was very courtly and wise.

9144   The king of Spain and his entourage

And the lady Queen Brande

She very gently commends to God,

Then she kissed her sister[102]

---

101. Verses 9114–9121 provide an echo of Guillaume's boyhood generosity — see vv. 371–380 — and function didactically within the narrative as they offer not only Guillaume's friends, but also the listeners/readers an example to follow.

102. Melior kissed Florence. Micha suggests that Guillaume is the sub- *(continued on next page)*

9148   And commended her to the Creator.
        Thereupon behold Alixandrine,
        She is getting her ermine all wet from her tears.
        She bids farewell to the queen,
9152   And Melior very sweetly
        With tender tears, with sighs
        Commended her to the Holy Spirit;
        Alphonse the king who was a werewolf
9156   She hugs and kisses in front of everyone.
        "My lord, said Melior,
        This God who with His body
        Redeemed the world, may He lead you to joy
9160   As I would truly like Him to do.
        —Amen, my dear," the king replied.
        Then they part, thus they leave,
        Everyone mounted their palfreys.
9164   The procession after them is immense
        Of King Guillaume and of his men
        And of the people all together.
        King Guillaume is grieving greatly,
9168   His eyes are wet with tears.
        He is holding his companion by the hand,
        Often he says to him: "Good sir Alphonse,
        My dear brother, my sweet gentle friend,
9172   By God the King of paradise,
        When you will be in your land,
        If any difficulty or war arises for you
        From a Saracen or from a pagan
9176   Or from any Christian man
        For which you want to take vengeance,
        Let me immediately know the situation.
        —My friend, says he, this we will do
9180   And you do the same with us."
        Then they came to their ship.

---

ject of the sentence. For this to be possible, there would have to be a lacuna prior to verse 9147, although Micha does not indicate the existence of such a lacuna, nor does Michelant. I would suggest instead that the poet refers to Florence as Melior's sister "seror," rather than as her sister-in-law "serorge," for the sake of rhyme ("seror / creator"). In verse 9171 the poet refers to Alphonse as Guillaume's brother "freres," not his brother-in-law as he does in verse 8303 "frere en loi" and again in verse 8891 "serorge." In verse 9291 he refers to Guillaume as Alphonse's brother "frere." It is therefore totally plausible that it is indeed Melior who kissed her "sister" Florence.

From their palfreys they dismounted,
They do not want to stay there very long.

9184   All their equipment they have brought on the ships
And their horses and their provisions
And the ladies and the lords.
Thereupon they went up onto the ship without waiting any
    longer.

9188   Very sad is King Guillaume,
When his companion parts from him.
He prays to God that He will protect him
And that He will lead them to safety,

9192   Then he raised his arm up,
And he made the sign of the cross with his right hand
And to the heavenly King commended him
And his sister and their entourage.

9196   Thereupon they move away from the shore,
They pull up the anchors; there is no more to be done,
And they raised the sails
Which fill with the wind and swell up.

9200   Then they leave; into the open sea they launch themselves.
King Guillaume did not move,
On the shore he remained standing so long,
And the barons who were there,

9204   Until they can no longer see the fleet.
When they no longer see it, then they turn back,
And the others do not stop or rest
Who are hastening greatly to get on their way,

9208   For they are very anxious about their return.
They sailed so long and they navigated so far
Until they returned to Spain.
It is not necessary to look for greater joy

9212   Than the joy that the people of that land showed
About their lord and about their friends
Who had returned to the country.
Everyone throughout the realm expresses great joy

9216   About the new king and about his wife.
They give them opulent and grand presents;
Everyone abandons themselves to their will
And to carry out their command,

9220   And the king gives thanks to everyone.
The dead are mourned and missed

By those who once loved them,
Nevertheless they are quickly forgotten
9224 For those who had returned
And for the thing they learned
That had happened to their lord:
How he was a beast and then he was a man,
9228 How he had abandoned his region,
How he was received in Palermo,
How he had become a man there
Because of Lady Brande the queen
9232 Who had made the remedy for him,
The magic spells, and then returned him to his natural state.
Never has anyone seen such happy people
As are all those throughout the realm.
9236 Now we will tell again of King Guillaume
Who has put his land back into such a good state
And reinforced it and fortified it,
Rebuilt the walls, erected the towers
9240 And put the cities back in order
That it does not fear any man alive.
The people who had been expelled, the fugitives,
Came back to the country.
9244 Everywhere he has assured the peace so well
That there is no man highborn enough or strong enough
Who might dare harm the weak.
The king makes justice so just
9248 That the poor and the rich are considered the same.
In that space of time and on that day
The emperor had departed this life.
Dead was the emperor of Rome,
9252 But the barons and the rich men
And the people of the empire
Make the king of Apulia lord,
For they do not know in what land
9256 They can seek or find anyone better than him,
Nor as strong or as helpful
Nor in the empire one as capable
Who might keep the empire on the right path.
9260 And especially since he had
Taken their damsel as his wife:
It is right that he should have the realm.

They have their letters made and written
9264   And sealed and put in wax;
Their messengers are prepared,
Wise and well instructed,
And they have two bishops of the country
9268   Sent with them to the king,
That he might come to Rome to be emperor.
The queen wept for her father,
When she learned that he was dead.
9272   But it was very comforting to her
That her lord the king will be emperor
Of all Rome and of the empire
And that she will be consecrated empress:
9276   This completely comforted her.
King Guillaume does not delay.
That same hour he selected messengers,
And he sent them to his companion
9280   In Spain, King Alphonse.
He asks him to come to him,
May no excuses hold him back,
And he should bring with him his wife the queen
9284   And his brother and Alixandrine
And his father, if he is alive;
But he was dead and lifeless.
Dead is the king and deceased
9288   And from this earthly life departed.
When King Alphonse learned this news,
Know this truly: it was very pleasing to him,
That his brother the king will be emperor
9292   And that he will rule Rome and the entire empire.
He does not delay at leaving,
With a marvelous entourage
Of his barons, of his friends
9296   The king set off on his way.
So much does the king hasten to travel
Both by land and by sea
That they came straight to Palermo
9300   There where the king of Apulia was.
When the two kings spotted each other
And the queens saw each other
And the ladies and the lords,

9304   Never has anyone seen greater joy.
King Guillaume does not delay
To give a good welcome to the whole entourage,
He takes great pains to honor them.

9308   That entire week
The king had them settled comfortably
And rested and adorned in finery;
Each had everything he or she needed.

9312   And when the king had to leave,
Throughout his realm he placed and put
Both his magistrates and his bailiffs
And ordered that they not harm

9316   The weak any more than they would the strong,
That everywhere they might have true justice,
For the poor as well as for the rich.
Afterward he immediately set off on his way.

9320   Everyone in the entourage is full of great joy,
They ride along very happily.
Never has one seen such noble people,
Very magnificent was the company.

9324   The king does not forget his mother,
Rather he takes her along with great honor
With his wife and his sister,
For she was so wondrously wise

9328   That her equal could not be found.
So much did the entourage travel together
And traverse the open country
That they came straight to Rome.

9332   They are received with such joy,
Never since Rome began
Has there been any as great nor will there ever be
Until the end of time, it seems to me.

9336   Never in any assembly
Have they seen so many noble vassals.
At the principal and most important palace
The king and the ladies dismount,

9340   And the others select their inns
Which they find in abundance,
Where immediately one puts at their disposal
Horses and palfreys,

9344   Clothing and equipment.

The Romans honor them very much,
Never were they low-born men,
Nor will they ever desire or long to be so,
9348   Thus they offer them what they have.
They stayed in the city until
The barons have assembled
From throughout the empire and the land;
9352   They made the king emperor
And his wife empress.
They are consecrated and blessed by
Pope Clement, a pope
9356   Who was between the two Gregorys.[103]
He was considered to be a very wise man
And he was the pope of Rome.
He anointed and crowned them
9360   And sung mass and marked them with the sign of the cross
And did the entire ceremony
And all that was part of the service.

When they were anointed and consecrated
9364   And crowned just as they should be
And they had heard the mass
That the pope had sung,
They returned to the great palace.
9368   Never has it been found or known
That at any other coronation
Have there been in Rome such grand people,
Such marvels or such finery
9372   As there were for this emperor.
I do not know what to tell you
About the meals or about the joy,
Or about the riches that are there.
9376   I do not believe there is any man in the whole world,
As wise as he might be, whether he is a layperson or a cleric,
Or prepared and sure in the seven arts,
Who would know how to speak about it or tell it.

---

103. Clement III (1187–1191) was the pope between Gregory VIII (1187) and Gregory IX (1227–1241). Although this verse might be seen as proof that the romance was written in the thirteenth century, it does not preclude it from being written between 1194 and 1197. The poet plays with names throughout the romance and he may have assumed or guessed that since there had already been eight popes named Gregory, there would eventually be a ninth. Moreover, there is no other name in the romance that matches a historic figure.

9380   Because of this, I want to be silent about it.[104]
         But before the court came to an end
         And the assembly of barons departed,
         The emperor did what a truly noble
9384   And kind and valiant sovereign would do.
         The cowherd who had raised him
         And the good lady as well
         He sent for and saw that they had
9388   Beautiful equipment and a very great fortune;
         He had them come before him,
         For he wants to see them very much.
         When they had come before him,
9392   With great honor they are received.
         The emperor said to both of them:
         "Good man, do you recognize me?
         — Do we know you? In truth, sire, we do.
9396   Formerly we considered you our son
         And we raised you, it seems to me,
         Seven years all together.
         Until you were such a fine young gentleman,
9400   That Emperor Nathaniel
         Took you away with him.
         Never have we had such great grief
         As we had because of you, good sir.
9404   Never could we resist it."
         The emperor responded:
         "It is true, it was exactly like that.
         You indeed raised me
9408   Loyally seven full years;
         But in the name of the lord Saint Peter,
         Never have you performed such an act of upbringing,
         Any work or toil or labor
9412   Which has brought you to such an honor.
         Know that because of the pain that you have endured
         Never from hunger or deprivation
         Will you suffer any day of your life.
9416   — May the King who has everything under His power
         Sire, says he, repay you

104. Here the narrator goes beyond the topos of inexpressibility as a rhetorical device and compares himself to other writers; no one is skilled enough to do this. Therefore he cannot be faulted.

And may He protect you from evil."
Then he sends them to a castle
9420 Which is situated so splendidly and beautifully,
With such abundance and with such wealth
I know only that nothing is lacking
That would bring pleasure to a valorous man.
9424 There they lived in great joy
And in repose all their life.
And the emperor ordered all his
Magistrates and his bailiffs
9428 To obey each one
Just as if they were his father and his mother,
If they value their lives.
Thus it was done. But now we will tell
9432 Of the barons and of the great court
That the good emperor held.
Such an assembly of barons came
From the neighboring lands
9436 That it was nothing but marvelous.
The plenary court lasted
A full fifteen days,
Never was there a court so honorable,
9440 So pleasant or so charming
Or so praiseworthy or so courtly;
Never has there been a court where there was so much wealth,
So much splendid new equipment
9444 Or so many warhorses strong and swift,
So many young nobleman or so many vassals
Or so many highly born princes by birth,
So many ladies, so many maidens
9448 So honorable or so beautiful;
Never has there been a court where there were so many rich
       gifts
Given by princes, by barons,
As there were in truth at this one.
9452 But they do not want to remain there any longer,
Because the court has lasted long enough
Both the expense and the assistance:
Each one wants to return to his land.
9456 The emperor said that his land

Should be put at their disposal immediately,
For him and his people as he wants
9460   And he said: "I want and I wish
Him to take them all as he pleases."
And the emperor of Germany
Thanks him with great dignity,
9464   Thus he promises each one his aid.[105]
But before the barons left,
The emperor took homage
From the lords who were at the court;
9468   They made homage to him just as they should.
Of Melior the empress
They all took leave together
Both the ladies and the lords
9472   And the worthy maidens.
To her came the king of Spain
And his companion to say farewell
And she rose to meet him,
9476   For she was very wise and good-mannered;
She put both her arms around his neck:
The king of Spain, in the presence of everyone,
She embraces and kisses at their parting
9480   With soft tears, with sighs;
(He was marvelously dear to her,
For he had been very useful to her in many times of need,
Just as I told you before),
9484   And she commends him to the Holy Spirit
To protect him and his people
And everyone all together.
Beside him she sees Alixandrine
9488   And her sister-in-law the queen
Who are ready to leave.
Their tender faces and chins
Are all wet from tears.
9492   By their long tunics of silken cloth
The empress pulls them to her.

---

105. The passage 9458–9464 is rendered unclear by the lacuna at 9457. It is Guillaume who is speaking, through indirect discourse, in verse 9456, but it cannot be him in verses 9460–61, since Guillaume is thanking that person in verse 9462. A likely speaker for verse 9460–9461 might be Alphonse, or possibly Brandin, but it is difficult to speculate what might have been offered to Guillaume (verses 9457–61).

Then they take each other arm in arm,
With great love they kiss each other
9496 And hug and embrace each other,
For they do not know, since they are leaving now,
If they will ever see each other again.
They say farewell with tender tears,
9500 Which are falling down their faces.
The good lady of Sicily
Takes her daughter by her right hand,
Very gently she implores her:
9504 "Daughter, says she, hear me:
You will go away to your country
Where you are the proclaimed queen.
Think about serving your lord
9508 And do entirely as it pleases him.
Above all else bring him honor
As a loyal lady does for her lord.
Honor what he honors
9512 And love what he loves.
If there is a baron with whom in error
The king, your lord, quarrels,
Think, my dear, that with love
9516 He might return to your lord,
For this is what a good lady must do.
So be wise and good,
Clever, courtly and perfectly behaved,
9520 Just as you should be because of your lineage."
She responds with a sweet manner:
"My sweet dear lady,
Very gladly, so help me God,
9524 I will do as you have said,
And even better, if I am able,
Because toward honor I must aspire."
Then they kiss each other gently;
9528 To God the omnipotent King
The ladies commended each other.
Then they mounted up on their palfreys,
Together with the king they set off on their way;
9532 And the emperor accompanies them,
His right hand is holding on to the pommel
Of the saddle of his friend

And tears are falling from his eyes drop by drop.
9536 He pulls him aside out of the crowd;
Then the emperor said to him:
"My friend and my brother,
By God who established everything,
9540 Be sure that you do not forget to see
That I receive letters often from you
And you will receive mine in the same manner:
By this means I will know and you will know as well
9544 How we are both faring,
Thus we will be comforted more.
— Indeed, I will do as you desire,
Responds the king, I am pleased about it and want to do it."
9548 Thereupon he wept
So that tears flowed down his face.
And he implores him to turn back,
For he had accompanied them a great distance.
9552 And when it came time for them to say farewell,
The two lords kissed each other
And say that they will never fail each other,
As long as God keeps them in life
9556 Each will come to the other's aid if he is needed.
Then they part from each other and traveled on,
The others said goodbye to one another,
To the ladies came the emperor;
9560 The queen kissed her brother
And the emperor his sister
And commended her to the Creator;
He kissed Alixandrine again
9564 And hugged her and embraced her.
"My dear, says he, you are about to leave;
But see that you do not forget me,
If you have any worry or need
9568 Where I might be of value to you and help you,
Send me word at once.
In the name of the Lord in whom I believe
I will not fail you any day of my life."
9572 And for this the lady thanks him very much.
At that moment they departed,
Each left for his land.
The king of Spain rode

9576   With his household and his entourage
Until they arrived in their land.
They are received with great joy;
Never has any man seen greater joy
9580   That what they show for their lord,
For their relatives and for their friends
Who have returned to their land.

Now we will tell of the king of Rome
9584   How he most courteously
Brought his situation to a successful conclusion.
He does not want to rest there a long time,
Thus he rides throughout his realm
9588   And with him he brings his wife
And he takes formal promises
From villages, from towns, from cities
And from castles and from castle keeps,
9592   From dukes, from princes, from barons,
And they make these oaths according to his will.
When he had the land submitted to him,
The countries and the fiefs
9596   And dukes and princes and lords,
Then he establishes such a peace throughout his realm
There is no one bold enough, man or woman,
As valiant or as brave as he might make himself,
9600   Who dares harm anyone.
In peace go the merchants,
The foreigners and the peasants,
They do not fear that anyone will steal from them
9604   What the emperor will not repay;
For whoever would attack the land,
No other guarantee would he offer,
Except to deliver his body to be hung,
9608   No one would ever be able to escape from that.
Everyone comes there with confidence;
May good come to he who maintains such justice.
The emperor was very valiant,
9612   A strong and powerful righter of wrongs.
He glorifies good according to his ability,
He suppresses evil and makes it fall,
The proud he subdues and restrains;

9616   The flatterers, the liars,
        From them he distances himself, and he is right to do so.
        He honors and believes honest men,
        He loves God and serves His holy church,
9620   He honors his mother and fulfills his duties to her
        In any way that she desires.
        Serve her he must and obey her,
        For she was a good and loyal lady.
9624   She was his private inspiration.
        She was generous and a good alms giver,
        She thanks God, as does her son,
        That he was emperor and consecrated
9628   And assured of the empire
        And king of Apulia and of Sicily;
        And that her daughter was queen
        Of Spain and wife of King Alphonse.
9632   Now she can see her vision,
        What she had dreamt, that her right hand
        Would extend over Rome and the left
        Over Spain, that is
9636   That her son is sovereign of Rome
        And king and emperor and lord
        Of all the realm and of the empire.
        The emperor was very courtly
9640   And fierce and noble and upright,
        He held his country very much in peace;
        No one quarreled or waged war,
        For he has no neighbor, know this to be true,
9644   Who does not fear and serve him according to his ability.
        He had two children by his wife
        Who were very powerful and fierce;
        Each in turn displayed all his life
9648   Marvelous lordship:
        One of them was king, the other emperor.
        About Guillaume and his mother,
        About his children and his offspring,
9652   About his empire and his realm
        The story draws to an end here.
        May He who always was and always
        Will be, may He pardon shortly
9656   And may He protect Countess Yolande,

The good and loyal lady,
And may He preserve her from evil.
She had this book written and made
9660   And translated from Latin into French.
Let us pray to God for the good lady
That He let her soul rest in peace
And that He give us this compensation
9664   So that we may come to a good end.
Amen.
      Here ends the romance of
      Guillaume de Palerne.

Bibliography

French Editions of Guillaume de Palerne

Guillaume de Palerne. Ed. H[enri]. Michelant. Société des Anciens Textes Français 5. Paris: Firmin-Didot, 1876.

Guillaume de Palerne: Les Versions en Prose. Ed. John C. Manolis. Diss. Florida State University, 1976.

Guillaume de Palerne: Roman du XIIIe siècle. Ed. Alexandre Micha. Textes Littéraires Français. Genève: Droz, 1990.

Other Editions of Guillaume de Palerne

EachtraUilliam: An Irish Version of William of Palerne. Ed. and trans. Cecile O'Rahilly. Dublin: Dublin Institute for Advanced Studies, 1949.

Guillaume de Palerne: The Ancient English Romance of William the Werwolf. Ed. Frederick Madden. 1832. New York: Burt Franklin, 1970.

The Romance of William of Palerne (Otherwise Known as the Romance of "William and the Werwolf"). Ed. Walter Skeat. Early English Text Society, Extra Series 1. 1867. London: Kegan Paul, Trench, Trubner, & Co., 1890.

William of Palerne: An Alliterative Romance. Ed. G. H. V. Bunt. Groningen, Neth.: Bouma's Boekhuis bv, 1985.

Primary Sources

Chrétien de Troyes. *Cligès*. Ed. Alexandre Micha. Classiques Français du Moyen Âge 84. Paris: Champion, 1957.

Énéas: Roman du XIIe siècle. Ed. J.-J. Salverda de Grave. Classiques Français du Moyen Âge 44, 62. 2 vols. Paris: Champion, 1925, 1929.

Les Lais anonymes des XIIe et XIIIe siècles: Édition critique de quelques lais bretons. Ed. Prudence Mary O'Hara Tobin. Publications Romanes et Françaises 143. Genève: Droz, 1976.

Lais féeriques des XIIe et XIIIe siècles. Trans. Alexandre Micha. Le Moyen Âge. Paris: GF-Flammarion, 1992.

Marie de France. *Les Lais de Marie de France*. Ed. Jean Rychner. Classiques Français du Moyen Âge 93. Paris: Champion, 1966.

[Renaut]. *Galeran de Bretagne: Roman du XIIIe siècle*. Ed. Lucien Foulet. Classiques Français du Moyen Âge 37. Paris: Champion, 1971.

Secondary Sources

Barber, Malcolm. *The Two Cities: Medieval Europe 1050-1320*. London: Routledge, 1992.

Berkvam, Doris Desclais. *Enfance et maternité dans la littérature française des XIIe et XIIIe siècles*. Essais 8. Paris: Champion, 1981.

Bloch, Marc. *Feudal Society*. Trans. L. A. Manyon. 2 vols. Chicago: University of Chicago P, 1961.

Born, Lester K[ruger]. Introduction. *The Education of a Christian Prince*. By Desiderius Erasmus. Trans. Lester K. Born. New York: Columbia University Press, 1936. New York: Octagon-Farrar, 1973. 44–130.

_____. "The Perfect Prince: A Study in Thirteenth- and Fourteenth-Century Ideals." *Speculum* 3 (1928): 470–504.

Cosman, Madeleine Pelner. *The Education of the Hero in Arthurian Romance*. Chapel Hill: University of North Carolina Press, 1965.

Curtius, Ernest Robert. *European Literature and the Latin Middle Ages*. Trans. Willard R. Trask. Bollingen Library 36. 1953. Princeton: Princeton University Press, 1983.

Dunn, Charles W. *The Foundling and the Werwolf: A Literary-Historical Study of Guillaume de Palerne*. Toronto: University of Toronto Press, 1960.

Fourrier, Anthime. "La 'Contesse Yolent' de *Guillaume de Palerne*." *Études de langue et de littérature du moyen âge offertes à Félix Lecoy par ses collègues, ses élèves et ses amis*. Paris: Champion, 1973. 115–123.

Frappier, Jean. "L'Institution de Lancelot dans le *Lancelot en prose*." *Mélanges de philologie romane et de littérature médiévale offerts à Ernest Hoepffner*. Publications de la Faculté des Lettres de l'Université de Strasbourg 113. Paris: Belles-Lettres, 1949. 269–278. Rpt. in Frappier, *Amour courtois et table ronde*. Publications Romanes et Françaises 126. Genève: Droz, 1973. 169–179.

Kelly, Douglas. "Fortune and Narrative Proliferation in the *Berinus*." *Speculum* 51 (1976): 6–22.

_____. *Medieval French Romance*. Twayne's World Author Series 838. New York: Twayne, 1993.

Kennedy, Elspeth. "The Quest for Identity and the Importance of Lineage in Thirteenth-Century French Prose Romance." *The Ideals and Practice of Medieval Knighthood II: Papers from the Third Strawberry Hill Conference 1986*. Eds. Christopher Harper-Bill and Ruth Harvey. Suffolk: Boydell Press, 1988. 70–86.

Kittredge, G[eorge] L[yman]. *Arthur and Gorlagon: Versions of the Werewolf's Tale*. [Harvard] *Studies and Notes in Philology and Literature* 8 (1903): 149–275. Rpt. New York: Haskell House, 1966.

McKeehan, Irene Pettit. "*Guillaume de Palerne*: A Medieval 'Best Seller.'" *PMLA* 41 (1926): 785–810.

Ménard, Philippe. "Les Histoires de loup-garou au moyen âge" *Symposium in honorem prof. M. De Riquer*. Barcelona: Universitat de Barcelona Quaderns Crema, 1984. 209–38.

Morawski, Joseph, ed. *Proverbes français antérieurs au XVe siècle*. Classiques Français du Moyen Âge 47. Paris: Champion, 1925.

Newman, Paul B. *Daily Life in the Middle Ages*. Jefferson: McFarland, 2001.

Otten, Charlotte F. *A Lycanthropy Reader: Werewolves in Western Culture; Medical Cases, Diagnoses, Descriptions; Trial Records, Historical Accounts, Sightings; Philosophical and Theological Approaches to Metamorphosis; Critical Essays on Lycanthropy; Myths and Legends; Allegory*. Syracuse: Syracuse University Press, 1986.

Paris, Gaston. "Le Roman d'aventure." *Cosmopolis* 11 (1898): 760–778.

Poirion, Daniel. "Le roman d'aventure au moyen âge: étude d'ésthétique littéraire." *Cahiers de l'Association Internationale des Études Françaises* 40 (1988): 111–127.

Sconduto, Leslie A. "Blurred and Shifting Identities: The Werewolf as Other in *Guillaume de Palerne*." *Romance Languages Annual (1999)*, XI (2000): 121–126.

_____. "Rewriting the Werewolf in *Guillaume de Palerne*." *Le Cygne: Bulletin of the International Marie de France Society*, 6 (Fall 2000): 23–35, addendum.

Sconduto, Leslie Ann. *Metamorphosis and Identity: The Individual in Society in Guillaume de Palerne*. Diss. Rutgers University, 1995.

Sturm-Maddox, Sara. "Arthurian Evasions: The End(s) of Fiction in *Floriant et Florete*." *"Por le soie amisté"*: *Essays in Honor of Norris J. Lacy*. Eds. Keith Busby and Catherine M. Jones. Faux Titre 183. Amsterdam: Rodopi, 2000. 475–89.

Uitti, Karl D. *Story, Myth, and Celebration in Old French Narrative Poetry: 1050–1200*. Princeton: Princeton University Press, 1973.

Williams, Harry F. "Les Versions de *Guillaume de Palerne*." *Romania* 73 (1952): 64–77.

_____. Review of *The Foundling and the Werwolf: A Literary-Historical Study of Guillaume de Palerne*, by Charles W. Dunn. *Speculum* 36 (1961): 123–25.

Index

(References are to line numbers of the poem)

9537, 9559, 9561, 9611, 9627, 9639; as
the king of Rome 9583

Heugot: the father of Martinet 596
Holy Mary: the Virgin Mary 96, 7644,
8611
Holy Spirit 5102, 5852, 9154, 9484
Huet the dwarf: one of Guillaume's
childhood friends 594
Hugenet: one of Guillaume's childhood
friends 595
Hungary 677

Israel (the people of) 3926

Jasan: a Palermitan 5765
Jesus 1186, 1672, 2840, 3129, 4014,
4551, 4627; the Son of Holy Mary
8611; the Savior 3198, 3383, 3756
Joathas: ambassador from the Greek
emperor 2605, 2621
Jonah: character in the Bible who was
swallowed by a whale 3139
Josson du Pré: one of the knights of the
duke of Saxony 2065

King of Spain: father of Alphonse and
Brandin, husband of Brande 281,
4417, 4655, 5244, 6570, 7012, 7060,
7108, 7261, 7569, 8323, 8523, 8579,
8671, 8745, 8769, 8840, 8961, 9083,
9117, 9144, 9287

Lertenidon: Felise's brother and the son
of Patrichidus, the Greek emperor
3362, 8690, 8710, 8841, 8947
Lombards: subjects of Rome 774, 1848,
1893, 1895, 1920, 3783, 8866
Lombardy: regions in both northern
and southern Italy in the twelfth
century 764, 982, 1935, 2414, 3879,
4860
Love: Love personified 1587, 1589

Marcon of Reggio: one of Guillaume's
knights 5753
Maron of Alidos: a Spanish warrior
6806
Martinet the son of Heugot: one of
Guillaume's childhood friends 596
Melant: town 6599

Meliadon: a Spanish knight 6707, 6731,
6747, 6816, 6825, 6835, 6842, 6849,
6865, 6893
Melior: the daughter of Nathaniel, the
emperor of Rome, by name 649,
658, 701, 714, 723, 817, 970, 984,
1013, 1022, 1079, 1082, 1093, 1100,
1136, 1154, 1340, 1373, 1405, 1410,
1433, 1438, 1452, 1465, 1467, 1563,
1676, 1689, 1730, 1739, 2453, 2519,
2805, 2808, 3075, 3079, 3176, 3314,
3358, 3502, 4025, 5178, 5195, 5357,
5554, 5566, 7042, 7159, 7593, 7811,
7890, 8152, 8286, 8430, 8647, 8655,
8657, 8840, 8843, 8955, 9139, 9142,
9152, 9157, 9469; as Roman maiden
7977; as daughter of emperor 4271,
4313, 5235
Messina: city in Sicily situated on the
Strait of Messina 4597
Morel: Guillaume's horse 2272
Moysant: priest, Felise's chaplain 4783,
4884, 5166

Nathaniel: Melior's father, the emperor
of Rome and of Germany, by name
1191, 2888, 3478, 3512, 3747, 3847,
8448, 9096, 9400; as the emperor
388, 411, 417, 428, 434, 441, 461, 463,
466, 471, 476, 486, 490, 512, 524, 534,
600, 606, 613, 621, 625, 630, 638, 642,
648, 656, 664, 691, 721, 782, 791, 1115,
1210, 1234, 1240, 1303, 1793, 1800,
1805, 1820, 1849, 1851, 1857, 1858,
1945, 1948, 1951, 1969, 1975, 2305,
2355, 2356, 2357, 2379, 2392, 2395,
2401, 2433, 2447, 2488, 2506, 2514,
2524, 2540, 2558, 2566, 2592, 2600,
2611, 2641, 2672, 2687, 2693, 2701,
2703, 2741, 2755, 2915, 2997, 3041,
3223, 3466, 3503, 3518, 3525, 3557,
3614, 3632, 3657, 3681, 3821, 3841,
3891, 3941, 3963, 4252, 4271, 4313,
5116, 5235, 5911, 8205, 8403, 8424,
8431, 8455, 8461, 8477, 8496, 8505,
8515, 8553, 8565, 8570, 8571, 8581,
8585, 8594, 8622, 8648, 8672, 8746,
8754, 8767, 8837, 8924, 8957, 9003,
9018, 9058, 9250, 9251

Paien: the father of Thumassin 598